THE
DIARY
THAT
CHANGED
THE
WORLD

THE REMARKABLE STORY OF OTTO FRANK
AND THE DIARY OF ANNE FRANK

THE
DIARY
THAT
CHANGED
THE
WORLD

—

KAREN BARTLETT

Biteback Publishing

First published in Great Britain in 2022 by
Biteback Publishing Ltd, London
Copyright © Karen Bartlett 2022

ISBN 978-1-78590-615-2

10 9 8 7 6 5 4 3 2 1

A CIP catalogue record for this book is available from the British Library.

Set in Adobe Caslon Pro and Futura

Printed and bound in Great Britain by
CPI Group (UK) Ltd, Croydon CR0 4YY

For my father

CONTENTS

CONTENTS

INTRODUCTION

'I identified with her situation, and therefore the lessons of that tragedy sunk more deeply in our souls and encouraged us. If a young girl of thirteen could take such militant actions then so could we...'

NELSON MANDELA, ON READING
THE DIARY OF ANNE FRANK IN PRISON

When Otto Frank unwrapped his daughter's diary with trembling hands and began to read the first pages, he was discovering a side to 'his Anne' that was as much a revelation to him as it would be to the rest of the world. It was late 1945, and in Amsterdam life was bleak: Europe had been torn apart by war; the city was recovering from a brutal Nazi occupation and years of famine and hardship. The few returning Jewish refugees straggled back to an unwelcoming country that had once been their home. For many the fate of their families was unknown. In unwrapping the package before him Otto must have felt he was handling a miracle – opening a portal to the past that offered the chance to reconnect with his lost life, and the people he had loved.

Otto read the first words and was quickly overcome with emotion. He did not know that he would take the bundle of handwritten pages before him and turn his daughter into an icon, placing a teenaged girl with dark hair, a fiendish temper and a lopsided smile at the heart of a debate about twentieth-century history – with themes about growing up, persecution, human values and religion still as contested today.

As a man who had survived Auschwitz only to discover that his entire family had perished, Otto Frank must have believed he had already experienced the worst that life could hold. Undoubtedly that must be true, but he had many painful struggles ahead. Little did he know that his desire to share his daughter's story with the world would spark a bitter battle over the nature of the diary and Anne's legacy that would embroil him in years of legal battles, driving him to a nervous breakdown and eventually into a new life in Switzerland.

Since Otto Frank arranged the first publication of *The Diary of Anne Frank* in 1947, it has sold more than 31 million copies and been translated into seventy languages. There have been five different editions of *The Diary of Anne Frank*, two graphic biographies, five books for children, seven feature-length documentaries, one BBC TV series and three feature films. An animated film, *Where Is Anne Frank* by Israeli director Ari Folman, debuted at the Cannes Film Festival in 2021, while books like Nathan Englander's *What We Talk About When We Talk About Anne Frank* continue the debate about Anne's legacy. In Amsterdam, 1.2 million people visit the Anne Frank House every year to see the secret annexe where the diary was written, while more than a million people in the UK have seen the touring Anne Frank exhibit. To those who weary of her singular fame, it sometimes seems like everyone who ever met Anne Frank has written about their acquaintance, however fleeting.

Anne's journey through adolescence, set against the backdrop of the Holocaust, quickly became an iconic text of the twentieth century, as widely read and resonant in Japan and Cambodia as in the US, Germany and the UK. Upon its publication, thousands of young people wrote to Otto to express how much the book reflected their own teenage years, while world leaders, including Nelson Mandela, who read the book during his incarceration on Robben Island, sought inspiration from Anne's message of hope and humanity.

This remarkable impact was driven by the determination of one man: Otto Frank. Once an ordinary loving father of two girls, Otto became the guardian of Anne's memory – overseeing every aspect of the diary's publication and its legacy to the point of obsession. From its inception, *The Diary of Anne Frank* would test Otto to his limits.

Hard as it now seems to believe, from the very first reading people opposed the publication of the diary. In Amsterdam the influential Rabbi Hammelburg called Otto 'sentimental and weak' and said all 'thinking Jews in the Netherlands' should oppose the 'commercial hullabaloo' of the diary and the Anne Frank House. Later, in 1997, Cynthia Ozick of the *New York Times* said, 'The diary has been bowdlerized, distorted, transmuted, reduced; it has been infantilized, Americanized, sentimentalized, falsified, kitschified, and, in fact, blatantly denied…' Criticism of how the diary was interpreted could be harsh and emotional – and sometimes justified.

Yet Anne's story touched a chord. Within three years the diary had been translated into several languages, with critics commenting on the 'mixture of danger and domesticity that has a particular poignancy...' Undoubtedly it was the publication of the diary in the US that would catapult the story of Anne Frank to worldwide fame, but this also marked the beginning of Otto's relationship with a supporter who would turn into a nemesis. Meyer Levin was an American writer who would go on to fight Otto over control of Anne's legacy in a series of bitter court battles and engage public figures on his behalf, including even Eleanor Roosevelt.

While Otto fought in the US courts to preserve his control of the diary and its dramatic rights, he was also forced to defend its authenticity in Germany, where Holocaust deniers brought a series of claims against him alleging that the diary was a fake that Otto had written himself. *The Diary of Anne Frank* was now at the heart of the battle over Holocaust denial, and controversy would rage for decades, exacerbated by the revelation in the 1980s that Otto had personally withheld five pages from publication. An unexpurgated publication of the diary in the 1990s prompted another round of soul-searching over Otto's editing of the original script.

One young girl's diary had touched millions of lives. Over the years thousands of readers wrote to Otto, seeing him as a father figure in their own lives and taking up long correspondences with him, which he meticulously answered sitting in his study in Switzerland, day after day. In Germany young people founded Anne Frank clubs and there was even an Anne Frank Village for refugees. In Japan the diary became a runaway bestseller, offering a chance to discuss a war which was largely taboo. The diary broke other taboos in Japan too – young girls read it as it was one of the first books to speak about menstruation, and soon girls began to talk about having their 'Anne Frank'.

Anne Frank and the diary meant many different things to many people – none of which Otto could have envisaged in 1947. By the time Otto died in 1980 he had become symbolic of one view of the Holocaust, and humanity, which downplayed – in some people's eyes – the full horrors that the Jewish people had suffered, the diary ending as it did before Anne's capture and death in Bergen-Belsen.

Otto, the saintly father figure, was as sanitised as Anne had become herself. The reality was more complicated, and more compelling. Otto lived many lives, enjoying a privileged childhood at the pinnacle of German society only to lose everything in the 1930s and restart his life almost as a door-to-door salesman in Amsterdam. He strove above all to protect his family but was powerless to prevent their horrible deaths at the hands of the Nazis. Returning to Amsterdam as a shattered man, he was gripped by the absolute conviction that his daughter's handwritten diary had a message for the whole world. He was a loving, sensitive and traumatised man who found happiness again with his second wife but was at the same time often overwhelmed with nervous exhaustion and fits of deep depression. He was driven by an obsession with Anne and Anne's legacy that overrode all else, and arguably blotted out even the memory of his other daughter Margot.

Today, almost eighty years after Anne's death, that battle to define what she means to the world is still intense, with the future of a multi-million-pound industry at stake as competing foundations, cultural critics and former friends and relatives clash over the legacy of Anne Frank – and who should control it.

This book goes beyond conventional biographies of the Frank family to examine the story of *The Diary of Anne Frank*, the highly controversial role it played in twentieth-century history and publishing and the fundamental role it has played in our understanding of the Holocaust. Moreover, this book will examine the way in which the diary holds a mirror to the second half of the twentieth century and how the ongoing conversation about its role and authenticity still has relevance to our discussions about religion; the rise in antisemitism; gender; culture and cultural appropriation; bias in the writing of history; the commodification of tragedy; and suspicion regarding corporate charitable fundraising. At the same time, the book will shed new light on the life and character of Otto Frank, the complex, driven and deeply human man who lived in the shadows of the terrible events that robbed him of his family while he painstakingly crafted and controlled his daughter's story.

In the end, it's arguable that, for Otto, his mission to spread awareness of Anne's diary was, if anything, too successful. His work resulted in an unstoppable momentum and appetite for her story, and her worldwide popularity has often rendered her an abstract symbol for a variety of individuals and interest groups. That may be its greatest weakness – or the source of its strength and enduring power. At the heart of *The Diary of Anne Frank* is the relationship between Anne and Otto, who together crafted a story that has been ceaselessly reimagined by successive generations of readers. All this makes it simultaneously one of the best-loved and most controversial – and certainly one of the most potent – books ever published. One young girl's diary changed the world.

CHAPTER 1

'QUITE CONSCIOUSLY GERMAN'

BASEL, DECEMBER 2014

The Christmas decorations and markets light up Basel, making this small Swiss city on the borders of both France and Germany seem uncommonly cosy and cheerful. Like many people in their seventies and eighties, two Basel residents, Buddy Elias and his wife Gertie, are downsizing – clearing out the attic and getting rid of several generations' worth of papers, clutter and possessions from their family home. Unlike most other pensioners, however, Elias is Anne Frank's cousin and one of the last living relatives who remembers her. The papers and artefacts are not family trivia, meaningful only to a few close relatives and destined for the dustbin, but an extensive testament to the Franks and the Eliases. They are a remarkable and rare history of a German Jewish family that will be part of a permanent exhibition at the new Frank Family Center, housed at the Jewish Museum of Frankfurt. Researchers from the centre have been staying with Elias and his wife for a week, sorting through final possessions, and now the removal trucks have arrived to take the archive north into Germany. 'When the chair goes, I will be sad,' Elias says, referring to a small chair that Anne used to sit on when she visited him as a girl on holiday. 'I was a lively boy, Anne was a lively girl and her sister Margot was a reader. I had a jack-in-the-box theatre at home, with a grandmother that popped out and a crocodile. I'd play it for her, and she loved that.'

Elias lived a double life for decades: on the one hand a successful German-speaking actor who made his name as an ice-dancing clown in *Holiday on Ice*; on the other president of the Anne Frank Foundation in Switzerland, where he fought numerous battles over the years to make sure his cousin's work was not exploited. The rehousing of the artefacts will turn out to be one of Buddy Elias's last acts as the keeper of the family flame – reminding the world that the Franks were once a proud German family. 'Amsterdam was an asylum for Anne and her family for eleven years during the Nazi time. But it cannot be regarded as their home. Now the artefacts have to go back to the place where the Frank family lived since the seventeenth century; that's Frankfurt.'

Buddy's uncle was Otto Frank. Tall, dashing and witty, Otto was, as his daughter Anne described him in her diary, 'extremely well brought up'. Radiating charm and kindness and drawing on an ample supply of money, he was perfectly well-placed to enjoy the life of a wealthy young man in the early years of the twentieth century. For upper-class Europeans, these were halcyon days – before wars, financial crises and social uprisings would irreparably alter their way of life. The Frank family were happily settled in a large suburban villa in Frankfurt, where Otto and his brothers and sister came of age, spending their days engaged in rounds of tea parties, dancing, horse riding and becoming embroiled in blossoming – and then failed – romances. Otto's life was particularly gilded in that it included university study in Heidelberg and the glamour of a first job with Macy's department store in New York City. The fact he crossed the Atlantic several times by ocean liner, something no ordinary German could have dreamed of, was testament to the family's wealth and position. For young Otto, the future looked promising, and the present was great fun.

Otto's father, Michael Frank, had left his hometown of Landau in 1879 at the age of twenty-eight and settled in Frank-furt. Seven years later he married 21-year-old Alice Stern, a member of a well-known and prosperous family, and moved into stockbroking and banking, as well as investing in various busi-nesses, including two health farms and a company that made cough lozenges. The Franks' first child Robert was born in 1886, followed by Otto on 12 May 1889, Herbert in 1891 and Helene (known as Leni) in 1893. In 1901, Michael Frank founded the Frank bank, specialising in foreign currency exchange, and then moved his wife and children into their family home – a large semi-detached villa at 4 Mertonstrasse with long balconies and landscaped gardens.

The Franks fitted into their place in the upper echelon of German society perfectly. Except for one thing, of course: they were Jewish. Frankfurt had long been a centre of Jewish life in Germany and was the home of great banking dynasties like the Rothschilds. Yet Germany in the late-nineteenth and early twentieth centuries was rife with antisemitism, as nationalist groups employed vile rhetoric and lies to try to force Jews from every area of public life. Jews were increasingly viewed as a race rather than a religious group, and in Germany antisemitism was flavoured with what historians like Daniel Goldhagen argue was a distinctly 'eliminationist' character that was entrenched in German culture. Between 1899 and 1939, Germany passed 195 laws, or acts of discrimination, against Jewish people, while Great Britain passed eight and France one.

If this encroached on Otto Frank's otherwise enjoyable life it was, at first, only dimly. 'There was at this time some anti-semitism in certain circles, but it was not aggressive and one did not suffer from it,' Otto remembered. Like many families in their economic strata, the Franks considered themselves German first, Jewish second, and Otto pointed out that he would not have become an officer in the First World War if he had not felt 'quite consciously German'. Later he admitted this had made no difference in the eyes of his persecutors.

Firmly non-religious, Otto did not have a bar mitzvah or learn Hebrew. While the family valued Jewish traditions, they ate pork and ignored religious holidays. His family, he later wrote, never set foot in a synagogue.

As a boy, Otto first attended a private prep school and then the local Lessing Gymnasium, where he was a popular student. His cousin remembered him as 'outgoing and fun and he became an accomplished cellist, enjoyed writing for the school newspaper, and developed a love of classical German literature'. Although he was the only Jewish student in his form at Lessing, this fact would not become important to him until much later in his life – when he angrily replied to a classmate who had written a book about their time at the school, stating, 'I was un-pleasantly struck by your apparently knowing nothing about the concentration camps and gas chambers, since there is no mention of my Jewish comrades dying in the gas chambers.' Otto reminded him he was the only member of his family to survive the horrors of the Holocaust.

At the time, however, Otto was only concerned with seeking out new and stimulating experiences. Bored with parties and balls, waltzing and dinners, a trip to Spain in 1907 sparked what would be a lifelong passion for foreign travel, and, after passing his Abitur in 1908, he left again for a long trip to England.

When he returned to Germany, Otto enrolled for a short spell studying economics at Heidelberg University, where he met and became close friends with Charles Webster Straus, a young American on a year abroad from Princeton. Although Otto left Heidelberg after only a couple of terms, his friend Charlie invited him to the United States for a year's work experience at Macy's department store, where his father was part-owner. Straus Senior assured Otto that if he enjoyed the job, a good career at Macy's awaited him. By this time Otto had already embarked on a training programme with a bank in Frankfurt and was engaged to be married – but he seized the new opportunity, sailing for New York in September 1909 on the *Kaiser Wilhelm der Grosse*. On board, Otto spent the long and rainy voyage enjoying the magnificently appointed accommodation and writing letters to his sister Leni to celebrate her sixteenth birthday. After only a few days in New York, however, his dream was shattered when he received news that his father was dead.

Michael Frank had died suddenly of a heart attack on 17 September 1909. He had said what turned out to be a final goodbye to his son Otto on the docks in Hamburg only a few weeks earlier. When Otto returned to Germany his carefree youth was over: Alice Frank had taken control of the bank, but without Michael the future of the family business seemed uncertain – and Otto's fiancée had spectacularly broken off their engagement.

Otto had been romancing a girl before his departure for New York and asked her to wait for him. She did not. According to Otto's cousin Milly Stanfield, he took the break-up of his youthful love affair 'very hard', and he withheld the references Anne made to his first failed love affair in the published edition of the diary. 'It can't be easy for a loving wife to know that she'll never be first in her husband's affections, and Mummy did know that...' Anne had speculated. Whether his disappointment really did stretch over decades is unknown (a later account by Stanfield suggested that it did not), but certainly by Christmas 1909, a dejected Otto returned to New York in very different circumstances to resume his work at Macy's.

Otto stayed in New York, off and on, for two years, socialising for the first time with other wealthy Jewish families, learning the ropes of working for a big department store, attending charity balls and immersing himself in local politics, when Charlie announced his decision to run for office. Eventually, though, he returned to Germany for good. In 1911, Otto took up a position with a metal engineering company in Düsseldorf and appeared to pick up his old life as it had been, with lavish lunches, trips to the circus, visits to his mother and family holidays in Switzerland. Milly Stanfield described a visit to the Franks after Otto's return where they held 'a big luncheon with an enormous ice-cream gateau decorated with fairy-tale figures, and Tanti Toni invited us all to the circus'. Despite outward appearances, though, the world was changing. When Milly returned on her next holiday from London in July 1914, she found the house convulsed in near hysteria at the prospect of the outbreak of war, and the French branch of the Frank family, Otto's Uncle Leon, Aunt Nanette and their sons Oscar, Georges and Jean-Michel, described the extreme antisemitism they suffered in Paris. By August, Milly and her family were advised by the British Consulate to return to England, and they departed from a chaotic Frankfurt train station feeling that a wall of fire now separated Germany from the Allies.

Like many young men on both sides, Otto entered the war with energy, excitement and the optimism of certain victory. Although German military academies had previously made it very difficult for Jews to enrol, the advent of the First World War meant that 100,000 Jewish men would be drafted into battle. After a year on loan to a company doing war work, Otto joined the army in August 1915 and wrote a cheerful letter to his family from the training depot in Mainz. 'All in all I think I've got it good,' he noted. Adding that the food was 'pretty good' and that he'd had to clean the windows and polish his boots, he concluded that he'd rarely spent a more amusing train journey than the one to the training depot. Some of the officers drank like fish, but he was quite content, even if not looking forward to the prospect of sleeping on a straw bed. He summed up: 'Everyone wants to join in the victory!'

In 1916, Otto was sent to the Western Front, where he was attached to the infantry as a range finder and survived the Battle of the Somme before being promoted to lieutenant in 1917. Throughout the war he would continue to write thoughtful letters to his family back home, usually offering advice on daily matters to his little sister and rarely, if ever, describing the horrors he witnessed. In June 1918 he told Leni he was in a good mood, sitting in fine weather looking at some roses – longing for the 'easy life' to start again.

As a surviving soldier from the Western Front, Otto understood perhaps more than anyone that, in truth, the 'easy life' had vanished for ever. He returned to the family home on Mertonstrasse in January 1919 to face his worried family, who had been expecting him weeks earlier. After listening to Otto's explanation that he had been honouring his word and returning two horses to a farmer in Belgium, Alice Frank flew into a temper and threw a teapot at his head. Life for the family had been far from easy in their years apart. The French part of the family had been decimated when Uncle Leon committed suicide by jumping out of a window after the deaths of his sons Oscar and Georges in the war. Aunt Nanette had been committed to a mental hospital – leaving only the one remaining son, Jean-Michel, behind. In Frankfurt the family bank was in severe trouble after Alice's investment in war bonds wiped out a large part of their wealth. Faced with such dire circumstances, Otto reluctantly took over running the bank and the family cough-lozenge business. For several turbulent years he steered the business, navigating the plummeting German mark, political instability, growing extremism and rising antisemitism.

In the early 1920s, Otto attempted to set up a foreign currency trading arm of the bank in Amsterdam, but when the attempt failed he returned to Frankfurt in 1925 and, to the astonishment of his wider family and friends, promptly announced his engagement to the unknown Edith Holländer, a young woman from a wealthy Jewish family in Aachen. At the relatively advanced age of thirty-six, Otto was finally getting the family he had told his sister he craved, but equally importantly, he would benefit from a large dowry that he hoped would help save the family business.

Otto had spent a romantic youth, but his marriage, which took place in Aachen on 12 May 1925, his thirty-sixth birthday, was a 'business arrangement'. Later he would admit that he had not been in love with his first wife, but they settled down together into a comfortable and secure union. The Holländers were a more religious family than the Franks and had founded their family fortune on a scrap-metal empire. On the eve of her marriage, at twenty-five years old Edith was described as shy, family-orientated and academic – yet she also had a wide circle of friends, played tennis, cut her hair in a stylish 1920s bob and danced the Charleston. While Anne was often tempted to muse over her father's passionless imprisonment – 'What kind of marriage has it turned out to be? No quarrels or differences of opinion – but hardly an ideal marriage. Daddy respects Mummy and loves her, but not with the kind of love I envision for a marriage ... Daddy's not in love' – Otto himself was more sanguine. He wrote to Edith on their wedding anniversary in 1939 that while they had been buffeted by the whims of fate, 'the most difficult situations haven't disrupted the harmony between us'. Commending Edith for her spirit and solidarity, Otto added, 'What is still to come nobody knows, but that we will not make life miserable for each other through little arguments and fights, that we do know. May the coming years of our marriage be as harmonious as the previous ones.'

After a honeymoon in San Remo in Italy, Otto and Edith returned to live in Frankfurt. At first they lived in the family home in Mertonstrasse, with Otto's mother, his sister Leni, now married to Erich Elias, and her family, including her second child Buddy. On 16 February, Otto and Edith's first daughter, Margot Betti, was born, and one year later the family took the unusual step of moving out of the family home and into their own large apartment on Marbachweg, which they rented from landlord Otto Konitzer, a Nazi Party supporter. Cementing their happiness, their second daughter was born at 7.30 a.m. on 12 June 1929 – Annelies Marie. Writing in Anne's newly started baby book, Edith says, 'Mother and Margot visit the baby sister on 14 June. Margot is completely delighted.'

Otto was a loving father to both girls, taking over bathtime and reading them bedtime stories when he returned from work – including one he invented himself called 'The Two Paulas', about two sisters, one good and one bad. From the beginning, though, he had a special bond with Anne, who was as wilful and lively as Margot was tranquil. Anne was 'a little rebel with a will of her own', Otto said. When she woke through the night it was Otto who would go to her, soothe her and sing to her.

Despite the injection of Holländer money, however, the Frank family bank and business was floundering due to the dire state of the German economy – and the Franks were finding them-selves subject to increasingly virulent antisemitism as the Nazi Party rose to power.

In 1929, Otto's brother-in-law Erich Elias left Frankfurt to open a branch of Opekta in Switzerland. Opekta was part of a company that manufactured pectin, used as a gelling agent in jam, and would play an important role in the Frank family – although Otto did not know it at the time. Leni and son Buddy joined Erich in Basel the following year.

Back in Frankfurt, the Frank family bank and the lozenge

business had seen an enormous dip in profit due to the Wall Street Crash, and Otto began what would become a familiar round of downsizing – moving both businesses into a smaller, cheaper premises.

To make matters worse, the following year Otto's brother Herbert was arrested and sent to prison for committing illegal foreign exchange transactions. Their mother Alice was forced to travel to Paris to ask her nephew Jean-Michel to lend her money to keep up mortgage payments on the house in Mertonstrasse. Although she had managed temporarily to keep the wolf from the door, Otto wrote to her and questioned whether it still made sense to hold on to the house 'from an economic and political point of view'.

The 'political point of view' was already impinging more significantly on the life of the Frank family. Otto had been forced to move his family from their spacious home in Marbachweg when his Nazi landlord decided he could no longer 'stomach' taking rent money from a Jew. The family had moved into a smaller apartment in Ganghoferstrasse, but in December 1932 they were forced to leave there too due to their dire economic circumstances, and go back to the family home on Mertonstrasse.

Otto understood he was merely playing for time. In July 1932, the Nazi Party (NSDAP) had won 230 seats in the Reichstag, and in January 1933 Otto and Edith were visiting friends when they heard on the radio that Hitler had been made Chancellor. Otto recalled that he looked across at Edith and saw her sitting as if turned to stone, but their host for the evening cheerfully piped up: 'Well, let's see what the man can do.' The Franks were already aware of what he could do. Their former domestic servant Kathi Stilgenbauer recalled asking who the 'Brownshirts' were in 1929, and while Otto had tried to make light of it, Edith had looked grave and said they would all find out the answer to that soon enough.

By the time Hitler took power, Otto and Edith had heard the stormtroopers marching past singing 'when Jewish blood spatters off the knife', and they were already discussing how to leave Germany. Yes, the scale of it was daunting, and Otto had already tried and failed to set up a business in Amsterdam in the 1920s. But a new law decreeing forced segregation in schools made the Franks determined to leave. Margot's teachers had been dismissed in favour of Nazi Party officials, and she was forced to sit apart from her non-Jewish classmates. Still, for Otto the question remained: how would he be able to support himself and his family if they went away and gave up more or less everything?

Otto turned to Erich Elias for help, and Erich suggested that he set up an independent branch of Opekta in Amsterdam, financed by an interest-free loan of fl. 15,000 repayable over five years. Otto accepted and the family prepared to leave Germany, with Otto travelling directly to the Netherlands while Edith and the girls stayed in Aachen until they could find a suitable home in Amsterdam. It was an enormous and emotional decision. 'My family had lived in Germany for centuries,' Otto recalled. 'We had many friends and acquaintances but by and by many of the latter deserted us, incited by the National Socialist propaganda.'

Otto took his last photo of his family in Germany in March 1933, using his trusty Leica camera. In the picture, Edith and the children look serious, clutching each other's hands as they stand in Hauptwache Square in central Frankfurt. Three weeks later, on 1 April, the Nazis incited a nationwide boycott of Jewish businesses and began to pass a series of laws banning Jews from most parts of business and social life.

By August, Otto and his family had left Frankfurt, the city of Otto's happy childhood and family life, and embarked on a precarious journey into the unknown. Otto wrote that when the people of his country had turned into nationalist hordes and cruel antisemites, his world had collapsed. He had to face the consequences, and though it hurt him deeply he realised that Germany was not 'the world' – and he left for ever.

For the first few months in Amsterdam, Otto rented a room and travelled to his small Opekta office by tram. During the autumn of 1933 Edith visited him often as they looked for a family home together – finally settling on a modern, light, three-bedroom apartment at 37 Merwedeplein in the Rivieren-buurt, where many other Jewish immigrants were settling. The Franks rented the apartment in December 1933, and by February 1934 both Margot and Anne had joined them. 'One must not lose courage,' Edith Frank wrote to Gertrud Naumann a few days after her arrival, for, unlike her husband and children, Edith was desperately homesick for Germany, lamenting the poorer quality of Dutch clothes, her smaller home, the superiority of German sweets and the hard-to-learn Dutch language. While Otto, Margot and Anne had the advantage of quick assimilation into Dutch culture through work and school and soon began speaking equal parts Dutch and German to each other, Edith struggled through unsuccessful Dutch lessons with a neighbour and began to lean more on her religion – paying weekly visits to the liberal synagogue.

The Franks were only four of the more than 25,000 German Jewish immigrants to enter the Netherlands between 1933 and

1938, and their arrival prompted often hostile and prejudiced reactions. Speaking German on the streets was discouraged. 'It was not about antisemitism then. There was a lot of anger and dislike towards us because we were German. It didn't matter that we were Jewish Germans arriving in the country for fear of our lives; we were simply Germans to the Dutch,' recalled Laureen Nussbaum, whose parents had known the Franks in Frankfurt before emigrating to the Rivierenbuurt in 1936. Nor were the immigrants always greeted warmly by the existing Dutch Jewish community, who often resented their more affluent homes and lifestyles. In the 1930s the Dutch authorities strongly pressured new arrivals to move on to a third country and be resettled elsewhere through the Committee for Jewish Refugees.

By 1939 the number of Jewish people in the Netherlands had grown to 140,000, 60 per cent of whom lived in Amsterdam. In that same year the Dutch government began constructing a large refugee camp, Westerbork, which was later to play a crucial role in the deportment of Jews to Nazi concentration camps.

Despite Edith's homesickness and an undercurrent of anti-German sentiment and antisemitism in Amsterdam, for a few years at least the Franks settled into a happy family existence. Still, it was certainly not the life they had been used to in Germany; Otto travelled constantly to grow his business, but it remained unprofitable until the 1940s, and for many years he relied on family loans. Friends reported that he often looked tired and exhausted. Edith worried about the looming Nazi threat on the border and urged Otto to consider emigrating to somewhere safer, but he did not want to. There were personal tensions too. In 1935 and 1936, Otto employed a Dutch woman, Jetje Jansen, as a tester at Opekta, and her husband Joseph to build display stands for trade exhibitions. In the course of their employment Joseph became convinced Otto and Jetje were having an affair, which sparked a deep hatred towards Otto that lasted for years. The couple divorced, Joseph joined the Dutch SS following the Nazi invasion, and his grudge towards Otto has been suggested, in an unproven claim, as a possible reason for the family's betrayal in 1944. Whatever the truth, it would not be the last time Otto's friendship with a woman led to unhappiness.

For the children, at least, life was less complicated. More families arrived in Merwedeplein, and the Franks made new friends and adopted a cat. Anne and Margot went on holiday to Basel, where their grandmother Alice now lived with Aunt Leni and cousins Stephan and Buddy, learning to ice skate in the winter and spending summer afternoons running around in mountain pastures. Edith's mother, Rosa, also visited from Aachen, and Edith took the girls into the city for visits to shops and museums. Margot was clever at school and wanted to grow up to be a nurse in Palestine. Anne, by contrast, hated mathematics and only worked at the subjects that interested her. 'Anne was a normal, lively child who needed much tenderness and attention and who delighted us and frequently upset us. When she entered a room, there was always a fuss,' Otto recalled. 'Margot was the bright one. Everybody admired her. She got along with everybody ... She was a wonderful person.'

Visiting relatives and friends remembered the sense of warmth in the family. Writing home, Anne and Margot's cousin Stephan reported that he slept very well in his fold-up bed, and that Anne would sit and chat with him at 6 o'clock every morning before Otto woke up and joined them and Margot jumped down from the top bunk. Anne's best friend, Hanneli Goslar, said Otto was 'a wonderful father' and remembered that he would sit with them every night, drinking a beer and tipping the glass up and up, and they would sit open-mouthed waiting for him to spill it – but he never did.

At work Otto had been joined by new employees, some of whom would become family friends and an important part of the Frank family story – most notably Miep Gies, who herself had emigrated to the Netherlands from Austria as a child in 1920. Miep and her husband regularly visited the Franks at home, and she remembered how the Opekta employees had stood silently around the radio when the Nazis swept into Austria and Hitler announced the annexation in 1938. For Edith Frank it was an ominous turning point, and she begged Otto to emigrate to America, where other members of the family had settled. Otto, however, took a more optimistic view and regarded Amsterdam as 'a haven', expecting that the Netherlands would remain neutral and untouched as it had in the First World War. By the time he was forced to face the truth, it was too late.

On 1 September 1939, Germany invaded Poland and two days later was at war with Britain and France. The Second World War had begun, and the Nazi invasion of Denmark and Norway in April 1940 meant that even the Netherlands could no longer ignore the threat on its borders. Otto's cousin Milly recalled getting a letter from Otto saying 'how terribly unhappy he was because he was sure that Germany was going to attack'. While the Franks put on a calm front for their children, they were now frantically working to get out of the country, with Otto using all his old contacts in New York to get immigration papers. His efforts failed. Edith's brothers Walter and Julius had emigrated to Massachusetts and found work with a box company. After growing close to the owner, they got him to agree to sign the necessary papers to bring the Franks to the US, but by the time this had been agreed time was short – and soon the borders had closed. Cousin Milly suggested they might at least send Margot and Anne to live with her in England but, after discussing it, Otto and Edith turned down her offer, saying they could not go through with it. Their daughters meant too much to them, and they could not bear to be parted.

It was a fateful decision. On 10 May 1940, Germany invaded the Netherlands. During four terrifying days of attacks by paratroopers followed by a bombing raid, thousands of Jewish residents tried every avenue of escape – running down to the harbour when they heard, falsely, that boats there would carry them to England. By 14 May the Dutch royal family, the Prime Minister and his Cabinet had fled to England in exile and the Netherlands had capitulated to German rule. The country was now to be governed by Reich commissioner Arthur Seyss-Inquart, who had formerly ruled the Nazi-annexed Austria and instituted a reign of terror against the Jews there.

For the first few months, however, the Nazis proceeded cautiously, not wanting to alienate the Dutch population, who they believed were naturally 'Aryan' and very similar to Germans. Gradually, though, a series of anti-Jewish laws were passed, each more punitive than the last. Jewish companies were required to register, and Dutch citizens were asked to pinpoint Jewish homes on maps. By 1941 Nazi laws prohibited Jews from participating in almost all professions and all areas of social life and entertainment, including going to the beach, the cinema and parks. Jewish children were expelled from their normal schools and sent to special Jewish schools.

During this time Otto and Edith tried to maintain a normal family life. Otto wrote,

> When I think back to the time when a lot of laws were introduced in Holland, due to the occupying power, which made our lives much harder, I have to say that my wife and I did everything in our power to stop the children noticing the trouble we would go to, to make sure this was still a trouble-free time for them.

As ever, he was closest to Anne, choosing to take her away with him for a few days to a hotel in Arnhem, where he could rest and recuperate. Edith held birthday parties for both girls, and they were encouraged to give whatever they could to poor beggars who came to the front door asking for food. At school, Margot continued to study hard, while Anne began to develop crushes on local boys.

Beneath the façade, however, life was becoming intensely difficult for the Franks. At home, Rosa Holländer, who was now living with them, developed cancer and died in 1941 – something Edith and the children found particularly devastating. Under the new laws the entire family was required to register as Jewish with the Nazi authorities, and Otto had been forced to 'Aryanise' his businesses, officially signing them over to the ownership of Dutch members of staff while he secretly continued to run them behind the scenes. Otto's companies were now supplying the German Army with the gelling agent pectin and other goods – but their lives and livelihoods were put under direct threat when Tony Ahlers, a violent antisemite and Nazi collaborator, appeared in Otto's office on 18 April with a blackmail letter.

The letter Ahlers carried was from Joseph Jansen, who had

been nursing his hatred of Otto since the suspected affair with his wife years earlier. In it, Jansen claimed that Otto was supplying the German Army but had been heard to say anti-German things in conversation, including that the war would last years and Germany would suffer terribly. Ahlers demanded a payment to stay quiet – which Otto handed over immediately, sealing the start of an ongoing blackmail relationship which would haunt him. Miep Gies recalled that after Ahlers left the office, Otto emerged looking ashen. According to biographer Carol Ann Lee, Miep said,

> Mr Frank read me the letter and I remember, still today, that it was written in the letter that the Jew Frank was still tied to his company and had expressed himself in an anti-German fashion during a conversation. I don't know who signed the letter, but I deduced from the content that it had been written by the Jansen I knew.

Under such pressure it was hardly surprising that Otto was beginning to crack. Writing in her diary on 7 May 1944, Anne recalled, 'I have never been in such a state as Daddy, who once ran out onto the street with a knife in his hand to end it all.'

It was becoming increasingly clear that the only option for the family was to go into hiding, and hopefully to remain there until the end of the Nazi occupation. It was an eventuality that Otto had been preparing for since 1941, identifying the upstairs annexe of his office at 263 Prinsengracht as the most suitable hiding place, papering out windows and doors and recruiting his trusted staff to begin carrying in supplies of food, plates, cutlery, linen and all that they would need to sustain them.

On 12 June 1942, Anne celebrated her thirteenth birthday, receiving amongst other gifts a diary from her parents. It was a momentous gift, although no one realised it at the time. During those weeks Otto and Edith began preparing the children for the fact they would soon be leaving their normal lives behind them. On 4 July, Otto wrote to his family in Switzerland that everything was fine, although they knew that day by day life was getting harder. 'Please don't be concerned,' he added, 'even if you hear little from us.' In another letter to Julius and Walter, he said he regretted that he would not be able to correspond with the family but was sure they would understand.

The day came on Sunday 5 July, when sixteen-year-old Margot Frank was ordered to report to the SS for deportation to a Nazi labour camp. Thousands of Jewish boys and girls in the Netherlands received a similar order that day, the first in the series of systematic deportations of Jews to the concentration camps that would continue, without pause, for the remainder of the war. Many complied with the order, afraid but not wholly understanding what a terrible fate awaited them.

Margot's friend Laureen Nussbaum claimed that some of her friends wanted to go when the call-up came. They did not expect anything too bad to happen, but their parents begged them to stay and hide. Other parents made their children obey the call-up, in order to save the rest of the family.

The Franks were in no doubt about what it meant, and Otto had already warned his friends about the true atrocities that were occurring in the concentration camps:

It was said that life in the camp, even in the camps in Poland, was not so bad; that the work was hard but there was food enough,

and the persecutions stopped, which was the main thing. I told
a great many people what I suspected. I also told them what
I heard on the British wireless, but a good many still thought
these were atrocity stories.

On the day after the call-up, the Franks decided that their only
option was to immediately go into hiding. Swiftly they left their
apartment at Merwedeplein for the final time, leaving behind
clues that they had fled to Switzerland – and abandoning, much
to her distress, Anne's beloved pet cat. On 6 July 1942, Otto,
Edith, Margot and Anne entered their hiding place in the annexe
of 263 Prinsengracht, and life for all of them changed irrevocably.

The family would live in the annexe for more than two years,
sharing five small rooms with four others – a family they were
already acquainted with, Hermann, Gusti and Peter van Pels,
who joined them on 13 July 1942, and then dentist Fritz Pfeffer,
who arrived on 16 November.

It is this group, with their daily activities, their hopes and
fears and the shifting dynamics of their relationships, that is so
evocatively chronicled by Anne in her diary. In it she writes of
her teenage troubles with her mother, her ever-closer relationship with Otto, her growing sexual awareness, the day-to-day
irritation of those around her – in particular Fritz Pfeffer, whom
she was forced to share a room with – and her blossoming ro-
mance with Peter van Pels. Yet her diary is far from just a record
of the minutiae of daily life; in it she notes down stories, edits
her own previous entries, plans to become a great writer and
looks out on the chestnut tree growing in the yard backing onto
263 Prinsengracht, with dreams full of freedom and the future.

Otto, who had previously been nervous and drawn, became a

supremely calm and unifying figure, structuring the days of the people in the annexe to give a feeling of purpose. Miep Gies noticed that he carried a new sense of composure and displayed a veneer of total control:

> Only with a certain time allocation laid down from the start and with each one having his own duties could we have hoped to live through the situation. Above all the children had to have enough books to read and learn. None of us wanted to think how long this voluntary imprisonment would last.

Under Otto's leadership, they followed a silent timetable of reading, writing and studying in the day. When the offices below were closed, they could then speak, play music and board games and recite poetry. Under the leadership of Edith and Fritz, the group celebrated the Friday-night Sabbath and religious holidays and cooked Jewish recipes.

'I have to say that in a certain way it was a happy time,' Otto later wrote. How fine it was to live in such close contact with the ones he loved, to speak to his wife about the children and future plans, to help the girls with their studies, to read classics with them and have discussions about all kinds of problems and all views about life. All this would not have been possible in a normal life, when he was working all day. 'I remember very well that I once said – when the Allies win, and we survive, we will later look back with gratitude on this time that we have spent here together.'

Those familiar comforts could not keep the world at bay, however, and as they crowded around the radio in the evening, they listened with trepidation to news about the war and Nazi atrocities. Otto said the radio connected them to the world, but prohibited BBC broadcasts told that Jews were regularly being killed by the Nazis by machine-gun fire, hand-grenades – and even by poisoned gas.

Nor was their family time free of the tensions and strains that might be imagined if eight people are crammed into confinement together for two years. Anne wrote unapologetically about her emotions at this time, and it was many of these entries that were controversially edited or excluded by Otto from the first versions of the published diary in the late 1940s.

In an entry on 3 October 1942, relatively soon after they entered captivity, Anne wrote,

> I told Daddy that I'm much more fond of him than Mummy, to which he replied that I'd get over that ... Daddy said that I should sometimes volunteer to help Mummy when she doesn't feel well, or she has a headache; but I shan't since I don't like her and I don't feel like it. I would certainly do it for Daddy, I noticed that when he was ill. Also it's easy for me to picture Mummy dying one day, but Daddy dying one day seems inconceivable to me.

Otto edited this entry substantially in the first published diary, wanting to spare his wife's memory and writing, 'In reality she was an excellent mother, who went to all lengths for her children.'

Other entries vanished completely, including this one:

> I used to be jealous of Margot's relationship with Daddy before, there is no longer any trace of that now; I still feel hurt when

Daddy treats me unreasonably because of his nerves, but then I think, 'I can't really blame you people for being like that, you talk so much about children and the thoughts of young people – but you don't know the first thing about them!' I long for more than Daddy's kisses, for more than his caresses. Isn't it terrible for me to keep thinking about this all of the time?

In the closing paragraphs of the diary, Anne expresses her fury at her mother:

I can't talk to her. I can't look lovingly into those cold eyes, I can't. Not ever! If she even had one quality an understanding mother is supposed to have, gentleness or friendliness or something, I'd keep trying to get closer to her. But as for loving this person, this mocking creature – it's becoming more and more impossible every day!

Despite Anne's teenaged tensions with her mother, Edith did support her daughter. It was Edith who sympathised with Anne's fears of being discovered when the others went downstairs in the evening to listen to the radio, and who supported Anne in wanting to keep a light on when German and Allied aircraft flew over, because she was frightened of the dark. Yet Otto was undoubtedly Anne's main source of emotional comfort, as evidenced throughout the diary. It is him she turns to to talk about other people in the annexe, her own growing sexual awareness – 'Daddy told me about prostitutes etc., but in all there were still a lot of questions that haven't been answered' – and her relationship with Peter van Pels.

These are issues that might have been more traditionally

shared between mother and daughter, but Otto and Anne had always been close. 'The one person who visibly meant something to Anne was her father. That was always apparent,' Miep Gies wrote. The feeling appears to have been mutual, as Otto's descriptions of his other daughter, Margot, always seem strangely wooden and one-dimensional. Margot is always described as studious, hard-working, almost perfect in her silent compliance. While Otto writes worryingly about his fears that Anne was too lively to adapt to confinement, he dismisses his elder daughter with the words, 'Margot, who was more mature, would come to terms with our situation.' After the war Otto discovered, to his amazement, that Margot also kept a diary during their time in the annexe, but as it was never found we know only a few of her thoughts and feelings that she exchanged with Anne and which Anne recorded in her diary. As Otto devoted himself with full energy and fervour to Anne's legacy through the publication of her diary after the war, Margot would recede further and further in his thoughts and comments. 'Otto never spoke much about Margot,' Otto's friend Father John Neiman commented in the 1970s.

Anne made her final entry in her diary on Tuesday 1 August 1944. In it she writes with characteristic insight about what she sees as the two sides to her personality – the light-hearted, 'boy crazy', flirtatious Anne who acts like a 'frolicsome little goat', and the other, deeper, more serious, quieter Anne. It is a topic she had explored in her previous entries – prompted by a book from the library called *What Do You Think of the Modern Young Girl?* On Saturday 15 July, Anne began dissecting her thoughts about the book and about herself, writing critically and at length about her relationship with her father, stating that she pushes him away and conceals her true feelings from him because he always takes an older, 'fatherly' attitude towards her and talks to her as if she is a child. 'Anyone who claims that the older ones have a more difficult time here certainly doesn't realize to what extent our problems weigh down on us, problems for which we are probably much too young,' she wrote on 15 July 1944.

Anne wrote that she saw the approaching thunder and felt the suffering of millions but concluded, 'If I look up into the heavens, I think that it will all come out all right.' In the end peace and tranquillity would return, and Anne could be once again a young girl able to hold on to her ideals, particularly that 'people are really good at heart'. That was the difficulty posed by the times they were living through, pondered Anne: 'Ideals, dreams and cherished hopes rise within us, only to meet the horrible truth and be shattered.'

After two years in hiding, the moment of horrible truth had arrived for the Franks. Three days after Anne locked her diary inside Otto's briefcase for the final time, the Gestapo raided 263 Prinsengracht on 4 August 1944.

'It was around ten-thirty,' Otto remembered. 'I was upstairs by the van Pelses in Peter's room and I was helping him with his schoolwork. I didn't hear anything. And then when I did hear something I didn't pay any attention to it.' The telephone call to SD headquarters had been made earlier that morning, notifying Gestapo officer Julius Dettmann that Jews were hiding behind an office building at 263 Prinsengracht. Dettmann instructed staff sergeant Karl Josef Silberbauer to lead an immediate raid on the premises.

The Nazi occupying forces in the Netherlands had offered payment in exchange for information about hidden Jews since the start of the deportations to the concentration camps, and betrayals were common. Of the 25–30,000 Jews who had gone into hiding, around 9,000 were caught, often stemming from information from the local Dutch population, neighbours, former friends and even family members with scores to settle. A group of so-called Jew hunters roamed the streets, making a living from ferreting out information and passing it on to the Gestapo. By the summer of 1944, the price of betrayal had gone up as the Nazis increased payments to try to catch the last Jewish families who had slipped through their net.

Over the years there have been many theories about who betrayed the Frank family. In her book *The Hidden Life of Otto Frank*, Carol Ann Lee makes the case that they were betrayed by Tony Ahlers. Others have claimed it was someone who worked at 263 Prinsengracht, perhaps in the warehouse. Or Ans van Dijk, a Jewish woman who, after being arrested herself, was given the choice between deportation and helping the authorities track down other Jews. She opted for the latter and disclosed the whereabouts of many Jewish families. And a recent cold-case investigation by a former FBI agent suggested Arnold van den Bergh from Amsterdam's Jewish Council was responsible. After many years of examination and debate, the truth of who betrayed the family remains unproven.

Whoever made the call to Julius Dettmann, what remains indisputable is that by the summer of 1944 many local people knew that there were Jewish people hiding at 263 Prinsengracht, and there had been several break-ins at the address and nearby buildings, widening the net of suspects even further. Otto didn't know who had betrayed them, but he understood that 'when the Gestapo came in with their guns, that was the end of everything'.

Hearing footsteps squeaking on the stairs that morning, Otto stood up from where he'd been working with Peter van Pels. The door opened and a man was standing in front of them with a gun in his hand. Otto and Peter were ordered downstairs, where they found Edith, Margot, Anne and the van Pels standing with their hands in the air. Fritz Pfeffer soon joined them, held at gunpoint by another Gestapo agent. An hour later, the families were led from the building into a waiting police van, each carrying a small bag of belongings. Otto remembered that Anne did not look at her diary, the pages of which were left scattered on the floor. 'Perhaps she had a premonition that all was lost now.'

After a terrifying interrogation at Gestapo headquarters and a night in the cells, the Franks were transported from Amsterdam Centraal Station to Westerbork, the former Jewish refugee camp that had become, since the Nazi occupation, an infamous holding camp for deportation to the concentration camps of the east. At Centraal Station, two sisters in the resistance, Lin and Janny Brilleslijper, noticed the Franks, in particular a very worried father and a nervous mother, and two children wearing sports clothes and backpacks.

Westerbork was a dusty wasteland where, under the guard of largely Dutch SS, Jewish men, women and children were imprisoned in barracks, fed poorly and forced to work in dirty and degrading conditions. At Westerbork, the Franks remained quiet and calm. According to Carol Ann Lee, Vera Cohn, who took down their details upon arrival, noticed 'their composure as they grouped around my typing desk in the receiving room. Despite the bitter and fearful emotions that welled in him, Mr Frank refused to compromise his dignity as a person.' Others remember that Edith, Margot and Anne clung to each other in quiet depression and desperation, while Otto, as ever thinking of his youngest daughter, managed to strike a deal to move Anne out of the filthy battery factory where the family had been assigned to work.

The conditions at Westerbork were terrible and utterly shocking – yet for all those who were arrested and taken there, the real fear was not the conditions in the camp but the weekly transport that left for the extermination camps in Poland. Those incarcerated in Westerbork would do everything and anything to avoid being put on the list of those to be deported, but few succeeded in escaping that terrible fate.

On the warm evening of 2 September 1944, the announcement was made of the following day's transport of 1,019 men, women and children. The Franks were on the list. Otto and the family had been eagerly listening to the news of the Allied invasion that summer, praying that their advance across Europe would halt the deportations in time. When he heard the news that the family had not escaped transportation, Otto ran desperately all over Westerbork, trying everything to save his family. 'Otto Frank went all over the place. He had the illusion he could go to Theresienstadt,' Janny Brilleslijper recalled, referring to the concentration camp that the Nazis had falsely held up as having 'model' conditions and where well-known German Jews and former German Army officers had been sent earlier in the war. But nothing could be done. On the morning of 3 September, Otto, Edith, Margot, Anne, the van Pels and Fritz Pfeffer were forced onto a locked cattle truck destined for Auschwitz. They did not know it, but the Allied advance would indeed stop the deportations. The Franks were on the last transport from Westerbork to Auschwitz.

Lin and Janny Brilleslijper were crowded into the same cattle truck, and Lin later recalled the terrible journey across Europe. Six prisoners sawed a hole in the floor of their truck to escape onto the tracks below. One was killed, and two more lost hands but were saved by local people. The others who had been in the escape truck were crushed back inside, where now no one could sit, and the smell was terrible.

After three burning-hot days and nights crammed together with no food or sanitation, the train eventually pulled to a halt in the middle of the night. Rose de Liema, who was in the same truck as the Franks, recalled the darkness. Outside they could hear shouts and screams, machinery and dogs barking. It was night, and the chimneys were burning with huge, bright flames. The SS beat everybody with sticks and guns. It was like arriving in hell.

Auschwitz, its neighbouring concentration camp for women, Birkenau, and its sprawling complex of satellite work camps was a vast city of death. At its heart, of course, were the gas chambers, where millions of Jews were sent directly to their deaths. Selection started immediately as disorientated families were herded off the trains and sorted into separate lines for men and women. At the head of each line, SS guards picked through the prisoners. Those who could work were pulled to one side, while the young, old and sick were immediately transported to be murdered in the gas chambers.

As the SS ruthlessly separated the men and women, Otto Frank managed one last look above the terrified hordes of people to see his family. He had done everything he could to save them, but there was nothing he could do now. Otto later told his relatives: 'I shall remember the look in Margot's eyes for the rest of my life.'

At fifty-five years old, Otto Frank was on the borderline for immediate removal to the gas chambers – but his strong demeanour saved him, and he was moved into the group allowed to live and work along with Fritz Pfeffer and Hermann and Peter van Pels. Edith, Margot and Anne were also allowed to live, but Otto did not know their fate. Instead, he began the 2-mile walk to Auschwitz Camp I, where he would be stripped, shaved and handed wooden clogs and a ragged striped uniform. Holding out his left forearm, he was branded with the prisoner number B-9174.

The average life expectancy for a Jew at Auschwitz was only six weeks, but Otto survived the terrible conditions, starvation, slave labour and crippling illness for five months – holding on against all odds until the liberation of the camp by Soviet forces in January 1945.

In that time, he developed a mental strategy for survival, much as he had done to steer his family through the difficult years of hiding in the annexe. Befriending a young man called Sal de Liema, who had arrived on the same transport, Otto asked him to call him Papa, something Sal initially refused as his own father had also been on the transport and was sent to the gas chambers. Otto explained, 'I'm the type of man who needs this, I need someone to be a Papa for.' Otto devised a mental plan never to talk about food or the terrible things happening at the camp – instead they would sustain themselves by talking about music and opera, even singing when they could.

As the months passed, each of Otto's friends from the annexe went to their deaths. Hermann van Pels was the first to die, about a month after their arrival at Auschwitz. Having snagged his thumb while digging a trench, he asked to work indoors. The SS agreed, but the next day Otto watched as Hermann van Pels was selected and led away to the gas chamber. Two hours later, a lorry drove past with their clothing.

Dentist Fritz Pfeffer was the next to go. Pfeffer volunteered to be one of sixty physicians in the camp to be transported to the Sachsenhausen concentration camp near Berlin. On 29 October 1944 he boarded the train, supposedly destined for Germany. He was never heard from again.

The last to go was young Peter. By early January 1945 Soviet forces were nearing the camp, planes circled overhead and prisoners could hear nearby artillery. In a panic the Germans had already begun to set fire to the paperwork that meticulously recorded their crimes in the SS administration block, dismantle the electrified fences and send back to Germany what supplies and stolen goods remained from their murdered prisoners. The SS were determined not to allow the surviving prisoners to be left behind, and on direct orders from Hitler they rounded up any fit men and women to embark on 'death marches' to other concentration camps deeper behind Nazi lines in Austria and Germany. In mid-January, Soviet planes attacked the Auschwitz area and destroyed the kitchen and food depot at Birkenau, and by 17 January Red Army units were approaching the nearby city of Kraków from the north and north-west. The following day, Peter van Pels visited Otto in the hospital barracks, where he was suffering from exhaustion. Peter was now eighteen and had become even closer to Otto during their time at the camp. 'Peter acted like a son to me,' Otto wrote. 'Every day he brought me extra food … We never discussed serious matters and we never spoke about Anne. I did not have the impression that he had matured much.'

Peter told Otto that the camp was being evacuated, and he was leaving. Otto had heard about the dangers of the death marches and begged him to stay, but Peter was convinced his best chance of survival was to leave rather than hide in the sick barracks. 'I'll make it,' he told Otto.

Peter van Pels left Auschwitz and walked to the Mauthausen concentration camp in Austria, notorious for its quarry and terrible conditions. Once there, he was put to work in the mines of the Melk satellite camp but fell ill from the hard labour and died on 10 May 1945, five days after the camp had been liberated by American troops.

On 19 January, the last able prisoners left Auschwitz and Birkenau, leaving behind 6,000 former inmates deemed too sick to travel or work, including Otto Frank. For the next few days those left behind struggled, alone, to survive. Bombing raids by the Soviets had cut electricity to the camp, and there was no food, water, heat or light. Trapped, the former prisoners scavenged what food they could find and broke the ice on frozen ponds to boil drinking water. For Otto, there was another terrifying ordeal to endure on 25 January, when a detachment of SS soldiers returned to the camp unexpectedly and dragged survivors outside, screaming and shouting at them. Otto feared that execution was imminent. 'We knew why we were there,' he said. 'We were finished.' The SS had received orders to return to the camp and liquidate every remaining prisoner, but just as they raised their guns to fire, a series of loud explosions filled the air and an armoured car with SS soldiers appeared at the gate.

'Return to barracks!' they shouted, and within seconds all the soldiers had disappeared.

Otto later found out they had received news that the Soviet forces were less than 10 miles from the camp. For two days the fighting continued, and the SS returned once more to blow up the crematorium at Birkenau. Then, on 27 January, the first scouts from the 60th Army of the First Ukrainian Front saw the remaining barbed-wire fences of Auschwitz. Like all survivors, Otto was indescribably relieved and grateful when the first Soviet soldiers, dressed in snow-white winter suits, arrived in the hospital barracks. 'They were good people. We did not care if they were communists or not. We were not concerned with politics, we were concerned with our liberation.'

Liberation had come, but the next few weeks remained incredibly perilous for the survivors of Auschwitz and Birkenau. Many more died due to weakness and disease. Some tragically died after eating food the Soviets gave them, as starvation meant their digestive systems were too weak to cope.

Soon the women from Birkenau were brought to the Auschwitz main camp for their own safety, and plans were made to evacuate them all further behind Soviet lines as fighting with the Nazis continued.

Otto's only thought at this time was to find Edith, Margot and Anne, and he asked every woman entering the building what had happened to his family. There was no news. One girl he recognised was Eva Geiringer, a teenager from a family of Austrian refugees who had lived across the square in Merwedeplein with her father Erich, mother Fritzi and brother Heinz. Eva had stayed behind in Birkenau with her mother, but her father and brother had left Auschwitz on the death march to

Mauthausen. Meeting Otto again, Eva remembered that he looked vaguely familiar. He was middle-aged with hardly any face left at all, 'just a skeleton's skull'. Still a gentleman, however, Otto stood and bowed to Eva.

As he searched for definite news of his family, Otto began keeping a simple diary in a small notebook the Soviets had given him. Preparing for evacuation from Auschwitz and what would become a long journey home across war-torn Europe, Otto finally found the strength to write to his mother in Switzerland. On 23 February 1945 he wrote,

Dearest Mother,

I hope that these lines get to you and all the ones I love the news that I have been saved by the Russians, that I am well, and full of good spirit, and being looked after well in every respect.

Where Edith and the children are, I do not know. We have been apart since 5 September 1944. I merely heard that they had been transported to Germany. One has to be hopeful to see them back well and healthy.

Please tell my brothers-in-law and my friends in Holland of my liberation. I long to see you all again and hope that this will be possible. If only you are all well. Indeed, when will I be able to receive news from you?

All my love,

Greetings and kisses,

Your son,

Otto

CHAPTER 2

THE DIARY

'Nothing of my household is left, not a photo,
not a letter of my children, nothing, nothing.'
OTTO FRANK IN A LETTER TO MILLY STANFIELD,
18 MARCH 1945

Otto Frank survived Auschwitz and returned to Amsterdam a shattered man. His one hope was that he would
see his family again – but as he journeyed across Europe, down
to the Black Sea and around by ocean to France, he discovered
the devastating news that his wife Edith had died of illness and
exhaustion in Birkenau.

Otto recorded the details of his long journey in his notebook.
On 3 March 1945, Russian troops had transported the camp
survivors by train to the Polish city of Katowice, where they
stayed in the Ferdinand collection centre in the middle of the
town. It was here that Otto had his first proper bath in eighteen
months and was given two shirts, a pair of trousers and food.
Otto reported that the local people were hospitable, and on his
second day he was invited to eat at a local woman's house. In

letters to his mother and to Milly Stanfield in London, Otto admitted that he now looked like a beggar and weighed only about 115 pounds. On 22 March, he learned the first piece of devastating news about what had happened to his family.

Sitting alone at a long table at the Ferdinand school, he recognised Rootje de Winter, whom he remembered from Westerbork. Rootje told him that on 5 September, she and her daughter Judith had been placed in a barrack with Edith, Margot and Anne. On 30 October, there had been a mass selection – those separated to the right would be gassed immediately, those on the left would be transported to another camp. Anne and Margot were chosen for the transport and left Birkenau believing that their mother had been sent to the gas chamber. But that was not her fate. While waiting to be taken to the gas chambers, Edith, Rootje and about twenty other women escaped to another barrack. Soon after, however, Edith fell ill with a high temperature and was moved to the 'hospital' barracks. At Auschwitz the hospital was a place to be greatly feared; patients received no medical help whatsoever and were often selected to be gassed, experimented on or directly murdered by the SS staff under the oversight of Dr Josef Mengele. A few days after Edith was admitted, Rootje saw her for the last time. She was, Rootje wrote, a shadow of herself. A few days later, she died, totally worn out.

Upon hearing the news Otto remained motionless and then laid his head on the table. In his diary he wrote, 'Mrs de Winter, Zutphen. Message of death of Edith on 6 January 1945, in the hospital from weakness without suffering. Children Oct, to Sudetenland, very brave, esp Anne, miss special Anne.' After waiting for a few days, Otto tried to compose a letter with the news for his mother, struggling to do so, as he told her, because the news had affected him so badly.

> She is another person murdered by the Germans. If she had managed to survive another two weeks everything would have been different after the liberation by the Russians. I have to ask myself whether we can get to Holland, I do not know. I hope, however, that we can still get there, in spite of the fact that Holland is still not liberated. I do not wish to write any more today.

Otto left Katowice on a Russian transport train on 1 April 1945, heading first to Czernowitz and then eventually to the Ukrainian port of Odessa – recording en route his observations on the shattered, war-ravaged landscapes and the local people who bartered with him for food. After a month in Odessa, Otto learned that finally he would be transported back to France by ship. He felt great joy at the news but also mistrust. So much had gone wrong in his life – could he allow himself to believe that he would finally return home?

Boarding the New Zealand ship the *Monowai*, Otto and other survivors left Odessa on 21 May, bound for Marseille. Otto awoke the following morning hopeful for the future, and longing for his children: 'My entire hope lies with the children. I cling to the conviction that they are alive and that we'll be together again, but I'm not promising myself anything. We have all experienced too much to pin our hopes on that kind of thing. Only the children, *only the children* count.'

Otto landed in Marseille on 27 May and travelled by train across France, arriving in Amsterdam on 3 June 1945. Upon arrival, a Red Cross worker marked his card 'Return!' and he went by car to Miep Gies's, where he discovered that his employees Kugler and Kleiman and Fritz Pfeffer's wife Lotte were all healthy. 'What a joy to see each other again, and how much grief!'

Miep Gies remembered that she opened the door to her apartment and found Otto standing there. 'We looked at each other. There were no words. He was thin, but he'd always been thin. "Miep," he said quietly. "Miep, Edith is not coming back … but I have great hope for Anne and Margot."' Overcome with emotion, Miep led Otto inside, where he would stay as a guest of the Gies family for seven years.

Otto returned to a city very different to the one he had last lived in as a free man. Only a quarter of the 140,000 Jews who had lived in the Netherlands before the war survived – a smaller percentage than any other West European country. Their transport to the death camps had 'worked wonderfully' according to Nazis like Adolf Eichmann, and had continued seamlessly and uninterrupted for years. Few had managed to hide, many had been betrayed. Those who did return discovered that they were no longer welcome. The Dutch 'hunger winter' in the last year of the war had hardened local attitudes to taking back returning Jews, and some found that local Dutch families had moved into their homes or wouldn't return possessions given to them for safekeeping before deportation. Antisemitism was rife. 'I'm sorry to say that the war and Hitler propaganda had a very bad influence,' Otto wrote with dismay.

After spending an evening with his friends, Otto got up the following morning on 4 June and went back to his office on Prinsengracht. It was almost unbearable, but Otto opened the door to the annexe and walked around the few rooms that had been the last home for his family. Anne's pictures of film stars and Princesses Elizabeth and Margaret were still on her bedroom wall. The map of Normandy where Otto had begun to track the Allied advance remained as it was, frozen in time. On the floor Otto saw a few brown beans that had spilled from a sack Peter had been carrying. Without a thought, he picked them up and put them in his pocket – where he would always keep them. For Otto, the task of finding his children and re-building his life had begun.

In the immediate aftermath of the war, the business situation in the Netherlands was terrible. Nonetheless, Otto had no choice but to return to work and find a way to make money and pay his loyal employees. His overriding obsession, however, was discovering the whereabouts of Margot and Anne. 'Everything is like a strange dream,' he wrote to his mother. 'In reality, I can't sort myself out yet ... I don't know where the children are, but I never stop thinking of them.'

Otto visited people he had known, scoured the lists of survivors printed in the newspapers, placed adverts asking for information about them and called the Red Cross for news. Anne's schoolfriend Jacqueline van Maarsen recalled being unsettled by Otto's visit. He came alone, his sad eyes staring out of his sunken face. Edith was dead, he told her, but he still knew nothing about Anne and Margot. Hope sustained him, but he was beginning to doubt. On 21 June, Otto wrote to his sister Leni that he had been convinced he would see the children, but now he wasn't sure. How could he go on without them?

It would be another agonising month before Otto discovered that both Margot and Anne were dead. Reading the Red Cross lists on 18 July 1945, Otto saw the names 'Annelies Marie Frank' and 'Margot Betti Frank', and next to both names – crosses. Otto found out who had reported the news and travelled to the home of Lin Brilleslijper. Lin and her sister Janny had been transported from Auschwitz to the camp at Bergen-Belsen. Lin and Janny had found two threadbare, scrawny girls wrapped in blankets at the water pipe. They looked like 'little frozen birds'. Those girls were Margot and Anne. Lin remembered seeing Anne and Margot a few days later in the sick barracks and begging them to leave as a typhus epidemic was ripping through the camp. Margot could not speak due to her high fever, but Anne said, 'Here we can lie together and be at peace.'

Within a few days Margot fell from her plank bed and died on the floor. Anne, wracked with typhus and hallucinations, met the Brilleslijper sisters again up on the open heath at Belsen: 'Anne stood in front of me, wrapped in a blanket … she told me that she had such a horror of the lice and the fleas that she had thrown all of her clothes away.' Anne died at Bergen-Belsen in March 1945, and Lin and her sister carried both Anne's and Margot's bodies to the mass graves for burial. Three weeks later the camp was liberated by the Allies.

Otto recorded the terrible news in his notebook only with a single * and the words Lien Rebling (a misspelling of Lin's name). He asked his brother Robert to write and inform the rest of his family. Two weeks later, Otto wrote to Milly Stanfield that he would never be able to bear the reality of his children's deaths. 'Nobody can really help me, although I have many friends. Useless to say much about it.' Although he did not know it, the only remaining item from his family life was Anne's diary, salvaged by Miep after the Gestapo raid on the annexe. Miep had not handed it over to Otto immediately, as she had still hoped that Anne would return and she could give it back to her.

'Miep by chance saved [a photograph album] and Anne's diary, but I don't have the strength to read it,' Otto told his mother. 'There's nothing of Margot's left anymore, only her Latin work, because our whole household was looted, and that's why everything we used so often and all Edith's and the children's lovely little possessions are lost.' Although he knew that there was no sense in thinking about them, he was a human being with a heart, and he couldn't help himself.

Otto's stepdaughter Eva Geiringer (later Schloss) recalled that Otto sat in their living room and unwrapped the diary with trembling hands.

Otto arrived carrying a small bundle wrapped up in paper and string. He was almost shaking with emotion as he told us that Miep Gies … had found the diary in the attic after they were arrested, and kept it waiting for Anne to return … Then with great feeling, Otto unwrapped the parcel and began to read some extracts to us. He read slowly, but he was trembling, and couldn't get far without breaking down in tears. He was astonished by the daughter he discovered in the pages, an Anne he did not recognize with deep thoughts and feelings about the world.

Eva and her mother Fritzi were astonished too. 'None of us could have imagined in our wildest dreams that the diary would be published – let alone that it would become an historic piece of literature that would change the world.'

For Otto, however, the discovery was his only reason to keep living, even if at first he could hardly bear to read it. In the weeks leading up to his discovery, Otto described his weariness, loneliness and sheer hopelessness in letters to his mother. He tried to keep busy and distract himself with friends and work, but business was terrible, he couldn't sleep, and he admitted that he was only skimming over the surface of life, trying not to think too deeply. In truth, he was a hollowed-out man, and he knew it. Writing to his mother about a children's festival at the synagogue Margot and Anne regularly attended, he said that while on the outside he was smiling, on the inside he was crying bitterly. Finding Anne's diary could not replace his lost children, but it was a living link to the past.

'What I'm reading in her book is so indescribably exciting,' Otto exclaimed to his family in late September 1946. 'I read on and on, I cannot explain it to you! I've not finished reading it yet, and I want to read it right through before I make some excerpts or translation for you. She writes about her growing up with incredible self-criticism.' Later he added, 'I can't put Anne's diary down. It's just so astonishing … I don't want to let it out of my hands for a moment, and it is being translated into German for you.' In his initial excitement to make excerpts for his family and create a first German translation, Otto could not have known that he was beginning the long process of shaping, editing and mediating the text from Anne's own varied notes, fictional stories and edits into a published work that would become *The Diary of Anne Frank*.

Miep Gies still resisted reading the text herself, but she remembered how Otto would spend hours after dinner in their shared apartment working on the diary, only to emerge, shaking his head in astonishment at what he'd read. 'He thought it was a war document, written by an intelligent child, during their time in hiding. At that time there was no talk of publishing ... It was private.'

Otto later wrote that reading the diary, slowly, a few pages at a time, was a revelation to him and uncovered a completely different Anne to the child he had lost. He had no idea of the depth of her thoughts and feelings. He was unaware that she knew so much of Jewish suffering over the centuries, or that the chestnut tree she looked at through the attic window was so important to her. These were emotions and ideas Anne had kept to herself, but through her descriptions, every detail of life in the attic became clear to Otto again.

Even at this early stage the development of the diary was a collaboration – and a mediation. Anne, of course, was the original writer, but Otto was now editing, choosing excerpts and typing up a Dutch text. This typed transcript was handed over to a friend of Otto, former journalist Anneliese Schütz, who attempted to recapture the spirit of a young girl in German. Schütz was about fifty years old and had been a journalist in Berlin before fleeing to the Netherlands in the 1930s, where she'd done various jobs, one of which was teaching literature to children including Margot Frank. Like the Franks, Schütz was deported by the Nazis to the Dutch camp at Westerbork, but was then sent to Theresienstadt where she survived the war and returned to Amsterdam in the summer of 1945. One of Otto's friends remembered she wore heavy glasses, had a Berlin 'snappiness' and carried herself with a strong sense of professional confidence. Otto's plan was to send the German excerpts Schütz translated and edited to his family in Switzerland, and at the same time he began typing another version of Anne's diary. This time, he had publication in mind.

Anne herself had undertaken the first edit of her diary after hearing a radio broadcast where the Dutch Minister for Education, Arts and Sciences, Gerrit Bolkestein, asked the people of the Netherlands to add documents, diaries and letters to a repository which would record life in the country during the war years. Bolkestein made the radio broadcast on 28 March 1944 and Anne began to rewrite her diary that month with the aim of publishing it herself. Otto's new transcript included those rewritten excerpts, the original diary entries which concluded three days before the family's capture, and four chapters from Anne's book of *Tales* which talked about their life in hiding.

Otto was conscious of his role as editor and the decisions he made. He shaped the text, cutting and pasting together excerpts and entries onto new sheets of paper, agonising as he went over what was too mundane, personal or hurtful to include.

In November, Otto wrote to his cousin Milly:

> It does not grieve me what she writes and I know quite well that there are several things she did not see right and she would have changed her ideas. In fact she was on very good terms with her mother at the camp later, but it is a disagreeable feeling to publish things against her mother, but I have to do it. There are passages I can scrape [*sic*], what she thought about my marrying Edith, our marriage, her views on politics … and others…

Otto was acutely sensitive to Anne's comments about her hatred for her mother, her suspicion that her parents did not have a passionate and loving marriage and her own romanticised feelings for her father. These comments were immediately excised.

Others, including potentially hurtful descriptions of the people Anne shared the attic with, remained.

Although Anne had begun editing her diary for inclusion into a Dutch post-war archive, Otto originally conceived of a published diary as an educational tool to teach young Germans about the persecution of the Jews and the Holocaust. As he prepared the text, he carried it around Amsterdam in a small case, showing it to various friends and acquaintances and asking for their opinions on the editing process and publication.

Writer Kurt Baschwitz, who lived near the Franks' old apartment on Merwedeplein, told Otto that the diary should be published as authentically as possible, and called it a literary masterpiece. Kurt's daughter Ida had bumped into Otto on the street.

> He cried when he saw me and said that at least I was still here. He had with him a little briefcase in which he kept Anne's diary, notebooks and loose papers. He told about how these were found after the raid of the annexe, that Margot had also kept a diary and that Anne and Margot wrote each other letters.

When Otto visited the Baschwitz house he gave the diary to Kurt and his daughter to read. 'Otto Frank came from a business environment and my father was one of his few intellectual friends, who even wrote books himself,' Ida recalled.

> I thought Anne wrote very unkindly about her mother and Margot and that that should be removed, also because it did not seem Anne's intention to make the diary public. Otto Frank and my father agreed. That also applied to Anne's passages of sexual

confessions. I remember one sentence in which Anne, very Oedipus-like, wanted more from her father than just friendship and I think Otto Frank destroyed that bit.

Above all, Otto told Kurt that he thought the diary should be published for children, especially German children, and he wanted to know whether Ida agreed that it would be popular with young people. Although Kurt strongly supported publication, neither he nor Ida believed it would have much influence on the mindsets of the German youth who were emerging from the Nazi years.

As he would do for the rest of his life, Otto took any divergence from his view of the diary as a deep personal slight and rejection. His disagreement with Kurt Baschwitz was the source of a falling-out between the two men – and was the first of many such disagreements that would overshadow the rest of Otto's life and frequently bring him to the point of emotional collapse.

Other old friends buoyed him with less critical responses, even if they were privately uncertain of the diary's worth.

Jacqueline van Maarsen was unsure why anyone would want to read the thoughts of a young child and was worried about the descriptions about herself, although Otto assured her she would appear under an assumed name. One of Anne's other close friends, Hilde Goldberg, bumped into Otto walking down the street in Amsterdam, and they both burst into tears talking about what had happened to their families in the war. Otto told Hilde about the diary, and she told him he should publish it. Why not, she mused; it was all he had left.

Otto also showed the text to his friends Werner and Jetty Cahn, who worked with the publisher Querido. Jetty had known

Otto since they had roomed in the same boarding house in Amsterdam upon their arrival in 1933. Werner, a German Jewish refugee and left-wing journalist for the newspaper *De Nieuwe Stem*, recalled how Otto would turn up with loose handwritten sheets from Anne's diary and read extracts to them. 'The diary made a great impression on us and I told Otto Frank that I would be willing to try to find a publisher. I advised him to keep hold of the original, and get it typed first.'

Getting the support of two people who worked in publishing boosted Otto's spirits immensely and suddenly made the prospect seem more than a dream. 'Next Friday is the big decision,' Otto wrote to his mother, 'but already I have the impression: publish without a doubt!' It was hard to take in what this really meant, Otto went on. The diary would come out in German and English, reporting everything that occurred when they were in hiding – all the fears, disputes, food, politics, the Jewish question, the weather, moods, problems of growing up, birthdays and reminiscences – in short, everything.

Otto's initial hopes, however, were dashed. Before the typescript was ready, Cahn approached her boss, Alice van Eugenvan Nahuys, at Querido about a possible publication, 'which she rejected haughtily'. The same happened with German publisher Gottfried Beermann Fisher (of S. Fischer Verlag), who was in Amsterdam at the time. Kurt Baschwitz sent the manuscript to publisher Blast, but they also turned the book down.

Amsterdam remained a city ravaged by the Second World War, with a poor and traumatised population. Otto wandered the streets, no more than another faceless returning refugee, sometimes bumping into familiar faces from the old days and bursting into tears over everything he had lost. His family was dead, his business on the brink of ruin. Relying on handouts from old friends, Otto was effectively homeless, living with Miep. Yet even at such a dire impasse – or perhaps because he had nothing else left of value – Otto was completely committed to the extraordinary idea that Anne's diary was worthy of publication and had a message the whole world could learn from. This would become his core, burning strongly in him for the rest of his life.

Undeterred by rejection, Otto pressed ahead and in December 1945 asked another friend, Ab Cauvern, a dramatist with the Workers Broadcasting Channel, to correct the manuscript for typing errors and remove Germanisms from the Dutch text. The Cauverns knew the Franks before the war, and Ab's wife Isa was Otto's secretary. 'Otto Frank came to see us in Laren – he was still living with the Gies family in Amsterdam – and my wife offered to type out the diary. And that is what happened,' Ab said. 'I read through the typescript and corrected typing errors in the margin. Finally, I added a closing word.' Cauvern's postscript read simply: 'Anne's diary ended here. On August 4th the Green Police [Gestapo] made a raid on the "Secret Annexe".'

As the new round of corrections was taking place, Otto was preparing to finally visit his family in Switzerland – a daunting process as travel in Europe in the immediate aftermath of the war remained a chaotic and almost impossible feat, especially for 'stateless' refugees and Jews. Yet he could hardly contain his enthusiasm for his work on Anne's diary, writing to his mother in mid-December that the Cauverns were making corrections as 'I have got so far with it now, and I would like to have it finished so I can show it to publishers … I can hardly get away from it all, and do not want to either.'

Otto finally arrived in Switzerland for the New Year of 1946 and spent almost a month surrounded by his closest family in the house on Herbstgasse in Basel. He later told them it had been wonderful to be with them again, but he avoided talking too much about the war years and the tragedies that had followed, for fear of reopening the wounds and breaking down. 'There is no point in wasting away in mourning, no point in brooding,' Otto told his nephew Buddy, although he would confess to friends that he often put on a brave face, while inside he felt that his life was entirely over.

When he returned to Amsterdam in late January 1946, Otto gave the revised manuscript of Anne's diary to Werner Cahn, who showed it to Annie Romein-Verschoor and her husband Jan Romein, the latter being another left-wing writer and highly respected Dutch historian who knew Cahn through his work at *De Nieuwe Stem*. 'After the typescript was finished, I wanted someone else's opinion,' Werner said. 'I took the typescript to Anne Romein-Verschoor, whose opinion I held in high regard. Jan Romein saw the typescript that night. He read it in one go and immediately wrote his article for *Het Parool*.'

Het Parool was an influential newspaper popular after the war for its allegiance with the Dutch resistance, and Romein's story appeared on the front page the next day, on 3 April 1946, titled 'A Child's Voice': 'By chance a diary written during the war years has come into my possession,' Romein wrote. 'The Netherlands State Institute for War Documentation already holds some 200 similar diaries, but I should be very much surprised if there were another as lucid, as intelligent, and at the same time as natural.'

Unlike Otto's previous attempts, this time calls from publishers immediately flooded in. 'Several publishing houses called Jan

Romein, and he referred them on to me,' Werner Cahn recalled. One was Fred Batten, from the publisher Contact, who was so enthusiastic Cahn gave him the typescript.

Batten had been sitting at his desk when his colleague Mr K. Lekkerkerker came in brandishing the newspaper. Lekkerkerker showed Batten the article and told him to discuss it with Contact's director G. P. de Neve – but at first Contact was not interested in the diary. Fred Batten's wife remembers that after receiving the manuscript from Jan Romein, her husband 'advised for it to be published. De Neve did not want to, but my husband pushed through.'

Some time later, Otto told Werner that he had received a contract from Contact, and Cahn looked it over, making several changes in Otto's favour. Despite their enthusiasm, there is a rumour that Contact only accepted the diary because they wanted to publish another book, which they anticipated would be more popular. Paper was rationed after the war, but Contact suspected the diary had the kind of political support that meant their paper order would be agreed by the government. Whether this is true or not, as soon as Otto signed the contract he was immediately thrust into a debate about further editing of the diary that would become familiar for almost every publication and dramatisation. It was one he engaged with intensely and with strong convictions.

Due to his religious affiliations, G. P. de Neve told Otto that Contact would like to remove passages Anne had written about menstruation, her dislike for her mother and her interest in her friend's breasts. De Neve was a pious Catholic and was so troubled by the passages that he discussed them with his priest. Later, de Neve's secretary said that he held a meeting in his office to discuss the 'unpleasant notes about Anne's mother as well as a passage about Anne's menstruation' with Fred Batten and an editor called Scheepmaker. Contact's business director also remembered various conversations about what to omit.

This hesitancy was not unusual. Translator Barbara Mooyaart noted that 'the Netherlands was much more puritan than England at the time', and the director of publishing house H. Meulenhoff later said they had rejected the manuscript 'because of the very personal nature of the diary and the sexual confessions … At that time people thought very differently about these things.'

On 16 October 1946, de Neve wrote to Otto: 'Hereby included I send you an overview of the shortenings that can be made according to my employee Scheepmaker and myself. Separately, I send several omissions which, in our opinion, could but do not have to be made.'

The letter goes on to discuss whether the book should be printed as part of their Prologue series, which they preferred but which Otto objected to as he did not like the format. De Neve added that they were still looking into publishing Anne's fairy tales. On the question of a foreword, Contact said they had permission from Jan Romein to publish an altered version of his article in the book, so there was no need for Annie Romein to write a preface. Instead, they would prefer a few words from Otto himself. A publishing date of late January or early February 1947 was proposed.

Otto replied three days later, on Opekta letterhead paper from the address at 263 Prinsengracht. He agreed with the numbers suggested for the first edition, and wanted to discuss illustrations for the book and what kind of prologue would be published under his name. On the matter of edits, he wrote, 'I would like to discuss the suggested omissions face-to-face. With some of them, I will accept without a doubt, whereas for some other omissions we may have a difference of opinion.' Otto's letter also refers to the early stages of a discussion about foreign rights and translations, and he reassured Contact that he would ensure future foreign editions credited the original Dutch, published by Contact.

After further chiding from Otto, the proposed, what he would later call 'unimportant', edits were agreed, and in total twenty-five different passages were removed.

Publicity for the diary was gaining momentum. Following the initial article in *Het Parool*, Werner Cahn's journal *De Nieuwe Stem* published five excerpts in June 1946. Finally, on 25 June 1947, the first edition of the diary was published, with 3,000 copies. Contact used the title Anne had chosen herself: *Het Achterhuis: Dagboekbrieven van 14 Juni 1942–1 Augustus 1944* (*The Back House: Diary Letters from 14 June 1942–1 August 1944*). Otto date-marked the momentous event in his engagement book with only one word: 'BOOK.'

'Astonishing' was how newspaper *De Groene Amsterdammer* described *Het Achterhuis* in its review of the book, complimenting 'the intelligence, the honesty, the insight with which she observed herself and her surroundings, and the talent with which she was able to depict what she saw'. Many other publications agreed, although some were more dismissive, saying the diary was by no means a war document 'but purely and simply the diary of an adolescent girl'.

An emboldened Otto followed up publication by sending copies of the first edition to the most prominent public figures in the Netherlands, including the Queen, most of whom replied with pro forma thank-you letters. As the second edition went to press later that year, Otto was delighted to report to friends that Anne's diary was a big success, with four book readings in the Netherlands and plans for English and German editions.

Otto had fulfilled the first part of his ambition: to share Anne's work with the world. Yet even in the early days of publication, not everyone shared his vision for her legacy. Otto believed that 'it is [for] Anne's spirit that the book should be read as widely as possible, because it should work for people and for humanity', but the Dutch greeted the story with some ambivalence. They believed that they too had suffered greatly under German occupation, yet little attention was given to their plight. Equally, Anne's story drew attention to the terrible treatment of their Jewish friends and neighbours in the war, and the fact that almost all had been betrayed and sent to their deaths by ordinary Dutch citizens.

Strikingly, however, the harshest condemnation of the book came from within the Jewish community itself. Rabbi Soetendorp told Otto 'there was no point in publishing as no one would be interested in the diary'. Others, like Mrs Blog, who was part of the liberal Jewish community with Otto, were shocked that he could reveal such personal things about his family life: 'I did not understand how he could show the world the things his growing daughter had written in these horrible circumstances. I was against publication, even if Anne Frank would have wanted it herself.' Rabbi Hammelburg, who served with Otto on the board of the Liberal Jewish Congregation in Amsterdam, went further, saying that Otto was a good man, but 'sentimental and weak'.

Hammelburg said Otto first told him about the diary when it was being edited by Contact:

> He told me about the passages concerning Anne and Peter 'making out' and that, as a father, he could not allow that ... I did not believe that that diary was Anne Frank's and thought, and I still do today, that a clever guy at the publishing house put it together to make it a bestseller. The subjects that are covered are within the realms of the imagination for a teenage girl, but the way in which they were described was not. The whole commercial aspect of it has never appealed to me and I have never appreciated the Anne Frank House. This goes for all practising Jews in the Netherlands.

Hammelburg's comments reflected a sense of unease in the Jewish community that persisted as Anne's story played an increasingly iconic role in the story of the Holocaust. The Frank family hardly represented the lives of most European Jews in the Second World War, very few of whom had the resources to hide from the Nazis. Nor did Anne's writing express the horrors she had experienced in the concentration camps, stopping as it did before her capture. Instead, Anne's story positioned her as the ultimate victim: a blameless and innocent young girl with no agency over her own life or the ability to defend herself. It was a position some parts of the Jewish community would become increasingly uncomfortable with.

References to the 'commercial hullabaloo' that resulted from the success of the diary and Otto's relentless promotion of it was also something even his earliest and strongest supporters would question. Annie Romein-Verschoor reflected:

The overwhelming success of the book exceeded all my expectations and even now I cannot really explain it ... Success breeds success and the desire for money. This is not an imputation against Otto Frank, who, when he came to tell me that the diary should be published, with tears in his eyes, assured me that he did not wish to profit from the suffering of his child, and I assumed he meant it as he has held to that ... Otto Frank was certainly opposed to the success and the subsequent myths and the speculative defilement which inevitably came with it, but he could not stop it.

In trying to share Anne's legacy as widely as possible, Otto had already significantly reshaped and recreated her diary – and published a new text. Anne's edited second text had removed some of her earlier indecision about who to address her writings to – in the first version she addresses various girl characters who were the popular heroines of Dutch children's novels at the time. It also cut many romantic passages about her relationship with Peter and some comments about her mother. Alongside the two diaries, Anne wrote several fictional stories. 'Just imagine how interesting it would be if I were to publish a novel of the Secret Annexe,' she wrote. 'The title alone would be enough to make people think it was a detective story.' In shaping a text, Otto borrowed from both parts of her diaries, restored passages about Peter, deleted parts about his marriage to Edith, incorporated parts of Anne's fictional stories and decided on a single focus whom the diary was to address – Anne would write to Kitty.

Otto would remain the ultimate arbiter and editor of the diary, yet from the beginning the published diary was a powerful tool for those with a political or social agenda. Those most instrumental in its initial editing, publication and promotion in the Netherlands, including Kurt Baschwtiz, Ab Cauvern, Jan and Annie Romein and Werner Cahn, were a dedicated and close-knit group of socialists. *The Diary of Anne Frank* was not only a beautifully written text about the life of a young girl but also a powerful propaganda weapon that emphasised their commitment to rejecting fascism in all its forms and reshaping Europe along socialist lines. Otto was never a socialist, but he believed in the universal appeal of Anne's work to increase understanding and fight discrimination and would collaborate with others who had political agendas if it furthered the aims of the book. He remained delighted with the success of the Dutch publication and pressed ahead with attempts to publish abroad.

In July 1949, Otto travelled to France and England to meet publishers. In Paris, he signed a contract with Calmann-Lévy, who would publish the diary the following year. As was so often true with relation to the diary, it was a deeply felt personal connection that led to publication. Calmann-Lévy was an extremely distinguished French publishing house whose founders had been interned during the German occupation. It was the son of the owners who picked up the manuscript, understood its potential and pushed for publication.

The French edition, known as *Le Journal*, would be based on a translation of the published Dutch edition rather than returning to the original source material written by Anne – but Contact was annoyed to note that the edition did not mention the Dutch edition or copyright. Otto's business dealings relating to the diary were often complicated and fraught, leading to tense accusations. G. P. de Neve wrote to Otto:

The mention of copyright in the French edition clearly claims that Calmann-Lévy is allowed the rights to foreign editions. This is explicitly against the agreement between Calmann-Lévy and yourself and yourself and publishing house 'Contact'.

Furthermore, we are disadvantaged as the condition you agreed upon in Article 5 of the agreement with Calmann-Lévy, i.e., the mention of publishing house 'Contact', Amsterdam, has not been published. I request you take the necessary steps towards Calmann-Lévy to mend the damage, which happened after not holding up their agreement with you, and to make them declare that in no way are they allowed to trade the foreign rights.

It was a sour note, but in August 1950 *Le Journal* was published to great critical acclaim and commercial success. One French reader was so moved and impressed she immediately passed the book on to her husband, Meyer Levin, an American Jewish writer whom Otto would soon know well, with long-lasting consequences for them both.

Meanwhile, Otto used the occasion of the French publication to send a German translation to a Mr Koretz at Fox Film in Paris, but this came to nothing. Soon after, he arranged for an advance copy of *Le Journal* to be given to Frank Price, head of US publishers Doubleday in Paris. Price said he thought the book was of little importance and told his assistant Judith Bailey to reject it. Bailey asked him to reconsider.

Otto's efforts in the UK took a little longer to come to fruition – partly because he was also juggling attempts to sell the book in the US and Germany and was deeply absorbed in every last detail of negotiations. British publisher Secker & Warburg asked for time to consider the book, but while they prevaricated a new publishing house called Vallentine Mitchell expressed a strong interest. Vallentine Mitchell was negotiating with Otto via Meyer Levin, who had immediately contacted Otto after reading the French edition of the book. Levin told friends he believed Anne Frank was 'the teller' for the story of the Jews of Europe and wrote to Otto to offer his services in translating and selling the book around the world. 'My interest in the diary is not commercial so much as one of sympathy and I would be glad of the opportunity to translate it.'

Otto asked Levin to stall Vallentine Mitchell until he had a definitive answer from Secker & Warburg, but Levin pushed him further, stating, 'They have had long enough on it.' His suggestion was to let Vallentine Mitchell have it.

After Secker & Warburg rejected the book, Otto did offer the British rights to Vallentine Mitchell and began to consider an English translation. As he had already discovered, creating a translation that was both technically correct and also captured the spirit and cultural references of a lively young girl was tricky. In France, the publishers had tackled the problem by creating two translations: the first written by someone who was fluent in both Dutch and French and could ensure technical correctness; the second by a young French woman who read the first translation and then imbued it with the spirit of a girl. 'This is essential!' Otto wrote, as he contemplated using the same approach for the English translation.

An English translation did already exist, written by a woman called Rosey Pool, but English and American friends advised Otto not to use this version. Instead, he accepted an offer from Vallentine Mitchell for a £50 advance and 10 per cent of royalties, and agreed that Barbara Mooyaart-Doubleday, a young British woman living in Holland, would undertake a new English translation. In March 1951, Mooyaart-Doubleday bought a copy of *Het Achterhuis* and started work. 'I was deeply moved by the diary. I read it in one breath – took it to bed with me and read it through,' she later recalled. After submitting an initial sample of her work, she discovered that an Englishman living in The Hague had also been asked to submit a sample, with highly unsatisfactory results. 'It's unthinkable really,' Doubleday said. 'Anne's diary translated by a man!'

Mooyaart-Doubleday took four months to finish the translation. Sitting at her dining-room table, she wrote in longhand surrounded by dictionaries. In the afternoon, her little boys played in their playpen while she turned out three pages per day, and then reviewed and continued in the evening after they were in bed. Many of the passages omitted from the Dutch edition were included for what was considered a more broad-minded British audience. When she was finished, Mooyaart-Doubleday sat on her balcony and read the proofs through with Otto, who had already shown her the annexe.

'I left my boys at home and travelled to Amsterdam by train. I remember walking from the station and seeing the church – Westerkerk – in the distance ... it was very strange ... I was charmed by Otto. He was tremendously courteous, old worldly in that sense.' While Otto remained focused on showing her around the annexe, he was composed, but once they left and walked across the street for lunch, he became emotional. 'Tears came into his eyes several times. He was a very sad man, at that time, it was all still very close.' After their meeting, Otto took Barbara to meet Fritzi Geiringer, whom he'd reconnected with after the journey back from Auschwitz, and told her that Barbara shared his vision for the book.

As Otto's friendship with Fritzi had deepened, he shared all his thoughts and feelings about the diary with her, and her opinions were important to him. He was now embroiled in all aspects of publishing the diary around the world, and the negotiations would dominate his thoughts and take over both their lives.

In the early 1950s Contact continued to negotiate with foreign publishers, working on Italian and Scandinavian editions. This often led to further conflict with Otto, who questioned whether the Italian publisher was of good enough stature and insisted that he only wanted a 'first-class publishing house'.

In Scandinavia, Contact argued bitterly with their agent over the handling of the publications, and then with Otto over an agreement with Swedish publisher Lars Hökerbergs Bokförlag. 'I would like to say clearly that the way in which you are dealing with the translations does not have my approval and I do not think this way of handling things is correct,' Otto wrote angrily. 'It was your duty to give me Hökerbergs's contract for approval *before* signing it.' Otto insisted that Contact write to Hökerbergs to tell them that he, not Contact, was the owner of the rights.

As the book approached publication in Britain, Vallentine Mitchell asked a child psychologist, Dr Emmanuel Miller, to provide his thoughts for publicity material. Miller noted that the book was 'exceptionally honest and intelligent', but he believed that 'although it was written by a young girl it is unlikely to be read by adolescents. We believe it will be of interest for parents and all those interested in the inner problems of growing children.' The publishers than asked a novelist, Storm Jameson, to write the introduction to the book – which again frustrated Otto, who had been hoping for a 'bigger name'.

Britain had a unique war story in Europe, one that involved the Blitz and fighting 'alone' against the Nazis. 'It was too precious', historian Tony Kushner argues, 'to have been brought into question by the experiences of another people whose suffering and losses made the British sacrifices pale into insignificance.' Moreover, Kushner adds,

> British Jewry internalized many of these tendencies, keeping the Holocaust at a distance. Peace and quiet and especially the suburban lifestyle was the goal and realised ambition of many. The Jews of Britain were engaged in what the writer Bernard Kops has called the 'post-war pursuit of the semi and the three-piece suite'.

Anne's story was one about puberty, not the Holocaust, Vallentine Mitchell's managing director David Kessler concluded: 'The fact that it records war-time experiences is, to my mind, far less important than its qualities as a remarkable document of a girl's adolescence.'

The first UK reviewers reflected thoughtfully on the book but with little passion. 'The chill of Belsen pervades these trivialities. "She'll grow out of it," one thinks. And then one stops and remembers that she was never given the chance,' commented the *Newcastle Journal*. It 'strikes very hard on the imagination', wrote Mary Stocks in the *Manchester Guardian*, adding, 'It may be that this particular mixture of danger and domesticity has a peculiar poignancy.' However, she went on: 'This book comes to us in translation fairly late in the day. We have begun to forget Belsen and the persecutions and the pogroms that led up to it. Later persecutions of different origin and claiming different victims have obscured those evil memories.'

Vallentine Mitchell's Barry Sullivan agreed, noting in a letter to Barbara Mooyaart-Doubleday that 'in England, Belsen is a "hazy", almost "historical" fact, and the word is often used in jokes'. Indeed, the reaction of the British public was cool. Vallentine Mitchell published 5,000 copies of *The Diary of a Young Girl* in May 1952, but despite the efforts of a large sales team it did not capture the public imagination and was outsold for the first few months by Florence Greenberg's *Jewish Cookbook*.

'The book was not selling very well in the provinces,' the publisher's representatives reported, with only two copies being sold over two weeks in September 1952.

When Otto complained to Kessler about the poor sales figures in Britain, Kessler replied that they had never anticipated that the book would be a bestseller, and selling 5,000 copies in six months was 'very creditable'. Kessler wrote, 'We took the book in the first instance because we believed it was one which ought to be read in England ... We had sufficient confidence to estimate that it would cover its expenses.' By late 1952, however, the publisher had concluded that the diary was coming to the end of its sales life and rejected a second print run. By 1953, *The Diary of Anne Frank* was out of print in the United Kingdom.

The situation was frustratingly similar in the Netherlands. Although the diary was in its sixth edition by July 1950, many believed that interest in the war years was waning there too. A time lapse between the publication of the fifth edition in February 1949 and the sixth in July 1950 led publishers to believe that the resonance of Anne's story had peaked, and the book was not reprinted in the Netherlands between 1950 and 1955. Otto wrote to Contact: 'It may be worth the effort to get rid of the idea of it being a "war book" amongst booksellers.' It was more than possible, he believed, to still sell the book if it was promoted with more value on 'the pedagogical and psychological side'.

Otto's frustration grew as his frequent letters to Contact, urging them to be more active in publicising the book, often went unanswered. 'I do not doubt about your activities, yet I want to point out that, in my opinion, the main reason for the sales is the many articles about Anne that have been published in all the newspapers lately,' Otto wrote in the autumn of 1955. 'I admit that a coloured advertisement board is not necessary at this moment to boost sales, but I hope it can be made at a later point, especially as that was the reason I was satisfied with a very low percentage for the licence.'

Soon he wrote again, saying, 'I would really appreciate to hear from you in response to my writing of the fifth of this month, as I'm not comfortable with *Het Achterhuis* not being available in bookstores, all the more because much has been written about it lately and this now cannot benefit the sales.' Otto suggested that Contact publish a cheaper pocket edition, and indicated that he was prepared to accept a lower share of the royalties if that made it more attractive to the publisher.

When Contact replied to discuss a dispute around payment from a serialisation in Sweden, Otto noted, 'I was happy to finally hear from you. I understand that you are busy at this time, but if you check our correspondence, you will find that very often answers to my letters take a very long time.' Contact tried to placate Otto, claiming it cared more about his interests than he suggested:

First of all, our apologies for the lack of response on your letters of 5 and 14 September this year. For publishing houses, these months are the busiest of the year, so much correspondence has to be temporarily delayed ... it is obviously unpleasant to read that you always have to use somewhat forceful language.

Otto was right, however, to note their often lukewarm responses and ambivalent attitude towards Anne and the diary. His fears that the diary was slipping into obscurity seemed justified. But nothing could have been further from the truth. Otto's determination to find a global audience for Anne's writing was about the bear fruit, as her work exploded into the consciousness of millions of people across the Atlantic. *The Diary of Anne Frank* was about to take America by storm.

CHAPTER 3

ALL-AMERICAN GIRL

*'Last winter in Paris I read the manuscript of a book, which I
had just received in bound form, called* The Diary of a Young
Girl *by Anne Frank ... I think it is well for those of us who have
forgotten so much of that period to read about it now, just to remind
ourselves that we never want to go through such things again if
possible. Her story ended tragically. She died in the concentration
camp at Bergen-Belsen. This diary should teach us all the wisdom of
preventing any kind of totalitarianism that could lead to oppression
and suffering of this kind.'*

ELEANOR ROOSEVELT, *ST LOUIS POST-DISPATCH*, 22 APRIL 1952

When Hasia Diner carried home a copy of *The Diary of
Anne Frank* from the public library, the book had become
imbued with so much meaning 'I felt like I could hardly hold it.
It was so auspicious.' For Diner, then a Jewish girl in early 1950s
Milwaukee and now an eminent historian at NYU, the diary
was almost a sacred text:

When I was a little girl I had an 'evil stepmother'. She was a

Holocaust survivor, and so all my knowledge and thoughts about Hitler were wrapped up in my experience with her. Then, one night, I sat in the congregation of a synagogue in Chicago and listened to the rabbi telling us about Anne Frank. My concept of the Holocaust shifted. Afterwards my father was very angry because he felt that the rabbi had not shown enough reverence in the way that he described Anne. 'She was a saint, she was a saint!' he kept saying. I thought: 'No – she was an ordinary girl.'

Otto Frank had begun discussions about a US edition of the diary shortly after the publication of the French edition, when he was also working on plans for a UK edition. In what would become a common occurrence, however, negotiations were fraught and prone to dispute, with misunderstandings and accusations of disingenuous behaviour made by all sides. Otto's letters from the period show that he was minutely involved in every negotiation and decision and quite capable of rejecting a writer, translator or publisher if he felt that he had struck a better deal elsewhere. From Otto's perspective, these decisions were never about financial gain but always about who shared his vision for Anne's legacy and who could best communicate it to the largest number of people. Often, however, those who worked with him would be surprised, and extremely disappointed, to discover that while they were proceeding on the basis that they had reached an agreement with Otto, he had subsequently reached another agreement with someone else without telling them.

One of the key contacts Otto made at this time was American writer Meyer Levin, who had been given a copy of the French edition by his wife Tereska Torrès. Otto's relationship with Levin would cast a shadow over the rest of his life – but that was yet to unfold. At first acquaintance, Levin was a 44-year-old novelist and writer who had served as a war correspondent in France and written searing first-hand accounts of the liberation of the concentration camps. As he witnessed the horror, he realised that he was not the person who should tell the story of the Jews of Europe – that some day, a 'teller' would arise from the survivors themselves. As he read the diary, Levin came to believe that the teller was in fact Anne Frank. Her voice, he said, had reached him from the pit of Bergen-Belsen, and he vowed to avenge her.

Levin was immediately captivated by the diary and contacted French publisher Calmann-Lévy to enquire about US and UK rights. Calmann-Lévy passed his letter on to Otto, and Otto replied on 19 September 1950 to say that his French agents Maison D. Clairouin were working on UK and US rights, and so he could not offer Levin an option 'at the present time'.

Maison D. Clairouin were indeed working on foreign rights for the diary. But Otto told neither Levin nor his agent that he had also asked his old friend Charles Nathan Straus in New York to find out if Random House would be interested in publishing the diary in the US.

Otto's response did not dissuade Levin, who immediately wrote back to state that he was also interested in translating the diary and asked for permission to speak to his contacts in film and theatre. This friendly correspondence framed what would turn into an all-consuming battle between the two men, but at the time Otto merely replied that he did not believe the nature of the diary lent itself to becoming a successful stage adaptation. He added, however, that if Levin had some ideas in this direction he was 'absolutely free' to pursue them.

Levin did just that, and proceeded to send out dozens of letters to agents, producers and directors. None were willing to commit at such an early stage, but Otto offered further encouragement, writing that 'you just go on and I shall not interfere'.

Focusing on the book, Otto began to involve Levin in his efforts to secure publishers in the UK and the US. In the US, Appleton Century, Harper and Harcourt, Knopf, Schocken, Scribner's, Simon & Schuster, Vanguard and Viking had all rejected the manuscript, while Random House stated they might consider publishing if a British company would do likewise.

In November, Levin sought to raise publicity around the diary, writing in *Congress Weekly*, a magazine published by the American Jewish Congress, that Europe was much more open to publishing books by Jews and accusing the American market of being too narrow-minded. In that same month, a 'Letter from Paris' by Janet Flanner, published in the *New Yorker*, also raised the profile of the diary, calling it 'one of the most widely and seriously read books in France', although she dismissed Anne in a patronising put-down as a 'precocious' and 'talented little Frankfurt Jewess'.

Reading both articles, US literary scout and Dutch refugee Dola de Jong was immediately intrigued and ordered a copy of the diary to read herself. Although she recognised its merit straight away, de Jong was surprised to discover that publishers did not share her opinion and had little interest in the book. Although she was well connected, all the publishers she approached rejected the book, including, initially, Doubleday. Eventually, de Jong found a junior editor at Little, Brown in Boston who shared her belief in the diary: Ned Bradford.

Bradford cabled Otto almost immediately: 'This is definite

offer to publish Anne Frank diary in the US. Excellent chance simultaneous British publication ... Prefer Dola de Jong to translate, much enthusiasm for book here. Little, Brown & Co.'

Otto was then undertaking negotiations with Vallentine Mitchell for the UK edition and wrote to Meyer Levin to say that he had accepted Little, Brown's offer but wanted the two companies to work together on a translation. By now Otto understood that getting the right voice for Anne's writing in a translation was crucial, and he doubted whether Dola de Jong, a native Dutch speaker, could find the right tone in English. Otto warned Little, Brown that the 'charm of the book could be spoiled' but told Levin on 10 December that his fears were obviously 'mistaken': 'Little, Brown want her to translate ... I had a pretty sharp correspondence with her, but I hope that she understood the situation now and that everything will be settled.'

Otto later admitted that he had agreed that de Jong could translate but had never urged her to start work. De Jong and Ned Bradford believed that, even without a written contract in place, they had secured Otto's word, and 'we trusted Otto Frank'. Rather foolishly, de Jong threw caution to the wind and began translation on spec, only to discover three months later, in an article in the *New York Times*, that Otto had in fact signed a contract for US publication with Doubleday. De Jong rang Bradfield immediately, where they commiserated but agreed that there wasn't a 'darn thing' they could do. De Jong was personally incensed with Otto Frank but decided simply to drop the matter. (As mentioned in the previous chapter, in the end Barbara Mooyaart-Doubleday translated the book into English for both the US and UK editions.)

De Jong and Bradfield admitted they had behaved

unprofessionally, but they were far from the only people to become so emotionally attached and enthusiastic about the book that they tried to force Otto into giving commitments he was not ready to make. When those commitments did not come to pass, they would often feel bitterly let down and deceived. For his part, Otto often shared detailed personal confidences with agents, possible publishers and many others about his thoughts on the diary and its legacy, without revealing that he was in fact in negotiations with many other people too. While he was usually technically correct that he had not signed contracts or given written agreements, reading the correspondence it is easy to see how many people could believe he had agreed in principle.

The question of translation was not the only issue that had plagued negotiations between Otto and Little, Brown. There was also disagreement about foreign rights (particularly Canadian) and, more crucially for Otto, dramatic rights.

On 14 March 1951, Frank Price from Doubleday wrote to Otto offering similar financial terms to Little, Brown. Otto replied stating that the reason he had not yet signed the contract with Little, Brown was a 'sentimental' one concerning the prospect of a film or play. 'I do not want a film to be made based on terror, bombardment and Nazis spoiling the base of the diary and therefore want to keep these rights under control.' How Doubleday responded to the question of a film would be crucial to Otto's decision, he insisted. After receiving reassurance from Price, Otto formally rejected the offer from Little, Brown on 27 March and signed a contract with Doubleday on 27 April 1951.

The final month of contract negotiations with Doubleday had not been smooth, however. Otto had upset his French agents by conducting the negotiations on his own, without involving them. As they had provided the initial contact with Frank Price at Doubleday, they demanded their fee – which Otto refused to pay. Eventually, Otto agreed to pay one third of the fee, but he was now also conducting double negotiations, with Frank Price at Doubleday and with Meyer Levin, over stage and film interest. In New York, however, Doubleday was thrilled to have secured the rights to the book, and those most closely involved in the purchase – Frank Price, Jason Epstein, Karen Rye and Barbara Zimmerman, who would become the book's editor – formed an 'Informal Society of Advocates for Anne Frank' and began work with great enthusiasm.

Even so, the sales team estimated that the book's potential was small and urged the marketing department to play down the 'grim aspects of the story' in favour of the 'beauty, humour and insight' of a sensitive adolescent.

Then 24-year-old Barbara Zimmerman, who was the same age as Anne would have been, formed a close partnership and friendship with Otto that would last for decades. In mid-October 1951, she started their correspondence by writing to Otto that, at his suggestion, they had begun discussions with Eleanor Roosevelt over writing an introduction. The fact that Otto considered Roosevelt a suitable figure to write an introduction to the diary demonstrates the unshakeable confidence and belief he had in the importance of what was then still a virtually unknown work by a teenage girl. It was crucial to him that those involved with the book were motivated by the same vision, and he replied to Zimmerman that he had the feeling 'that the matter of Anne's book is not only a commercial question for you, but also a personal one'.

By February 1951, Zimmerman was able to send Otto the text of the introduction written by Eleanor Roosevelt (although most likely it was a draft written by Zimmerman herself and signed off by Roosevelt), and Otto was pleased to note that it was a 'splendid piece' which showed that Roosevelt had 'understood Anne' and 'picked out her ideals in many of the letters Anne was writing'. Rejecting commercialism and upholding those ideals was paramount to Otto, who wrote to Roosevelt to thank her. Reading her introduction had given him comfort and the conviction that Anne's wish 'to live still after her death and to have done something for mankind' was fulfilled.

Meyer Levin had organised serialisation for the book in *Commentary* magazine, an intellectual post-war Jewish journal, in May 1952. However, it was his review in the *New York Times* that truly launched *Anne Frank: The Diary of a Young Girl* in the US, and subsequently around the world:

The Diary of a Young Girl by Anne Frank – Meyer Levin
New York Times Review of Books, 15 June 1952

Anne Frank's diary is too tenderly intimate a book to be frozen with the label 'classic', and yet no lesser designation serves. For little Anne Frank, spirited, moody, witty, self-doubting, succeeded in communicating in virtually perfect, or classic, form the drama of puberty. But her book is not a classic to be left on the library shelf. It is a warm and stirring confession, to be read over and over from insight and enjoyment...

There is no lugubrious ghetto tale, no compilation of horrors. Reality can prove surprisingly different from invented reality, and Anne Frank's diary simply bubbles with amusement, love, discovery. It has its share of disgust, its moments of hatred, but it is so wondrously alive, so near, that one feels overwhelmingly the universalities of human nature. These people might be living next door; their within-the-family emotions, their tensions and satisfactions are those of human character and growth, anywhere.

'I want to go on living even after my death,' Anne wrote ... There is anguish in the thought of how much creative power, how much sheer beauty of living, was cut off through genocide. But through her diary Anne goes on living.

The review was sensational. Barbara Zimmerman wrote to Otto: 'This is one of the most important things to happen to any book, especially since the *Times* is the most influential paper in the country ... The review itself is a beautiful one.' Zimmerman was already reviewing her estimate of what she had previously thought might be a 'small classic' and told Otto she now thought sales would be extremely good, adding that Anne would receive a wonderful reception in America.

Later, even after much bad blood had flowed between Otto and Meyer Levin, Zimmerman admitted that she still had to give Levin every credit for his review. 'It was damn good, very dramatic and really hit hard. It struck a chord with people and made them race out to read the diary.' Zimmerman stated that there had not been a book like the diary before: it was devastating and it was immediate. And it was in the voice of a child, which made it both more unbearable and yet more accessible.

Foreshadowing the schism to come about whether the diary should be interpreted as a Jewish story or simply a human one, Levin wrote a second review for the Jewish *Congress Weekly*, this time highlighting the diary's relevance as a part of Jewish history and its relevance to the Holocaust. The diary, he claimed, was the most important document to have come out of the 'great catastrophe'. The Holocaust had, at long last, come home, 'and our defences are shattered. We weep.'

In Amsterdam, Otto was overwhelmed by the sudden prospect of the diary's success and the attention this would surely bring. Still suffering enormously from the loss of his family, Otto was on the brink of a complete nervous breakdown and wrote to Barbara Zimmerman to express his fear that Doubleday would want him to travel to America to promote the book. 'It would be terrible for me to have to speak to someone interviewing me, I have to get out of a situation of that kind. I could not bear it.'

Despite his intense efforts to promote the diary and control every aspect of publication, Otto was still shocked by its immediate immense success in America. On 16 June 1952, *Anne Frank: The Diary of a Young Girl* went on sale in the US, and that same afternoon every one of the first 5,000 copies had been sold. A print run of 15,000 copies was rushed through, while massive advertising campaigns, promotional material and syndication rights were hurriedly agreed. Within two years the diary would sell 80,000 hardback editions and 200,000 paperbacks in the US.

Hasia Diner says it is impossible to over-estimate the importance of *The Diary of a Young Girl* to the Jewish-American community: 'In the early 1950s it was a sort of "golden-age" for Jewish America.' Jews, who accounted for no more than 3 per cent of the total population, were still discriminated against in every aspect of American public life: private employers could, and did, refuse to hire Jewish applicants; real-estate agents conspired with local communities to refuse to sell houses to Jewish families; and universities employed quotas to curtail the number of Jewish students. Yet it was also the start of the civil rights era.

The first civil rights legislation, passed in 1957, may have been weak, but it was the first such legislation to be introduced in America since the end of the Civil War around a century earlier. Old restrictions against Jews were still in place but were starting to crumble. Jews were comfortable in America – but not too comfortable. Jewish men had gone to fight for America in the Second World War and returned victorious. They were benefiting from the economic boom, their children were going to college and families were moving to the suburbs. Once there, on pretty tree-lined streets, Jewish community groups urged them to get to know their neighbours and share a little about what being Jewish meant.

'The years after WWII indeed represented a sort of high watermark for synagogue membership and Jewish supplementary school enrolment and summer camp attendance,' Diner writes. 'Never before in American Jewish history had such a large percentage joined congregations and exposed their children to some kind of Jewish education. And in those places, the tragic story of European Jewry under the heel of German Nazism reverberated deeply.'

Contrary to a belief that Jewish-Americans did not like to talk about the Holocaust in the years after the Second World War, or did so in a way that stripped it of its Jewishness, Diner's research, documented in *We Remember with Reverence and Love*, discovered that from the mid-1940s until the 1960s, diverse Jewish communities and groups across America found their own languages, memorials and texts to remember the 6 million Jews who had been murdered by the Nazis. Diner says,

American Jews, journalists, rabbis, writers, educators, camp counsellors, youth group leaders, functionaries of communal agencies, and the many others, including 'ordinary' Jews who wrote letters to the editor, sent their children to the camps, attended meetings, sat in the audiences, listened to the concerts, and contributed money to the causes promoted in the name of the catastrophe – all these wove the cataclysmic slaughter of the six million European Jews at the hands of the Nazis into the lived texture of their communities ... In every sector of the American Jewish collectivity, Jews told the story.

One example was the Jewish teenagers at the Reform movement's Camp Institute in Oconomowoc, Wisconsin, who edited a literary magazine about the summer of 1956. The magazine included a piece by young Sharon Feinman, who wrote about the theme of their summer, 'Naaseh v'nishma', 'We will do and we will hear'. Feinman wrote that even during 'the dark reign of terror when Hitler and the Nazis ruled Germany and plunged the world into a catastrophic war, when the people who called themselves the "master race" murdered six million Jews', the light of 'Naaseh v'nishma' burned mightily and against all odds 'the nation of Israel was born'.

Not only does Feinman's essay show that the Holocaust was woven prominently into Jewish life, but that remembering the horror and anguish of the crime was followed by a forward-looking contemplation of what this might mean for the future and all of humanity. Hasia Diner notes that such liberalism dominated American Jewish life at the time. With a few exceptions, 'Jews subscribed to a political vision that stressed a belief in progress and a commitment to Western values.' They believed in America, in pluralism and in the idea that good people could come together to tackle prejudice and discrimination.

Supported by publicity from more than 250 Jewish magazines, newspapers and journals active in the post-war years, mainstream and Jewish publishers had been printing a steady stream of books relating to the Holocaust since the end of the war – beginning with Doubleday, who published *No Traveller Returns: The Story of Hitler's Greatest Crime* by Henry Shoskes in 1945, telling the overall story of the Holocaust with a particular focus on the Warsaw Ghetto. Beechhurst published *The Buried Are Screaming* by Helen Waren in 1948, about her journey as a Jewish-American coming to Europe in the immediate aftermath of the war, while Viking published Bernard Goldstein's *The Stars Bear Witness* about his five years in the Warsaw Ghetto. In addition to reportage and memoirs, novels like *The Wall*, set in the Warsaw Ghetto, were widely read but criticised for factual errors and because the author was not Jewish.

Yet in spreading the story about Jewish culture and life to liberal America, Diner says, 'The biggest propaganda tool at their disposal was *The Diary of Anne Frank*.' Jewish community groups had been buying up books that spread the story about Jewish life and donating to them to local libraries since the early years of the twentieth century. Post-war, they went out of their way to include books that told the story of the Holocaust and often deliberated at length about which were best suited to a non-Jewish audience. In 1958, the Cincinnati Jewish Community Relations Committee debated the merits of a number of books they were considering for donation. The committee decided to purchase *Notes from the Warsaw Ghetto* for college libraries but rejected

Gerda Weissmann Klein's memoir *All But My Life*, which was an account of a young girl living through Polish ghettoes and the slave-labour camps of Nazi Germany. Although the committee commended the book as 'remarkable' and 'deserving of our attention', they considered it 'too tragic in its presentation … for us to use it as an item for placement in the school libraries'. Unsurprisingly, they decided instead to donate free copies of *Anne Frank: The Diary of a Young Girl*, which had 'superior public relations usefulness'.

Invariably, the first book Jewish groups bought was *The Diary of Anne Frank* – her innocent face, those big eyes, her family background and her dreams for her future melding so perfectly with the American dream of that era. The real life-and-death battles of the Jewish ghetto fighters of Poland made Americans feel uncomfortable with vivid depictions of the blood, gore and poverty in East European Jewish life – but Anne Frank offered the perfect antidote. A story of a middle-class girl from a loving nuclear family who enjoyed wholesome vigorous activities was the kind of tale most Americans enjoyed watching at the movies. Anne was a sort of Jewish Velvet Brown from *National Velvet*, who went ice-skating instead of horse-riding, bought pretty dresses, rode her bicycle and had birthday parties. She was feisty and fought with her mother. She liked boys. But undoubtedly, she was a good girl who could always rely on the wise counsel of her father. As the editors at Doubleday had rightly realised, Anne's positive message for the future and uplifting ending was crucial.

Yet if the phenomenon of Anne Frank had taken white America by storm, it did not seem to resonate in the same way with black Americans, and the diary was rarely referred to by black newspapers or staged as a play in black theatres. One person who sought to change that was a Dutch Jewish woman who had taught Anne in Amsterdam before the war, Rosey Pool.

Rosey Pool was a fascinating character. Born on the edge of the Jewish quarter in Amsterdam in 1905 and called 'Roosje' by her family, she developed a teenage passion for literature and socialism, got married and lived in Berlin during the rise of the Nazis in the 1930s, divorced and began dating women, and then returned to Amsterdam, where she joined the Jewish resistance, briefly encountered Anne Frank at the Jewish school and was then transported to – and escaped from – the Nazi camp at Westerbork. A recent study of Pool by Lonneke Geerlings summarises her extraordinary life. After the war Pool moved to London, where she devoted her considerable energies to promoting black literature and actors – something she continued to do in the southern states of the US at the height of segregation, and in Africa. Geerlings tells us: 'She witnessed independence movements in Nigeria and Senegal; and she was involved in the American Civil Rights Movement ... each of these moments would have been sufficient for a book in itself.'

As an obese woman, a Jew, a lesbian and a sometime socialist, Pool could never fail to be aware of her 'otherness'. She was an outcast, and on one of her American travels in the early '60s, one poet was amazed that 'one so removed' was interested in the black cause. Lonneke Geerlings notes that Pool's response was swift: 'Believe me: since 1933 I was anything but "removed" from all that,' she wrote, 'and the years 1940–45 in Holland under Nazi occupation when the yellow Jew stars were our darker skins completed my education.'

Pool had first encountered Anne after she returned to

Amsterdam from Berlin in 1933 and taught at the Jewish Lyceum, where all Jewish children in the city were eventually sent to study during the Nazi occupation. Anne did not make much of an impression on Pool, and she later remembered that Margot was in fact the more brilliant daughter who gained the most attention. Anne, she said, was 'your ordinary, pleasant girl to have in the classroom', though she did have a surprising ability to mimic the teachers and could impersonate almost anyone with merciless caricatures. Pool also gave private English lessons and sometimes visited the Franks at home to teach Edith. On these visits, she remembered, Anne would awkwardly scrutinise her 'with a large pair of eyes'.

Like most Dutch Jews, Pool was deported to the Nazi transit camp at Westerbork but avoided transport to the concentration camps of the east first by working as part of the camp administration, adding names to the transport lists, and then by escaping during a sanctioned day out to Amsterdam to get books for the camp library – such days out seem remarkable but were occasionally allowed for trusted inmates. Pool had been working as part of a Jewish resistance group, and as such had the contacts to go into hiding in the countryside, where she remained for the rest of the war.

In the aftermath of liberation, Pool found herself back in Amsterdam, as lost and shattered as other survivors. Walking down the street one day, she bumped into someone she recognised: Otto Frank. Like Otto, Pool had lost her entire family in Auschwitz. Otto told her that Anne had written a diary and implored her to read it. Pool did read it and could not imagine that the book would become a published bestseller – but she did translate the text into English. Rosey Pool's work was the first

English translation of the diary, but Otto was not impressed, believing Pool had not captured Anne's spirited way with words. As was often the case with Otto, though, he did not tell Pool he thought her translation wasn't good enough. Instead, he paid her and avoided answering her letters. In the meantime, Otto sent Pool's work around to publishers and agents so they could understand the substance of the book – before commissioning the translation they actually wanted to use.

Like many others involved in Otto's convoluted negotiations over the diary, Pool was puzzled and hurt but let the matter drop, watching from the sidelines as Barbara Mooyaart-Doubleday's translation was published. According to the archives, there is no evidence that Otto and Rosey ever corresponded again, but Pool would later find that her life once more intersected with Anne Frank – this time when she was commissioned to give a speaking tour in the United States. Lonneke Geerlings writes,

> Rosey Pool was received like a rock star when she travelled across the United States in 1959 and 1960. In eight months she passed through twelve states, held over eighty lectures, was interviewed on radio and television, posed for photographs, and handed out signatures. It was not her Fulbright scholarship or her research on African American poetry that sold out venues. It was her experiences with Anne Frank.

Pool was a hard-up freelancer living in London when she applied for the Fulbright scholarship for the humanities in 1959. As she was no longer living in the Netherlands, the Dutch committee puzzled over what to do with her application. At the ripe old age of fifty-four and with a very eclectic CV, Pool was not like the usual array of scholars and academics who won such grants, but when another applicant pulled out she was thrilled to receive the award. In October 1959, Pool arrived in Detroit, Michigan, ostensibly to research African American poetry, but she soon discovered that the Fulbright grant only covered travel costs and she would need to find other ways to make ends meet. The first obvious source of income for someone as lively and charismatic as Pool was to organise a lecture series, where she proceeded to give advice on a wide range of topics, from African poetry to European education to marriage guidance. Once her audiences discovered a little more about her, however, Pool found there was only one topic they were interested in: Anne Frank.

Pool's visit coincided with the launch of the Hollywood movie *The Diary of Anne Frank*, starring Millie Perkins, Joseph Schild-kraut and Shelley Winters, and millions of Americans flocked to the cinema to see a story they had already read as a book and often seen as a stage play. 'You came not to hear me speak,' Pool said in Kalamazoo, Michigan, in October 1959, 'but to hear a person who knew a child who means very much to you. It is still a miracle to me.'

This miracle clearly had commercial advantages for Pool, who understood that her experience had enormous value. And it was something her audience was clamouring for. They did not want to hear Pool's thoughts about black poets – they wanted to meet 'the teacher of Anne Frank'.

Pool began her tour in the north, speaking to largely white American audiences of school children and to Jewish groups. In the course of the events, she seemed ill at ease – sometimes making warm comments about Anne but often critical ones too. Although she used Anne's name to pull in a crowd, Pool sometimes seemed reticent when it came to talking about Anne – perhaps because she knew that in truth their connection was very slim – and most puzzling of all, she denied that she was also Jewish. Pool spoke to thousands and thousands of youngsters and liked talking to young teenagers in particular, as they were the same age as Anne had been and often wanted to think more deeply about the story. To begin, Pool would describe what Anne was like, and what it had been like teaching her before comparing Anne's situation to American school children in the present day, imploring them: 'Please, don't let her down a second time!' Afterwards the children were asked to write a report on the talk, and they often sent these to Pool, reflecting back the main points of Anne's story and thanking her for reminding them of the terrors of Nazi rule.

Pool herself was not unaware of the strangeness of the situation. Often she spoke in schools that were preparing to stage school versions of the play, and was not only asked to meet the actress playing Anne but sometimes a lookalike too. In Wyandotte, Detroit, a local newspaper reporter and the audience of 200 waited with bated breath to see if Pool would burst into tears and seemed disappointed that she did not.

Such meetings were awkward to put it mildly, and the young actresses later recalled that Pool was often reserved and uncharacteristically silent. As she admitted in her sessions with school children, she had not seen either the play or the film, and although she might be making money out of her association with Anne, coming face to face with the reality of the Nazi past was still very traumatic for her. She told a reporter from Ypsilanti High School: 'I am completely unable to go and look at a portrayal of things still so much a painful reality to me.' Maybe she would watch it someday, 'but I am not yet ready'.

Furthermore, when actually addressing her audiences Pool was faced with a dilemma. Should she burnish Anne's legacy with 'memories' of a saintly and brilliant little girl and give the people who had paid to hear her speak what they wanted, or should she be honest about the fact she barely knew Anne and had never paid much attention to her? This very same dilemma would challenge everyone who chose to speak and write about Anne from the publication of the diary until the present day. To reap the financial rewards and fame of an association with Anne Frank meant signing up to a hollowed-out script of well-worn, anodyne clichés. Pool muddled her talks with a little bit of everything. Lonneke Geerlings writes,

> Pool said that she refused 'to interpret something into now immortal Anne that isn't there', including saint-like qualities that she was attributed because of her suffering. She was not a saint, she was an ordinary girl ... There had been many who lived just like her and died the way she did. And if there was one message in her diary, it was that 'suffering is not a virtue'.

However, insisting that Anne was not a saint did not stop audiences from being shocked when Pool told them she barely remembered Anne, whom she considered an unremarkable child who 'wasn't charming', nor pretty, but instead a 'catty' little imp who was jealous of her sister Margot and whose head often appeared to be too big for her body. While such nasty remarks may have reflected Pool's true feelings about Anne, mixed in with ongoing resentment at her treatment by Otto over the translation of the diary, they did not sit well with describing a wholly innocent young girl who had been forced to spend years of her short life in hiding, only to be caught, starved and murdered – a victim whom Pool was exploiting as a meal-ticket at that. To combat this, Pool began sprinkling her talks with some of the forgiveness and optimism Americans had ascribed to Anne and the diary, through the play and then the movie version of her life. 'Sunshine, not poison, comes from the pages,' Pool told audiences, adding that Anne Frank 'never uttered a word of hatred'.

While Otto must have known of Pool's tour, he never commented on it or corresponded with her about it. But even if he did not write to Pool directly, he must have been deeply hurt and disappointed by some of her remarks. They would only cross paths on one more occasion (and even then not in person), when Otto endorsed an event in December 1959 in support of raising money for shelters for the young children of Israel. Pool spoke at the fundraiser, while Otto sent a message of support for the cause saying that Anne would have 'wholeheartedly endorsed it'.

At the end of her speaking tour in the northern states, Pool had made the equivalent of $10,000 in today's money – enough to propel her onwards to the next stage of her tour in the American south. Pool wanted to travel across the southern states to promote her interest in black literature and scout for talent for a poetry anthology she planned to publish. Much to her delight, she discovered that the UNCF, a philanthropic group funding scholarships for black students, was prepared to fully sponsor a three-month trip zigzagging across ten southern states and visiting twenty-two colleges. The trip was unprecedented for the

UNCF in both scope and cost, but Pool represented the ideals of racial equality and emancipation that the organisation championed – and she had the double pulling power of being able to speak about both black poetry and Anne Frank. 'The fund probably hoped that "Anne Frank's teacher" who criticized segregation would be an instant success,' Geerlings notes, and the many headlines she made were proof of this. Carefully staged photos of Pool speaking with small groups of students were requested by the UNCF and used for PR purposes long afterwards.

Pool immediately noticed the similarities between the segregated south and living in the Netherlands under Nazi occupation – with the 'whites only' signs only one superficial indication of this. 'Prejudice doesn't only hurt,' she told her audiences. 'It can kill.' And referring to the Holocaust, she exclaimed, 'It can happen here!' Now that she was in the south, Pool found a sense of urgency in her work. She actively linked Nazi oppression with the 'segregation, persecution and racial discrimination' she saw all around her.

Pool's attempt to combine the issues facing black Americans with the persecution Jews had faced under Hitler was problematic, however. Jewish-Americans faced serious antisemitism at the time and were often excluded from sports clubs, jobs and homes – but to black America they were still white people who were not sharing the same struggle. *The Diary of Anne Frank* seemed to resonate little in the black press or in the black community; Anne's story was not an obvious source of inspiration. In the language of the civil rights movement, the Frank family had not engaged in direct action but had taken a path of hiding and passive resistance that had ended in their destruction. Anne was a victim, not an icon of liberation and triumph. Pool was in a sense trying to create the 'universal' narrative of Anne's story that Otto himself so much wanted to create – but it was a stretch too far.

Sometimes Pool's lectures struck deeply. At Fisk University in Nashville, one student, Julius Lester, who heard Pool speak wrote,

> As I listen to her talk of a child hiding in an attic ... I understand [Pool's] accented words, but they do not make sense. I do not know how to live with the knowledge of such evils and such suffering ... I think about gas chambers and furnaces into which human beings were shoveled like waste paper ... Being forced to ride at the back of a bus is not in the same realm of human experience.

On other occasions students would be moved but puzzled, believing on one occasion that Pool had written *The Diary of Anne Frank* herself.

As her tour progressed, Pool was not only forced to correct such misconceptions but also to wade into larger controversies surrounding the diary. In the south, Pool had to confront Holocaust deniers for the first time. These were not just antisemites but people who were questioning the truth of the diary as a way to cast doubt over the mass murder of the Jews and the existence of the concentration camps. This was a battle that Otto was engaged with on the front line, and since she had also attached herself to Anne and the diary, Pool found herself on the fringes of some of these debates too.

One of the main assertions Holocaust deniers used to challenge the diary was that it had been written after the war by

Otto himself. Otto would prove this to be untrue in court, but Pool was often questioned about it by southern newspapers. At Xavier University in New Orleans, reporters asked her if the diary had been written by someone else, to which Pool replied, 'I can vouch for every word of it ... I made the first English translation of Anne's notes.' She also waded into the debate about how such a young girl could write such a mature and thoughtful text. Anne had grown up very rapidly, Pool told them, especially confined to the attic for such a long time with so many older people. Americans simply did not understand, she added, that European children had a much more advanced education.

In Mississippi, Pool was also forced to answer antisemitic slurs that Otto Frank was greedily exploiting Anne and the diary for money. Pool adamantly denied this, stating that it was 'far from true' and that the proceeds from the diary went to charity. She was less successful in defending herself against this allegation, as she did not donate her proceeds to charity or to the Anne Frank House or Foundation. Pool was not a mercenary character, pursuing financial gain – she spent decades working for racial equality and creating opportunities, particularly for black writers and performers. To do this, however, she had to make a living, and using her association with Anne Frank was an uncomfortable way of doing so: 'You trade a lot on Anne Frank's name,' one poet angrily wrote to her. 'I hope you have something of her soul and [that] all my suspicions are invalid.'

Rosey Pool's trip to the American south had changed her life, and she would soon return for an even more extended period to work for racial justice. On that occasion, though, there would be no mention of Anne Frank. In Lonneke Geerlings's study on Pool, she notes, 'Pool would rarely speak ever again about her former pupil in public. Later in life she even described Anne Frank's fame as the result of "a morbid interest" and "sensation-alism" that had little to do with sincere human interest.' As Pool had realised, within a few short years Anne Frank had become an American phenomenon. More than 200,000 copies of the diary had been sold, tens of thousands of people had seen the play and now a Hollywood movie reached millions. By 1960 the US had enshrined Anne in history, decreeing that all future Americans would know *The Diary of Anne Frank* by adding the book to the school curriculum. Writer and educator Ilana Abramovitch notes in her essay 'Teaching Anne Frank in the US':

> Anne's diary has a singular place in American education. Adopt-ed by teachers within a few years of its publication in English translation, it soon became the first widely taught text about a victim of the Holocaust. *The Diary of a Young Girl* also became the most widely read diary in American schools and the most widely read work written by an adolescent girl.

Within thirty years, half of all American high-school students had *The Diary of Anne Frank* on their required reading list, with most first encountering it in class at age twelve – just younger than Anne was when she wrote it. Using age as an entry point, teachers encouraged students to think about how they would feel if they were in hiding in a small space, angry at their parents or discovering romantic feelings towards someone. Abramovitch says, 'Teachers report that girls often connect more directly with the diary's female narrator, whereas boys often relate more to Anne's relationship with her parents or accounts of war.'

In the 1970s, one teacher listed more than twenty topics that they touched on through the diary, including history and historical people, thoughts for the future, understanding parents, race relations, self-expression and sex education. Other areas of the curriculum where the diary appeared included genocide studies, peace studies, conflict resolution, respecting differences, the importance of democracy and even health education. In Utah, an Anne Frank unit in health education for eight-year-olds pulled out quotes from the diary relating to nutrition and exercise. 'We have nothing but endive for a long time, endive with sand, endive without sand, stew with endive,' Anne wrote in 1944. When she enthused that she had 'a craze for dancing and ballet' and explained that 'one terrific exercise is to sit on the floor, hold a heel in each hand, and then lift both legs up in the air', teachers instructed their students through a series of exercises they said Anne could have done quietly in the attic without attracting attention.

Using the diary to support such a wide variety of topics also meant creating teacher guides explaining how to use the diary to approach each one. While in the 1960s and 1970s these were booklets and work plans, the way in which the diary is taught has also now evolved to include the internet and, controversially, student simulations. As early as 1993, English teacher Scott Christian set up an online literary forum called the 'Anne Frank conference', where middle-school students from across the US used the study of Anne as a writer to discuss growing up, human nature, 'literature, life, and more'. More recently, Jim DeLong, a language teacher in San Jose, California, built an online 'Anne Frank wall', where teenagers from around the world could post photos of themselves and their friends prominently holding up copies of the diary. At first DeLong used the photos to circle the walls of his classroom, but it grew into a virtual community of students from more than forty countries who were encouraged to 'discover how alive Anne's spirit is today throughout the world ... Anne Frank wrote, "I want to go on living even after my death." In a single glance this wall shows both the power of her teenage writing and the triumph of the human spirit over adversity.'

Taking this a step further, students were sometimes asked to imagine how Anne might have felt and then write their own responses. A fifteen-part lesson plan by the University of North Carolina directed students to write their own journal entries on subjects like, 'Pretend you have one hour to go into hiding. You can NEVER return to your home. You cannot carry a suitcase. What would you take with you and how would you disguise it en route?'

More extreme were lessons where students were asked to simulate experiences of their own to try to replicate elements of what Anne endured. On 14 October 2009, the *South Florida Sun Sentinel* reported, 'Florida students live like Anne Frank', explaining, 'Eighth graders at Florida's Bethany Christian School, which promises "academic excellence in a Christ-centered environment", traded their iPods and cell phones for potatoes, bread and carrots, in an attempt to turn their classroom into Anne Frank's attic for a strangely ascetic sleepover over the weekend.' Other simulations involved locking groups of students into fake classroom 'cattle cars' for an hour or asking them to spend two hours at home without wearing shoes, talking or flushing the toilet to 'live like Anne'.

As *The Diary of Anne Frank* expanded into more and more

areas of the school curriculum, historians and Holocaust memorial organisations criticised such attempts for failing to create any meaningful understanding of or empathy with Anne's experience. Two hours in a bedroom could not really compare to Anne's months hiding in fear in the annexe. How could a general dilution of her words sprinkled over every imaginable subject convey the true history of the Holocaust and the murder of millions? Anne was not 'bullied'; she was the victim of antisemitic persecution by a ruthless fascist regime. She was not on a 'diet' but desperate for any food that could be smuggled in by helpers risking their lives. Using Anne's diary might be a useful entry point for understanding a subject as difficult and traumatic as the Holocaust, but without its historical context it sometimes fell flat. One student wrote, 'Knowing Anne, she was happy in the concentration camps. She didn't have to be quiet anymore; she could frolic outside. She could be in nature. She loved nature. I think this was a welcome relief for her.'

Sometimes students completely misunderstood the diary, and some were too wrapped up in their own types of misery to comprehend another. Elaine Culbertson, a high-school English teacher in Philadelphia in the 1970s, decided to stop teaching *The Diary of Anne Frank* when her students revealed that they did not have any compassion for Anne 'because she had her family with her, as well as some food to eat and a cute boy to flirt with'. For her students, their own lives were much more stressful and dangerous.

If methods of teaching of the diary were controversial with historians and Holocaust memorial organisations, its substance became provocative after the publication of the *Critical Edition* of the diary in 1989. This edition explained the various stages of editing that the text had undergone and reinserted passages Otto had originally decided to remove. Parents, particularly from Christian communities, protested and demanded censorship of the pages where Anne discussed intimate and sexual matters.

In 2010, parents in Culpeper County, Virginia, petitioned the school board to remove passages 'inappropriate for classroom discussion'. School superintendent Bobbi Johnson explained, 'The essence of the story, the struggle of a young girl faced with horrible atrocities, is not lost by editing a few pages that speak to adolescent discovery of intimate feelings.'

The subsequent furore led the school board in Culpeper County to decide that they would allow the full text to be taught but only to older students – but the issue raised its head again in Michigan in 2013, when a mother complained that passages in which Anne describes her clitoris and labia made her young daughter uncomfortable. 'It's pretty graphic and its pretty pornographic for seventh-grade boys and girls to be reading,' she said, adding that it was her own job as a parent to give that information to her daughter. Her bid to get the district to review use of the diary failed when the school board voted unanimously to keep the unexpurgated version on the curriculum. Assistant superintendent Robert Behnke wrote to concerned parents: 'The committee felt strongly that a decision to remove the use of *Anne Frank: The Diary of a Young Girl – The Definitive Edition* as a choice within this larger unit of study would effectively impose situational censorship by eliminating the opportunity for the deeper study afforded by this edition.'

Buddy Elias had himself claimed that the *Critical Edition* was imperative in showing Anne 'in a truer light, not as a saint, but as a girl like every other girl'. But it was a dilemma that Anne, and Otto, had also wrestled over – taking the question of the interpretation of *The Diary of Anne Frank* full circle.

Americans had adopted Anne, flocked to the diary and expressed many of their deepest feelings through their identification with her. Success had sent the diary soaring on a global trajectory that turned its author into a global icon. But America had also turned Anne into a political pawn – and would be the setting of Otto's biggest battle to control her legacy.

CHAPTER 4

THIS IS MORE THAN
A SHOW

'If you really love me you would take a gun and shoot Otto Frank!'
Meyer Levin to his wife Tereska Torrès, from *An Obsession with Anne Frank* by Lawrence Graver

Otto had succeeded is making *The Diary of Anne Frank* one of the most widely read and admired books in the world, but by the early 1950s his life was tipping into personal and professional turmoil.

In New York, writer Meyer Levin, one of Otto's closest advisers and the man who had brought the diary to national prominence through his *New York Times* review, was becoming a mortal enemy, determined to pursue his own vision for a stage adaption of the book at all costs. Meanwhile, in Amsterdam Otto's life had been turned upside down. Old wounds, including the shattering loss of his family, the struggle to maintain his business and his vision for his daughter's legacy, had taken a huge personal toll. But as he teetered on the brink of nervous collapse, something else was transforming his life – new love.

Now facing the glare of publicity and complicated personal relationships, Otto considered escaping the city that held so many memories and starting again in Switzerland.

In September 1952, Otto embarked upon a much-anticipated trip to New York, where he would meet the team at Doubleday, including Barbara Zimmerman; his late wife Edith's brothers Julius and Walter; and Meyer Levin. For a man who had pleaded with Barbara Zimmerman not to arrange any interviews for him and who found even talking about the diary overwhelming and emotional, the trip seemed daunting and nerve-racking. His strength and source of solace was Fritzi Geiringer, the woman who had once lived just across Merwedeplein and whom he had reconnected with on the Soviet transport from Auschwitz. Fritzi and her daughter Eva had survived Auschwitz, but her husband and son had not. Otto had spent time with both Fritzi and Eva in Amsterdam after the war, and they had been amongst the first people to see Anne's diary when Miep returned it to Otto.

Now, his friendship with Fritzi had deepened into love, with Otto addressing long letters to his '*Putzeli*' or '*Sugarli*' from New York. In page after densely packed page, Otto poured out his thoughts and feelings about every aspect of the diary and day-to-day events. Fritzi considered them and replied seriously as a true partner. But more than that, Otto revealed that he was a man in love:

I'm looking forward to seeing you as much as you are with me. In my head you're always with me. I don't think you will have anything to complain about in the future. I haven't experienced real femininity until now. I want to send the letter quickly. Do the kisses do the trick? (They're included.)

Most striking of all in the letter is the line, 'I haven't experienced real femininity until now,' which seemed to sum up everything that had been lacking in his relationship with Edith. Otto felt passionately about Fritzi, and he wasn't afraid to show it.

As usual with Otto, however, there were complications – mainly caused by the hangover from his previous relationships with other women. 'Before he married Fritzi, Otto had other relationships, of course he did,' Laureen Nussbaum recalled. Otto had returned to Amsterdam in 1945, and in those years he had formed strong friendships with several women and romances with some. Otto was tall and dapper, educated and charming, as well as sensitive and respectful to women. Above all, he had shown that he was more than capable of sustaining a long marriage with a happy and loving family life. Nussbaum went on: 'Although it took him a long time to recover from his experiences, he was a very handsome man with a lovely personality. A lot of women were widowed during the war. He really did his best for people. Women liked him and why not!'

Nussbaum went on to recall that a Mrs van Collem, Anneliese Schütz and Lotte Pfeffer all had their eye on him. Lotte was the common-law wife of Fritz Pfeffer, the much-maligned dentist who had shared Anne's room in the annexe. Pfeffer was originally from Germany and had served in the First World War and worked in Berlin before fleeing to Amsterdam with Lotte in December 1938. After divorcing his first wife, Pfeffer had raised his son Peter alone before he was able to send him to safety in England in 1938, to live in the care of his brother. Although Pfeffer and Lotte had lived together as man and wife since 1936, they were unable to marry as Lotte was a Catholic and Germany's Nuremberg laws forbade marriage between a

Jew and a non-Jew. After setting up his dental practice in Amsterdam, Pfeffer became acquainted with the Franks and Miep Gies, who became his patient and arranged for him to go into hiding in the annexe.

After the war, Lotte connected with Otto in Amsterdam. Both of them were searching for information about their loved ones and soon Lotte was joining Jan and Miep Gies to play canasta on Saturday evenings, where Otto would sit alongside them and talk. As the relationship between Lotte and Otto developed, Otto helped Lotte get posthumous recognition of her marriage to Fritz and advised her about her difficult relationship with Fritz's son Peter.

Otto began writing to Peter Pfeffer before they had confirmed that Fritz was dead, saying they still held out hope and he had every sympathy with Peter. The thorny issue between Lotte and Peter seemed to concern payments that Peter believed he was entitled to as Lotte was not actually married to Fritz during his lifetime. Otto wrote,

> I on my part know nothing about your mother, your father never spoke about her and he introduced Charlotte [Lotte] as Mrs Pfeffer to all his acquaintances. Nobody knew that he was not really married to her, and it was not his fault that it was not done, but the laws prevented it being done. For Charlotte this situation is a very difficult one. She did everything possible for your father, she was the greatest support for him, and I know and admire her. I would do anything to help her, she is worth it.

Fritz Pfeffer was transported to Auschwitz with the Franks in 1944, and Lotte later discovered that he had died in Neuengamme concentration camp, near Hamburg, on 20 December 1944, with the cause of death listed as gastrointestinal infection. Otto's letter did nothing to reconcile her with her stepson, although Otto and Peter continued to write to each other for many years after Peter emigrated to the US, where he set up a successful office furniture company called Peter Pepper, which is still in operation today.

As time progressed, friends noticed that Otto and Lotte were becoming closer, and eventually expected to hear that they were getting married. When Otto asked Lotte to accompany him on a visit to his family in Switzerland, Lotte was thrilled and bought a new outfit – but upon their return it was obvious that things had gone wrong. 'We were all sure that Otto would marry Lotte,' Hilde Goldberg said, 'but sometimes things just don't work out.'

At the same time as he maintained his relationship with Lotte, Otto was also growing close to Fritzi – and decided that she was the woman he loved. The break with Lotte was painful and difficult. As time progressed Lotte would become bitter and unhappy about her relationship with Otto and the depiction of her former husband in Anne's diary and the play. For Otto, the situation with Lotte and the increasing public scrutiny he faced in Amsterdam was driving him to the brink of nervous collapse. Hilde Goldberg said,

> I could understand him moving to Switzerland. He was living with Miep and Jan and they had a little boy, but mostly I think it was the situation with Lotte that brought matters to a head. It was a bad time for him as far as Lotte was concerned – he really needed to put some space between them. She was madly in love with him, but he wanted Fritzi.

Trouble also loomed on another front. Otto's letters to Fritzi from his visit to New York chronicled not only his passion for her but also the complicated and deteriorating situation with Meyer Levin.

Levin was living above a bus driver's cottage in Antibes in the south of France when his wife, Tereska Torrès, gave him a copy of *Le Journal* in 1950. Levin had already published several novels and was a fairly well-known newspaper correspondent at this point, but despite the disparity in age and experience, he immediately saw himself as the spiritual guardian of Anne Frank.

Assigned as a writer to the 9th Air Force and the 4th Armored Division of the US Army between September 1944 and June 1945, Levin had seen the terrible suffering and piles of corpses at five Nazi concentration camps, including Ohrdruf, Nordhausen, Buchenwald, Dachau and Bergen-Belsen.

Shocked, Levin moved around the camps, writing down the story of 'the greatest systematic mass murder in the history of mankind' for the American public and trying desperately to account for the names and identities of those he encountered – both alive and dead. Later he recalled that for the first few weeks he groped around, 'beginning to apprehend the monstrous shape of the story', but 'I knew already that I would never penetrate its heart of bile, for the magnitude of this horror seemed beyond human register.' Although he had often written about the Jewish experience in America, and latterly in Palestine, Levin now had an epiphany: 'I realized I would never be able to write the story of the Jews in Europe. This tragic epic cannot be written by a stranger to the experience, for the survivors have an augmented view which we cannot attain.' Instead, a 'teller' would arise – and from the moment he first read her diary Levin was convinced that 'teller' was Anne.

There is no doubt that Meyer Levin understood the profundity and power of *The Diary of Anne Frank* – and his understanding was immediate, at a time when few others realised its potential. At the same time, Levin was afflicted with some of the same issues faced by Rosey Pool; he was a jobbing writer, and he needed to make a living. But more than that, Levin was plagued with a need to establish his reputation as an important writer after his previous work had received a mixed reception. So, just as Levin promoted the diary as a true believer, he also sought to tie himself to it commercially, trying to force Otto into agreeing that he had a role to play in either translating the book or writing the play. His mixed intentions had already caused trouble and discredited his reputation after the *New York Times* angrily discovered that, far from writing his now famous review of the book as an unbiased journalist, Levin was putting himself about town as some sort of agent for Otto Frank, trying to strike deals with producers.

As soon as the book was published in the US, Barbara Zimmerman wrote in an internal memo at Doubleday that Levin's machinations seemed to be screwing up the whole deal. On the day of publication, Zimmerman and Levin had jointly cabled Otto to state that they wanted to act together in representing dramatic rights. Levin then wrote another letter to Otto stating that he had in fact resigned as co-agent for dramatic rights, leaving it to Doubleday – he wanted only to write the adaptation. He added, crucially as matters would turn out: 'Of course, should the situation arise where a production by a famous playwright is possible only if I step aside, I would step aside.'

By now Cheryl Crawford, a famous Broadway producer, had already contacted Doubleday about dramatic rights and, not knowing about Meyer Levin's involvement, suggested Lillian Hellman or Clifford Odets as writers. Crawford had produced *Porgy and Bess*, *Brigadoon* and *Paint Your Wagon*, while Lillian Hellman was the acclaimed author of *The Children's Hour*, *The Little Foxes* and *Watch on the Rhine*, and Clifford Odets was considered one of America's most important playwrights, with works including *Awake and Sing!* and *Paradise Lost*. Otto was conflicted. Although he had never expressly agreed to Meyer Levin's demands, he had certainly acquiesced. Now America's most famous playwrights and producers were knocking at his door.

A few days after the diary was published in the US, Otto cabled Doubleday to agree that they could handle film and play rights, providing that such rights 'be approved by Meyer Levin and myself, as desire Levin as writer or collaborator'. Otto added that he had all confidence in Levin, who 'did a lot for the book, and is entirely filled with it'. Nonetheless, 'I understand that no one who buys the rights will want to have a prescription for what he has to do. How do we get over this point?'

The honest answer was: with great difficulty. Doubleday and Levin seemed to carry on with their separate negotiations for producers, but on 25 June Cheryl Crawford met with Doubleday and agreed that Levin could have the first opportunity to write a script within two months. If at the end of that time Crawford felt it was not completely ready, another writer would work alongside Levin to improve it. She said,

I have read Meyer's plays and think he has talent. I know that he wants very much to dramatize the Diary. I told him I would be willing to give him eight weeks to produce a draft. If it turns out well, I would produce it. If, on the other hand, it does not seem satisfactory, I would engage another playwright and compensate Meyer for his work. It would be splendid if Meyer could write a good dramatization as I know how close he feels to the book, but he is willing to take the chance I have suggested above.

Levin agreed to Crawford's proposal and received a reassuring letter from Otto immediately afterwards, stating, 'Let us hope the results will be gotten and of course I want you to have a share both financially and as a writer.' This would later turn out to be a key piece of correspondence. From the beginning, however, Levin worked on the assumption that if his draft was not deemed stage-worthy, another writer would collaborate with him – not that he would be removed from the project altogether.

Otto's correspondence shows that Levin demanded moral ownership over Anne's diary, and it seems unlikely that another writer would have been able to work successfully with him as a collaborator. Otto was forced to placate him and constantly smooth his ruffled feathers – even though it was Otto who was Anne's bereaved father, the editor of the diary and a Holocaust survivor himself.

From day one, Levin suspected plots against him. On 28 June, Levin's wife Tereska wrote a furious letter to Otto claiming that she knew Doubleday was conspiring to find 'a big American name for the big public', and that it was fascinating to watch 'the big company against the writer who was not *their* writer'. Explicitly, she asked Otto if he wanted Levin to write the play and ended with, 'Your decision at this point is indispensable.'

The barrage of passionate letters to and from all the actors in the saga only hastened the sense that Otto was now a man in emotional crisis. On 7 July, he wrote back to Levin to tell him, 'I am a terribly nervous man, near to a breakdown and must be careful not to hasten matters.' As Levin plotted and fumed, Otto was making arrangements to move back to Basel to be near his family. In Amsterdam, as he explained to Barbara Zimmerman, the past followed him everywhere: 'The most important part of my life I spent in this town, all the past is in some way connected with the city and her inhabitants.' As Anne's diary became a sensational success, he found himself constantly approached in the street by people who wanted to speak with him. While he never refused – he admitted that it was exhilarating to talk about Anne – it was a huge strain on his nerves.

In the summer of 1952, Otto moved into the attic rooms of his family home in Herbstgasse in Basel – an arrangement which others noted was curiously like the physical arrangement of the secret annexe – and thereafter returned to Amsterdam only for a day or two at a time. 'I can no longer live in Amsterdam,' he confided to Barbara Zimmerman. 'I can't stand it for more than three days.' Sometimes Otto returned to the annexe in Prinsengracht, which remained unchanged. 'I look around and then I leave. I cannot bear the sight any longer.'

In the face of so much emotional turmoil, Otto returned to Tereska Torrès's question. Did he want Levin to write the play? It was something he felt unclear about and unable to pass judgement on. His answer was both yes – and no. After long talks with Frank Price at Doubleday, Otto admitted that he was coming round to the idea of another writer working alongside

Levin. After talking with Price and reading Barbara Zimmerman's 'beautiful letters', Otto said he had faith in both Levin and Doubleday to sort things out.

At this point, however, Otto and Levin began to clash over the latter's insistence that only a Jewish writer could adapt the diary – something that would turn into a bitter disagreement between them. Levin was the author of six novels, including *Frankie and Johnny*, a story of two lovestruck teenagers in 1920s Chicago; *Yehuda*, set on a kibbutz; *The New Bridge*, about the life of an unemployed construction worker in the Depression; *The Old Bunch*, about the lives of Jewish families on the west side of Chicago; and *Citizens*, about a strike and the shooting of workers at a steel factory.

Lawrence Graver notes in *An Obsession with Anne Frank* that Levin 'seemed to be on the verge of shaping "a career" as an American novelist writing frequently and convincingly about the tensions of Jewish life'. Yet, while his books showed promise and often received favourable reviews, none of them were financially successful, and Levin himself admitted that his readership was 'faithful but not too numerous'. After his devastating epiphany in the war, Levin made two films in 1947–48: *My Father's House*, about a child who goes to Palestine hoping to find the father he had been separated from in a concentration camp; and *The Illegals*, a documentary about a ship secretly transporting Jewish survivors to Palestine. These films convinced Levin that his destiny was now to tell the story of Jewish life and modern America, and in 1948 he embarked upon an ambitious memoir, *In Search*. It divided his life into three sections, dealing first with his childhood in Chicago, secondly with his experiences in the war and finally with his efforts in print and in film to draw attention to the struggle of European Jews and their lives in the new state of Israel.

'Levin wrote *In Search* as if his life depended upon it,' Lawrence Graves notes, 'and in important ways it did.' *In Search* was supposed to be Levin's 'big book', the culmination of all his previous works and the vindication of his years of effort on behalf of the Jewish people. Much to his despair, publishers did not share his vision. 'From the moment he submitted *In Search* for publication … Levin's worst suspicions about his place in the literary scene in America were confirmed and intensified,' says Graves. Editors complained about Levin's focus on the victimisation of the Jews and his chronicling of his own numerous quarrels with the publishing industry. The book was 'overburdened with resentment and a conviction of having been wronged', wrote Random House, while Viking said it was verbose and self-indulgent. When Levin complained to Random House, editor Saxe Commins replied that while the book was written with a sense of urgency, the reading public would not be interested in Levin's grudges against publishers and film producers, concluding that the manuscript 'leaves the impression that a particular person, yourself, had a hell of a time with everybody'.

Although *In Search* was finally published in France, and then in the US in 1950, Levin was now convinced that he was engaged in an epic battle against people who refused to recognise his talent. Publishers, by their account, described him as suspicious, obstinate and incredibly difficult to work with.

Otto Frank could hardly have imagined that he was entering into this toxic stew when he first struck up correspondence with such a seemingly devoted fan of his daughter's work. But the progress of negotiation around the diary seemed only to confirm Levin's deepest fears. Not only was he in danger of being evicted from his own project (as he saw it) – but also in favour of a more famous writer, and one who had no interest in the Jewish essence of the work. Otto, for his part, used this moment to explain to Levin that he had never shared Levin's vision of the diary as a Jewish text, and reiterated his belief that its meaning was universal.

At the very beginning of negotiations for dramatic rights for the diary, Levin had sent Otto a list of the various playwrights who had expressed an interest in the play, including Maxwell Anderson, who Levin told Otto was wrong for the project for several reasons – not least because he wasn't Jewish. 'All literature, all art, in an expression of the soul; no stranger can as well express the soul of a people as someone from that people,' Levin concluded. But Otto did not agree and laid out his thoughts on the meaning of Anne's work in the starkest terms:

> As to the Jewish [issue] you are right that I do not feel the same way as you do. I always said that Anne's book is not a war book. War is the background. It is not a Jewish book either, though Jewish sphere, sentiment and surrounding is the background. I never wanted a Jew writing an introduction for it. It is (at least here) read and understood more by gentile than in Jewish circles. I do not know how that will be in the USA, it is the case in Europe. So do not make a Jewish play out of it!

As contract negotiations between Levin and Cheryl Crawford became more tense, this issue became paramount in Levin's mind.

He had spent the summer of 1952 working on the script for the diary on Fire Island. And he had squeezed in writing a radio play of an extract of the diary, which was broadcast on CBS during Jewish New Year and received good reviews from *Variety* and *Billboard*. After delivering a draft of the play in late September, Levin was buoyed by a call from Cheryl Crawford, who agreed that the script was 'promising' and good enough to proceed.

Yet all summer disagreement and mistrust had rumbled beneath the surface. Levin had frustrated Doubleday by conducting his own negotiations with producers and directors since the very beginning, often telling the publishers nothing about his manoeuvres. In August he had written to Otto, including a draft contract between them to agree rights and royalties. The contract took Otto aback, however, especially as it seemed very different to the agreement he believed Levin had reached with Cheryl Crawford. He asked Levin to wait until he arrived in New York in September, so they could all discuss the matter in person.

After the hugely successful publication of the diary in the US, Otto must have hoped to return to New York in a swathe of good publicity and support for Anne's legacy, as well as taking the opportunity to reconnect with old friends like Charles Nathan Straus and his late wife Edith's brothers. Accompanied by his cousin Milly Stanfield, he arrived on the *Queen Elizabeth* ocean liner on 29 September and was swept off in a huge Cadillac to the Madison Hotel, where he found whiskey and a bouquet of flowers waiting for him. Doubleday had arranged for him to sign for everything or ask for more money – which, being ever frugal and proper, he did not do.

Almost immediately the visit verged on overwhelming Otto's precarious emotional defences. Edith's brother Julius was, Otto reported, 'a wreck about the past' and 'very depressed and nervous'. At the hotel he hardly had a moment to himself, with hordes of people wanting to speak or listen to him. 'I've had no peace and quiet, and I'm quite excited, although I try to remain calm,' he wrote to Fritzi on 30 September. Otto had seen *The Diary of Anne Frank* in many bookshop windows and had visited Doubleday and spoken to the sales agents. Meyer Levin had also delivered a first draft of the script to him, and Otto was reading it slowly as it 'excites me terribly and I have to cry all the time'. Cheryl Crawford agreed in principle with the script, Otto wrote to Fritzi, and he hoped that only a few changes would be necessary.

A few days later, on 3 October, a bombshell struck: Cheryl Crawford told Otto and Levin that she had re-read the play and thought the script lost touch with the characters; they no longer moved her. She did not think the script had enough dramatic potential to continue or to engage another writer as collaborator. She now wanted to commission a new writer, with no input from Levin.

Levin was shocked and aghast. Crawford's rejection was full and final – and seemed to come after she had made such encouraging noises about the draft only a few days earlier. Crawford explained that she had come to her decision after carefully re-reading the play, but later evidence showed that she had in fact been swayed by other playwrights, including Lillian Hellman. Reluctantly, she agreed to allow Levin a month to rewrite the play, and to get a second opinion from another producer, Kermit Bloomgarden. However, Bloomgarden's opinion was even more damming, and he told Otto and Crawford that 'a producer would have to be crazy' to stage Levin's work.

Rather than encouraging Levin to accept the rejection of his play, Crawford's behaviour only confirmed to him – perhaps with some basis – that there was a plot against him by more famous writers who wanted to steal the project for themselves. While Levin ran around whipping up support for his script from other well-known critics, agents and producers, he contested that Crawford had never intended to produce his script but had only created the agreement between them to secure dramatic rights. In the face of her refusal to honour the agreement, Levin told Otto he should cancel the contract with Crawford and find a new producer to stage Levin's version of the play.

Otto was distraught about the awful and unpleasant situation he now found himself in. While he understood and appreciated the role Levin had played in publicising the diary, he had a legal contact with Crawford – and his confidence in Levin's script was vanishing. 'I'm getting impatient,' he wrote to Fritzi on 20 October. He had met with both Crawford and Levin but understood that Levin was not happy with the idea of making changes to his script. 'I told him that Bloomgarden and Miss Crawford didn't think his script was dramatic enough.' Levin did not want to engage with the conversation. He still had hope, Otto said, which he found very uncomfortable, describing the Levin disagreement as 'a knot that needed undoing'.

At the suggestion of Charles Nathan Straus, Otto appointed Myer Mermin, an attorney at Paul, Weiss, Rifkind, Wharton and Garrison, to take over the contract negotiations. After reading through the correspondence and the informal agreements that had been struck up by various parties at different times,

Mermin concluded that without formal contracts the case was not clear-cut. 'I had a meeting with my lawyer who sees great difficulties ahead,' Otto told Fritzi. 'The real problem is that Crawford didn't arrange a real contract with him and now it's too late.' Otto now wished he could drop 'the whole show business' and met with Levin to tell him, 'It's not right for the ideals of Anne to do something that might end up in a court case, and it's better to do nothing than for that to happen.'

Working with Levin's agent Miriam Howell, Mermin drew up a new agreement. Levin would have one month to submit his script to a list of agreed producers and see if they would agree to stage the play. If they did, Crawford would withdraw from the project. If they did not, Levin would lose his claim as the preferred writer and Otto and Crawford could proceed with a new writer. Two important supplements were added to the agreement: first, if Levin could not stage his script, Crawford would pay him $500 for his work; second, subsequent to a New York opening, Levin would have the opportunity to stage a Hebrew version of his play in Israel.

For a month Levin scrambled to get a producer on the list to agree to stage his script – but despite some praise, he was unsuccessful. By 21 December it was clear that Levin had lost whatever rights he had to the play. His involvement with *The Diary of Anne Frank* had reached a professional dead-end. This was a bitter pill and, predictably, Levin refused to swallow it. Instead of unhappily accepting the terms of the agreement, he struck out in a public legal battle to claim what he believed he had been unjustly denied.

First, he wrote a long and impassioned letter, outlining his complaints and alleging threats and deceit, to Brooks Atkinson, drama critic at the *New York Times*. Atkinson replied, advising him that it was not a topic for the *New York Times*, but he should try *Variety*. Levin did this, but the letter was not published after Crawford issued an angry denial of all the charges.

Levin was further enraged to discover that Crawford was considering asking novelist and playwright Carson McCullers to write the play, and in December he wrote to Otto Frank, who had now returned to Basel:

> I am disgusted and enraged at the thought that a non-Jew has been selected to write the play ... You may say it does not matter and all the rest of it, but after the way my work was treated to bring in a Gentile writer over the dozens of excellent Jewish writers, to have it produced by a Gentile when important Jewish producers who were eager to do it were ruled off the list, is scandalous beyond measure. I will not stand for this. I will write about it wherever I can.

Carson McCullers was indeed considering adapting the play and had written an emotional letter to Otto comparing Anne to Mozart, Keats and Chekhov. Ultimately, however, she was deterred by the vitriol and bad publicity associated with Meyer Levin's campaign. Despite meeting Otto Frank, she withdrew from the project in early 1953, fearing her health could not withstand the strain. Cheryl Crawford felt the same way, and also feared that after the financial failure of *Camino Real* she did not have the monetary resources to fight a possible lawsuit against Levin. By the spring of 1953, she had withdrawn too – and Otto was left with neither a writer nor a producer.

Upon hearing that Levin was considering bringing a lawsuit, Otto lashed out in anger:

I told you that it is against the ideas and ideals of Anne to have disputes and quarrels and suing ... I start to see you as a different person ... I would be very much pleased if you could stop with every kind of trouble making as this is unjust and below your standing.

In a second letter he added that every contract was sacred to him, even if it ended up to his disadvantage, and he told Levin: 'You are a bad loser.'

His letters to Barbara Zimmerman at the time reflect his anguish, however, and his nagging uncertainty that in many ways Levin had been treated unfairly. Although he stood by their contract, Otto believed Cheryl Crawford had behaved badly, and he questioned the role Doubleday had played in the negotiations too.

Levin was rash and untrustworthy, obsessed only with staging his own play and dishonestly determined to twist every fact to suit his own argument, Zimmerman replied. 'His bitterness has no basis in fact,' she told Otto, dismissing Levin's assertion that only a Jewish writer could convey Anne's story. As a Jew herself, Zimmerman admitted that she could understand why a Jewish writer might feel more strongly about the work, but 'the wonderful thing about Anne's book is that it really is universal, that it is a book, and experience, for everyone'.

Zimmerman believed that Meyer Levin was in danger of destroying both himself and Anne's play, and increasingly others in Otto's circle agreed with her. Myer Mermin was now on the front line of the dispute in New York. He believed that Levin's original genuine enthusiasm for the diary had been overtaken by his desperation to get his own script staged. Over the summer of 1953 Zimmerman and Mermin worked to replace Cheryl Crawford with Kermit Bloomgarden, constantly reassuring him that Levin's accusations were baseless and having him indemnified against any legal claim Levin might make. On 1 October 1953, Bloomgarden signed the production agreement, and work on the Broadway play was finally underway. For Levin, however, this did not signify that his war against the New York literary world was over, only that a new stage in his campaign had begun.

Bloomgarden considered a series of writers, including Carson McCullers, but finally decided on Frances Goodrich and Albert Hackett, a married couple and the biggest screenwriting team in Hollywood. Their work included the screen versions of *The Thin Man, Easter Parade, Father of the Bride, It's a Wonderful Life* and *Seven Brides for Seven Brothers*. Goodrich was the daughter of a wealthy Jewish family from New Jersey who had graduated from Vasser and was twice divorced by the time she met fellow actor Albert Hackett, and they teamed up together to write the 1931 play *Up Pops the Devil*. Hackett was from a show-business family and was the son of stage actress Florence Hackett and the brother of matinee idol Raymond Hackett. Together Goodrich and Hackett had written Hollywood classics with a formula that appealed to millions of Americans. But the prospect of adapting *The Diary of Anne Frank* left them daunted and apprehensive.

Accepting the commission, Kermit Bloomgarden told them the project was a tense drama that offered intimacy and 'moments of lovely comedy' that only heightened the tragic situation. The comedy was essential, Bloomgarden told them, as the only way to get people to sit through the show would be if it was funny. After the intense negative coverage of the row with Meyer Levin, Goodrich and Hackett also felt they needed to prove they were serious writers. They began studying European and Dutch history, as well as Judaism, visiting Jewish bookstores and even consulting with a rabbi over the correct ritual for celebrating Hanukkah.

Although the project would be tremendously challenging, Goodrich and Hackett told Otto, they were determined to catch Anne's indomitable spirit. Otto replied reassuring them that his vision for the play was one that focused on Anne's universal appeal. The people who had hidden in the annexe came from diverse Jewish backgrounds, he explained, ranging from the Orthodox Fritz Pfeffer to the more liberal but deeply spiritual beliefs of his wife and Margot. Otto admitted that while he had become a more conscious Jew because of his marriage to Edith, he had no religious background whatsoever. Anne, he added, was inscrutable on the question of her Jewish faith – although she did stand next to him when he lit the Hanukkah candles.

Goodrich and Hackett were relieved to hear this, as they'd heard that Levin's version of the play had been sunk by 'solemn breast-beating' about the fate of the Jews. Instead, they wanted to write an intimate and inspiring story that would leave the audience feeling uplifted. Even so, deference to Anne's and Otto's innocence and suffering left them timid and constrained, and they struggled through four unsuccessful drafts that included long passages of direct narration from the diary and little dramatic action. Finding the right note for a Broadway play about residents of what Anne herself had called 'a very peculiar board-ing house', who would share tense moments and hijinks before being murdered, was extremely difficult.

In an attempt to help with the script, Otto sent them a copy of Anne's writing *Give*, a work he belied typified her naïve and childish idealism. Goodrich replied that while it might be naïve, its message of love and understanding was what the world needed in such chaotic times. But Goodrich and Hackett had failed to make a personal connection with Otto – something he held great store by. Everything linked to Anne and the diary was personal to Otto; it was his real life, not just a business deal. When he received the second draft of the Goodrich and Hack-ett script, he hated it.

In comparison to Meyer Levin's script, which Otto believed had psychological development and good characterisation, the Hacketts' work was 'routine', 'not working up to the high spirit of Anne and in its present form would never convey the mes-sage which the book contains'.

Bloomgarden and Lillian Hellman also responded with nega-tive criticism of the early draft, claiming the Hacketts had stuck too closely to the written diary and failed to flesh out or dram-atise the characters out of sympathy for their fate. Anne was a saint but superficial. Margot was too 'snappish' in Otto's opinion, and she and Edith were portrayed as distant background charac-ters instead of forming the crux of dramatic tension with Anne as she entered puberty. While Otto was uncomfortable with the humour in the script, Kermit Bloomgarden told the Hacketts he would not produce the play unless it had more 'spiritual lift' for Anne. Frances Goodrich ruefully reflected that in trying to do justice to the characters while making them sympathetic, they had not made them human.

Disheartened, Goodrich and Hackett retreated to Martha's Vineyard in September 1954, to work on the script with Hellman. Their sixth draft, submitted after their stay, transformed the play. With reduced narration, it now had a satisfying rhythm that carried the story from scenes of tension and fear to life-affirming warmth and hope. Hellman had particularly advised heightening the drama in moments like the arrival of Fritz Pfeffer and the Hanukkah scene, where the inhabitants of the attic must decide whether and how to celebrate the holiday while in hiding. In October, Garson Kanin joined the team as director and focused further on the universal appeal of the play, adding Anne's voiceover of diary entries as a bridge between scenes.

Comparing Anne to the *Mona Lisa*, Kanin decreed that the play should not be depressing but instead an exaltation of her 'life force' and human spirit. Although he later claimed that the project was less of a theatre job and more of a 'rare religious experience', it was Kanin who stripped many of the Jewish references from the play, substituting Anne's words about how Jews had suffered through the ages with a more anodyne reference to the fact that people of all faiths had suffered at different times in history. He also replaced Fritz Pfeffer's comments about the persecution the Jews by the Nazis with the phrase: 'No one in Holland has enough to eat.'

'The fact that in this play the symbols of persecution and oppression are Jewish is incidental, and Anne, in stating the argument so, reduces her magnificent stature,' Kanin wrote. 'In other words, at this moment, the play has an opportunity to spread its theme into the infinite.'

Otto agreed with all efforts to make the play as universal as possible and welcomed the Hacketts and Kanin to Amsterdam for a week on 6 December 1954 to see the locations and atmosphere themselves. Together, they visited the area around Merwedeplein, Anne's old school and her favourite ice-cream shop. While the Hacketts met a Dutch historian and bought books about the city, Garson Kanin photographed everything necessary to recreate the annexe on stage, including windows, door handles and stairs. He even taped the sound of the church bells and the tram cars and the bicycles riding past. All were moved by the 'very harrowing' moments they spent in the room Anne had shared with Fritz Pfeffer, never more so than when they looked at the wall and saw a photo she had pinned there of Ginger Rogers starring in *Tom, Dick and Harry* – a film Kanin had directed.

Frances Goodrich wrote in her diary that she spent the entire week in tears and had 'thought that I could not cry more than I had'. She added that she had heard the strain had been so great that Otto had been ill for a week after their departure. Kanin recalled that he had found Otto 'a cold fish', who had shown them around Amsterdam without an ounce of emotion – until he found out that after their departure Otto had collapsed: 'He had been crushed, but he had not shown it.'

Otto wrote to his lawyer Myer Mermin that spending the week with the Hacketts and Kanin was a 'wonderful experience' and opportunity to discuss the play, but it had been 'very exciting too' – a term he often used to signify something that caused him extreme nervous distress rather than happiness.

Over Christmas, the Hacketts continued to refine the script while the casting of the main characters was finalised. After much debate, the young and relatively untested Susan Strasberg was cast in the central role of Anne. At seventeen, Strasberg was the daughter of legendary drama coach Lee Strasberg and had appeared in off-Broadway productions and sitcoms. She would star with Joseph Schildkraut playing Otto and Gusti Huber as Edith. While Schildkraut, a longstanding character actor, told Bloomgarden that the play gave him an 'almost sacred' feeling inside, and he wrote to Otto that he believed Anne was an immortal heroine like Joan of Arc, his outbursts and tantrums during rehearsals made the experience intensely difficult for Strasberg. Schildkraut was upset about having to shave his head to look like Otto, Strasberg wrote in her diary, and wanted her replaced because she was upstaging him – he was 'even unhappy because it was called *The Diary of Anne Frank*'. Almost every day 'he threatened to quit, accompanied by torrents of tears, which I later learned he could turn on or off at will'.

More public controversy was stirred by the casting of Gusti Huber, however. While Susan Strasberg, Joseph Schildkraut, Frances Goodrich and Garson Kanin all came from Jewish families, Gusti Huber was an Austrian actress who was accused of being a Nazi sympathiser close to Joseph Goebbels. Huber had married an American officer after the war and moved to the US, where she starred on Broadway in *Flight into Egypt* and *Dial M for Murder*. The accusation had been made by another actress, Lotte Stavisky, who refused to work with Huber, and was backed up by a 1935 Viennese newspaper article sent to Kermit Bloomgarden, in which Huber stated she would not associate with non-Aryan artists, who would 'endanger her stature in Nazi Germany'.

Although Otto was extremely worried about the accusation, it seemed that nothing could derail the production, and Huber went ahead to play the role of Edith both on stage and in the 1959 film. As rehearsals entered their final, frenzied stage, even more Jewish references were stripped from the script, including Peter's plaintive cry that they were being imprisoned 'because we are Jews!' and, most notably, the traditional Hanukkah music, the 'Ma'oz Tzur', was replaced with a far less solemn American song, 'O, Hanukkah'.

With opening night approaching, Otto fretted over whether 'the spirit of Anne's book will be transferred to the public'. Yet Anne's transformation into a 1950s American teenager was almost complete. Frances Hackett described Anne as a 'captivating, bright spirit', who might have been 'your neighbor's teenage daughter – or your own', while Garson Kanin added, 'I have never looked upon it as a sad play. I certainly have no wish to inflict depression upon an audience; I don't consider that a legitimate theatrical end.' Rather than viewing her death as a waste, the audience should instead see her life as part of a 'breathlessly exciting story'.

After years of wrangling, *The Diary of Anne Frank* premiered at the Cort Theatre in New York on 5 October 1955 – and it was nothing less than a staggering success. Marilyn Monroe graced the opening with star power, while a series of ecstatic reviews put Susan Strasberg on the cover of every American newspaper and magazine. If Dutch critics moaned that the play was 'kitsch' and had turned Anne into a 'thing of amusement', it was just what the American public wanted.

Brooks Atkinson in the *New York Times* called it a 'lovely, tender drama', while William Hawkins of the *New York*

World-Telegram reported that there was 'nothing grim or sensational about it'. Richard Watts of the *Post* wrote, 'There isn't a Nazi in it,' adding to the comments of the *Herald Tribune*, which stated, '*The Diary of Anne Frank* is not in any important sense a Jewish play'; instead, 'Anne Frank is a little Orphan Annie brought into vibrant life.'

Otto could not bear to attend in person but rather sent a letter to the cast that was pinned up backstage: 'You will all realize that for me this play is a part of my life, and the idea that my wife and children, as well as I, will be presented on the stage is a painful one to me. Therefore it is impossible for me to come and see it.' Instead, he wished them every success and that the message of the play would reach as many people as possible and 'awaken in them a sense of responsibility to humanity'.

The success of the play ensured that Otto's wish became a reality. *The Diary of Anne Frank* ran for 717 performances and was attended by 1 million people in New York. Soon, the play would tour more than twenty cities in North America and open across Europe and the world. In each new country the opening night was often attended by royalty and celebrities, keeping the play in the public eye, while in small towns amateur groups would stage their own versions, as well as there being school productions. In 1956 the play would win both the New York Drama Critics Circle Award for best American production and the Pulitzer Prize for drama. No wonder Frances Goodrich wrote that she was 'walking on air' at the play's success.

For Otto, however, there was much more at stake than a successful production, and the controversy caused by angry and distraught relatives upset by the characterisation on Fritz Pfeffer and the van Pels family, combined with an ongoing battle with

Meyer Levin, would almost tear him apart. Otto's careful editing of the diary and his extremely detailed notes to producers
and writers show that he was always understandably concerned
about presenting his family in the best light. When Anne talked
too much about her sexual feelings, those passages were crossed
out. If Edith seemed uncaring or overbearing, Anne's harsh descriptions were moderated. If writers like the Hacketts implied
Margot was snappish or unsympathetic, Otto quickly wrote
a letter insisting they correct the impression. As the ultimate
editor of the diary, Otto's opinion was paramount when it came
to the book. But he had far less control over a stage or film version, as writers and directors argued for more 'dramatic tension',
often at the expense of the truth.

Otto had agreed with all attempts to strip passages from the
text relating to the persecution of the Jews, but he also wrestled
with the representations of others in the annexe, which were car-
icatured for dramatic effect but extremely hurtful for remaining
family members. Many were already upset that their relatives
and loved ones were presented in the diary only through Anne's
eyes – the lens of an adolescent girl who sometimes lacked ma-
turity and sensitivity. When Frances Goodrich had toured the
annexe as part of her research for the script, she had marvelled
at Anne's bedroom, noting in her diary that this was the space
she had shared with 'the crotchety dentist'. But Fritz Pfeffer
was far from a bad-tempered religious irritant in the eyes of his
wife Lotte or his son Peter. As Otto was already struggling with
own relationship with Lotte Pfeffer, he forbade the Hacketts
from inventing a scene in the play where Pfeffer stole bread.
The scene went ahead, however, with Hermann van Pels as the
thief – an inclusion that he feared would upset van Pels's brother

so much it might lead to a lawsuit. As we will see later, for her part Lotte could not be pacified, and Otto found that many of his other friends in Amsterdam were questioning why he had allowed hurtful characterisations and untruths to be included. As the Hacketts immediately shifted their attention to turning their hit play into a Hollywood film, the problem intensified.

One month after the play had opened on Broadway, the Hacketts visited Otto in Basel, where he was now settled and happily married to Fritzi Geiringer. Knowing that Otto was apprehensive about a film, the Hacketts employed a three-pronged approach, combining their own visit with a letter from a mutual friend, Calvin Fox, and pressure and persuasion from their agent Leah Salisbury.

The correspondence between the Hacketts, Fox and Salisbury shows the crafty way they attempted to manipulate Otto's emotions, first sending Fox out to tell Otto that the Hacketts were also 'insecure' about the prospect of turning the diary into a film, as they shared Otto's 'intense emotional involvement' with the project. Salisbury followed with a letter offering to represent Otto in film negotiations, as she too had loved and suffered with him and taken the Franks to her heart. Yet when Otto politely rejected her offer, Salisbury and Frances Goodrich exchanged letters musing on the idea that Otto did not want to pay an agent's 10 per cent commission because he was too 'frugal' and suggesting he was a 'curious mix of great emotion and business', giving money away while 'securing its source'. Goodrich went on to add, callously, that she'd noticed Otto couldn't speak of the diary without crying but was always quite happy to invent scenes and change Anne's words at the same time.

While Otto fretted over every detail, producers, agents and

writers had long learned that they could easily manage his re-quests by appealing to their own personal attachment to Anne and their commitment to spread the message of her legacy. Behind Otto's back they often showed little sympathy for his loss. 'I thought I was the only one who dreaded his visit,' Albert Hackett wrote to Leah Salisbury when he heard that Otto might visit America. 'He lives in the past, and once he gets talking about the diary, the play, or Anne, he has very soon reduced Frances to tears.' The Hacketts, Kermit Bloomgarden and Garson Kanin were in full agreement that they would do everything in their power to deny Otto 'too much control' over the play or proposed film.

As pressure to agree to a film intensified, Otto expressed his fears that a movie would be even less true to the book, writing to his lawyer Myer Mermin that he feared some of the charac-ters would be represented in the wrong way, and he would be unable to face 'the reproaches of my conscience, of my family, or Miep, Kleiman and the others, who never understood that I gave away the rights to get money without any promise from the producer to respect the quality of the material'. Mermin, however, was working closely with Salisbury and the Hacketts to get Otto to agree to a film and without his knowledge passed on all of Otto's correspondence for them to read.

By the autumn of 1956 Otto had been persuaded of the bene-fits of turning what was now a hit play into a film, and he cabled the Hacketts in October to tell them he would he like to go ahead with them as writers – as long as he maintained a con-sulting role. For their part, the Hacketts were desperate to be rid of Otto and what they saw as his constant interference, made more complicated by the previously mentioned bad feeling the play had engendered from the people in his life and their fears that their representations in a film would be even worse.

No one was more upset than Lotte Pfeffer, who accused the Hacketts of portraying her husband as a 'psychopath' and a ridiculous loner. Specifically, she called out the fact that the play showed Pfeffer being educated about the Hanukkah ceremony as a means of educating the audience, when he was in fact the most religious person in the annexe and took his Jewish faith extremely seriously. The Hacketts batted away her complaint as well as her demand to see a screenplay in advance, telling Lotte that such plot devices were necessary and 'a play cannot mirror reality'. Unsatisfied, Lotte took up the matter directly with Otto, who wrote to Frances Goodrich: 'She is demanding from a film historical truth. This she cannot ask, nor does the public expect it.' His response seems remarkably unsympathetic given that he sought to exert his own tight control over the material and the characters he most cared about. Otto replied to Lotte telling her not to be so childish and that the Hacketts had the legal right to write what they wished.

Not only was she deeply unhappy about the portrayal of her husband and the breakdown of her romantic relationship with Otto, who had now chosen to marry Fritzi, but Lotte was also struggling with the news that her own son had been killed in the war. She wrote to Otto: 'I still quietly hoped that he would be in Estonia with farmers and I believed I would hear from him one day. Another illusion lost.' Carol Ann Lee includes in her biography of Otto an unexplained contract between Otto and Lotte, drawn up in 1956, in which Otto renounces 'repayment of all the sums of money he has given so far to Mrs Pfeffer'. In return, Lotte agrees to renounce all claims to *The Diary of Anne Frank* in book, play or film form.

Any remaining friendship between Otto and Lotte had been snuffed out, and she remained bitter about his treatment of her for the rest of her life. Other friends of Fritz Pfeffer shared her sentiment, with one writing to Otto: 'I will do my utmost to tell everyone who I speak to about the play how Fritz really was. Do you actually believe that an idiot could ever become a doctor or a dentist? I don't. Have you ever thought about why Fritz became a complainer during the hiding period?' Fritz Pfeffer was a stranger amongst them, all alone and worried about his family and his wife, the letter went on. 'Friends and acquaintances of myself and Fritz are enraged about the way in which the character of Fritz was portrayed.' Pfeffer had been reduced to a mere laughing stock and was now 'dead and unable to defend himself'.

If such words wounded and upset Otto, they had no effect on the Hacketts, who resisted his every attempt to recast Pfeffer in a more favourable light. Nor did it stop Otto from signing a contract for a film version with 20th Century Fox on 20 May 1957, with Goodrich and Hackett as the writers and George Stevens as the director. Stevens was another Hollywood giant, responsible for films including *A Place in the Sun, Shane* and *Giant*. His own experience as a young US soldier who had liberated Dachau made him enormously sympathetic to the story of Anne Frank, and his films thereafter were more serious. Otto liked him and felt their discussions showed their mutual understanding for the project.

When filming began in the spring of 1958, Joseph Schildkraut and Gusti Huber reprised their roles as Otto and Edith, but, as Susan Strasberg had announced she did not want to play Anne in the film, excited rumours and suggestions swirled about who would win the legendary role. For Otto, one actress stood out above all the rest – Audrey Hepburn. Hepburn had lived through the war in the Netherlands and bitterly remembered the Nazi occupation and the 'hunger winter' of 1944. She had seen Jews being shunted onto railway cattle trucks to be deported to concentration camps and had nightmares about it: 'All those faces peering out. On the platform, soldiers herding more Jewish families with their poor little bundles and small children … It was very hard to understand.'

After the war, Hepburn had lived in Amsterdam and read *The Diary of Anne Frank* in galley form in 1947 – which reduced her to floods of tears and made her hysterical. When George Stevens asked her to consider the role, she read the book again and wrote that she had to take to her bed for an entire day. As Hepburn and her husband Mel Ferrer were then living in Switzerland, Otto and Fritzi visited them to discuss the film. Hepburn remembered that Otto and Fritzi 'both had the numbers on their arms. He was a beautiful-looking man, very fine, a sort of transparent face, very sensitive. Incapable of talking about Anne without extreme feeling.' Otto seemed 'purged by fire', she added, saying that there was something spiritual about his face. 'He'd been there and back.'

Hepburn formed a lasting friendship with the family that even included Otto's sister Leni and meant that she later joined the Anne Frank Educational Trust in the UK as a patron. But in truth, at almost thirty she was too old to play a teenaged Anne. Regretfully, she turned down the role, telling Otto that in addition to her age she didn't want to exploit Anne's life and death just to get another salary and be praised in a movie. After Natalie Wood also turned down the role, the producers undertook a highly publicised national search for 'Anne' – finally casting an unknown nineteen-year-old model from New Jersey: Millie Perkins.

George Stevens had gone to great lengths to recreate the setting of war-time Amsterdam, filming exterior shots in the city and building a replica of the annexe on Stage 14 of the 20th Century lot. Props including pencils, milk bottles and bags were sent from the Netherlands to Hollywood, and the crew even bought bread from a Dutch baker in California. Stevens put up bulletin boards around the set so the actors were constantly reminded of photos of Anne and images of the terrible treatment of the Jews during the war.

Despite this and his own first-hand experience of the horrors of concentration camps, Stevens felt he had to reassure the American public that the film would be 'valiant' and 'humorous' and would emphasise Anne's 'magnificent triumph over fear'. He added, wrongly, that 'Anne didn't know anything about the camps'. Her diary was less a book about a girl facing death than the story of 'someone facing life'.

The Hacketts, Bloomgarden and Stevens did their utmost to portray the diary as an uplifting story, and if they did not reflect the true horror the situation, they probably did ensure its commercial success. Stevens's original ending for the film, set in Auschwitz, tested badly with audiences and was replaced by shots of floating clouds, overlaid with Anne's voice stating, 'In spite of everything, I still believe people are really good at heart.'

Barbara Zimmerman from Doubleday wrote that no one

wanted to have a sad, hopeless ending. It needed to be uplifting. The Hacketts 'weren't Shakespeare', she admitted, but they had made a good effort. Perhaps the refrain about people being good at heart was unfortunate, but the Hacketts helped sell a lot more books.

Still, after the astonishing success of the play, the reception of the film was disappointing. Critics pointed to the somewhat superficial characters and the narrative that had been stripped of most Jewish references. Audiences were smaller than expected. One cinema manager reflected that people were getting weary of hearing about the Holocaust and the war. Or perhaps, coming in at under three hours, the film was just too long. Yet despite the disappointing performance of the film compared to the play, *The Diary of Anne Frank* was nominated for eight Academy Awards and won three – including an Oscar for Shelley Winters, who had played Mrs van Pels (van Daan in the film).

Otto had been well compensated for the success of the play and the film. He was no longer the hard-up businessman who had moved into his family's attic in Basel, but he still lived like a frugal and careful man. In truth, he needed all his money to finance his new philanthropic venture – setting up the Anne Frank House in Amsterdam. Unfortunately, his financial and emotional resources had been sorely tested fighting a series of court cases, beginning with one against the increasingly irate and litigious Meyer Levin.

Levin had been predictably horrified by the appointment of the 'Hacketts of Hollywood' as screenwriters, and he had shared his anger and dismay as widely and publicly as possible. Sitting in the audience for a preview of the play at the Walnut Street Theatre in Philadelphia, Levin was struck not only by what he felt was the ongoing injustice being perpetrated against him but also by the familiarity of the material. Writing to Otto, he said, 'I have seen the play, and need hardly tell you that it is very much like the play I wrote.' All the torment and unpleasantness of the previous three years had been unnecessary, if only Otto had allowed him to produce his play which was so similar – only his had better characterisation. Levin's initial sadness and dismay soon turned to anger as he became seized by another conviction: the Hacketts had plagiarised his work. And this time, he would take his case to court.

Otto was convinced that Levin was deeply neurotic, in the grip of an obsession from which no one could free him. Even so, he was keen to avoid a legal battle and often raised with Myer Mermin the prospect of reaching a settlement with Levin that would remove him from their lives. Such a possibility must have been tantalising for Otto, who had been bombarded with distraught and abusive letters from Levin for several years – but it was impractical. The Hacketts held firm against any settlement that might be seen to acknowledge, even indirectly, that they had plagiarised material. Similarly, they blocked all Levin's efforts to stage his play in any form, even in Israel, which had been part of an earlier agreement but which the Hacketts claimed would decrease interest in the play in Europe.

As the court case loomed, Levin intensified his attacks, appearing on TV on *Newsbeat*, on the radio and in person at synagogues, ostensibly to talk about his new book but in reality to turn every discussion around to the injustice he had suffered as his play had been replaced by a version stripped of all Jewish meaning. Writing to Eleanor Roosevelt, who had penned the introduction to the American edition of the diary, he blackened

Otto's name, alleging that he had moved to Switzerland to avoid high taxes in the Netherlands.

A concerned Roosevelt wrote to Otto to query the situation with him and advised him to settle the case 'to avoid a court case which would bring out so many disagreeable things … and would be harmful to the feeling people have for you and for the play and particularly the diary from which the play was written'. Distraught, Otto was forced to reply explaining his business affairs in detail and pointing out that he had moved from Amsterdam to escape sad memories and be closer to his family: 'I am not led by financial interest. It always has been and still is my financial intention to give all the net profits of the play and the film to institutions in Holland and Israel in memory of Anne.'

Otto's old friend in New York Charles Nathan Straus backed him up, writing his own letter to Roosevelt to say that Otto was being besmirched and had 'suffered enough' without being forced in his old age to endure character assassination and slander. Eleanor Roosevelt reviewed the letters and coolly replied, 'I have read the material you sent and think you are probably right in your stand.' The exchange of letters, however, demonstrated that Levin was prepared to go to any length to win support for his cause. He continued to try to gather information about what Otto had been doing at Auschwitz and the background of actress Gusti Huber as a means of discrediting the play by any means.

The trial opened before Justice Samuel Coleman at the New York Supreme Court on 13 December 1957 and lasted for three weeks. Levin alleged that he had been defrauded of his rights to write the play by Otto Frank, and that Otto and Cheryl Crawford had used deceit to obtain the agreement of November 1952 by which he surrendered his rights. He also alleged that ideas and material from his script were used by Goodrich and Hackett for the Broadway version of the play. Levin sought $600,000 in damages from Otto Frank and Kermit Bloomgarden, and $450,000 from Cheryl Crawford in a consolidated suit.

For twenty-one days the all-male jury listened to angry accusations and inconclusive testimony about agreements and possible plagiarism. On 6 January, Judge Coleman dismissed the charges of fraud and breach of contract because there was no legal cause for the action. The jury was asked to consider the remaining charge of whether the Hacketts had used any characters, situations or plot created by Levin. After deliberating for ten hours, they returned a verdict in Levin's favour, awarding $43,750 damages and 25 per cent of future royalties from the play or film. Judge Coleman rejected this and asked the jury to agree a fixed amount – which they did, awarding Levin damages of $50,000.

Otto, the Hacketts and Bloomgarden were shocked by the decision and believed the jury had failed to understand the issues involved in creating two plays from the same source material. Moreover, the truth would always be ambiguous, because even if the Hacketts had not seen Levin's script, it was entirely possible they had heard his radio play, or that someone else – like Bloomgarden – who had read Levin's script might have suggested ideas and improvements based on material they had inadvertently absorbed. Although Judge Coleman agreed to set aside the verdict one month later and call a new trial based upon the 'complete failure of proof as to damages', the whole matter would drag on for over a year more, with Otto trying and failing to reach an agreed solution and Levin continuing to blacken his name in every public setting he could.

Levin now claimed that Otto hated him and recast their battle as the equivalent of Levin as the persecuted Jew, with Otto as his 'Nazi' persecutor. Their campaign against him was, he wrote, a 'shield for a bitter vendetta against a Jewish writer'.

In October 1959, Otto's legal battle with Levin reached its conclusion. Desperate to end the strain and to get Levin to renounce all rights to his daughter's work, Otto agreed to pay Levin $15,000 on the basis that Levin would give up any claim to royalties and assign any rights he believed he had back to Otto. The agreement had been reached with mediation by a rabbi, and both Otto and Levin 'approved the settlement recommended by the committee. They consider it an honourable and final solution of the dispute.'

The text read on that Levin 'believes that both Otto Frank and Kermit Bloomgarden are honorable men', and that nothing Otto or Bloomgarden had ever said was a reflection on Levin's talent or capacity as a writer. It concluded, 'All parties regret that the Hacketts received unfortunate publicity as a by-product of the dispute.'

By 1 November both parties had signed the agreement, but for Levin the end of the court battle was only one stage in his fanatical crusade. Three months later he wrote again to Otto, telling him: 'While the legal phase of our encounter is over the moral phase is not done. Your behavior will remain forever as a ghastly example of evil returned for good, and of a father's betrayal of his daughter's words.'

Believing that no good could come from engaging any further

with Levin, Otto proceeded to return his letters unopened. But while Levin continued with his own very successful writing career in Israel – where he wrote some of his most accomplished and popular work, including the novel *The Settlers*, which received excellent reviews and sold hundreds of thousands of copies – he continued to re-argue the case for his version of the diary for the rest of his life.

As he admitted, it cost him his marriage and drove his wife Tereska Torrès to attempt suicide. Friends and peers who had once respected him now saw him as mentally unstable, engaging in behaviour that demeaned him. When Levin finally staged a version of his play in Israel, the actors remembered him becoming red-faced and hysterical in the dressing room when the discussion turned to Otto Frank. It was another battle he lost, as Otto's lawyers soon stepped in and closed the production down. Levin's rage and bitterness remained undimmed until the end of his life, and he tragically spent his last few months on earth circulating hundreds of copies of what he termed his 'ethical will', titled: 'The Suppression of Anne Frank'.

For Otto, the long saga was deeply depressing, wounding and unnecessary. Years later he told friend Rabbi Bernard Heller: 'I never in my life got so disappointed by the character of any man as Meyer Levin's.'

CHAPTER 5

A TERRIBLE BURDEN: ANNE FRANK IN GERMANY

'Once again, the unspeakable guilt of the persecution of the Jews descends upon us, a terrible weight. We tremble with those poor, confined people forced to conceal themselves in the hiding place provided by magnanimous Dutch friends in order to escape the grip of the henchmen. We breathe with them the prison-like air of the annexe in the Prinsengracht in Amsterdam that they can never leave, feel with them the daily deprivations, the gnawing hunger and the strain and what they mean for eight suffering people in daily, all-too-close contact, with all their agitation, fear and concern for one another, and finally discover that it has all been in vain.'
MARIE BAUM, FOREWORD TO THE FIRST GERMAN EDITION OF *THE DIARY OF ANNE FRANK*, 1950

On Sunday 31 May 1959, Otto Frank joined European dignitaries to commemorate the life of his daughter Anne. It was the first such event he had ever accepted an invitation to – and it was in Germany. Organised by the Belgian Dominican friar and Nobel Peace Prize-winner Father Dominique Pire, on the day Otto joined a host of other European dignitaries on a barren brownfield street on Carsonstrasse in Wuppertal, to dedicate the foundation stone for the 'Anne Frank Village'.

The Anne Frank Village was part of the European Village project dreamed up by Father Pire, where small villages would house political refugees escaping primarily from Soviet Eastern Europe. Local newspapers speculated that industrial Wuppertal, a Rhineland city previously more famous for its elevated trains, had never seen such an auspicious gathering. Otto was joined by Bishop Friedrich Karl Otto Dibelius, president of the Evangelical Church in Germany; former Belgian Prime Minister Paul van Zeeland; the Belgian and French ambassadors to Bonn; Ambassador Felix Eliezer Shinnar, head of the Israel Mission in Cologne; Dr Weitz, the president of the German Red Cross; and senior British and Belgian army officers stationed in West Germany.

After opening comments by Mayor Hermann Herberts, who reminded everyone that the idea of a 'social security system' had actually been invented in Wuppertal 100 years earlier, Paul van Zeeland invoked the memory of Anne, claiming she was a symbol whose spirit was necessary

to launch an attack on every injustice to the ends of the Earth. And finally, the people of our time must put an end to the drama of the refugees, once and for all. Only then will Anne's words take on meaning and confirmation, namely her last wish, that the world should once again know order, tranquillity and peace.

Finally, Father Pire stood to speak. As was now so common,

he immediately drew attention to one of the final passages in Anne's diary, where she stated her belief that people were good at heart, and urged the audience to

> understand one another, so that young girls shall never again be murdered; build a fraternal world in which the basis of life is not fear, but trusting co-operation. Fighters of yesterday, from both sides, allies and enemies, you have come today to perform together a symbolic act. This act would be meaningless if it were not to be sustained.

Turning to Otto, he described his presence as an example of forgiveness on the part of the person who had suffered most from Anne's death, and described it as an 'honest continuation of her life'.

Students from Ghent High School then read out the official declaration of the foundation stone ceremony in French, Dutch, German, Italian, English and Norwegian:

> On this day, Sunday 31 March 1959, a new European Village rises from the earth, bearing the name of Anne Frank. It was built by Aid to Displaced Persons with the help of friends from the whole of Europe, in order to give our uprooted brothers a new home, new work and new joy.

Then, as Beethoven's 'Ode to Joy' rang out, Otto, dressed in his usual grey flannel suit, dedicated the foundation stone. A host of international press filmed and photographed him, ready to beam the latest images of this now world-renowned figure around the globe. Surrounded by the flags of European nations and under the watchful eyes of the 5,000 local people who had gathered to observe, Otto had brought with him a small box containing a handful of soil from the Bergen-Belsen concentration camp, to bury along with the foundation stone.

Wuppertal may have seemed like an unlikely spot for an event of huge international significance, but on the same day, several hundred miles to the south in Geneva, fraught negotiations were coming to a close between the Soviet Union and the US over the future of Berlin.

After the Second World War Berlin was divided between the four Allied powers, but on 10 November 1958, Soviet Premier Nikita Khrushchev delivered a speech demanding that the Western powers of the United States, Great Britain and France pull their forces out of the city within six months. As tensions escalated, the United States was heavily invested in the success of a democratic West Germany, facing off against the Soviet-controlled German Democratic Republic (GDR) across the border in the east. On 5 May 1959, the US signed an agreement with West Germany to share classified information about American nuclear weapons and train the Germans in their operation.

On 11 May, the two sides met, with the foreign ministers of Britain, France, the Soviet Union and the United States convening in Geneva for a seventeen-day conference on the reunification of Germany. The talks failed to reach agreement but temporarily halted the ticking clock on Khrushchev's ultimatum to close off access to West Berlin if Allied forces were not withdrawn.

Thus, the Geneva Conference of 1959, an exercise in real-world politics, coincided with the most symbolic of events: the founding of a refugees' village in the new West Germany for those fleeing Soviet oppression. Nothing could have demonstrated more starkly that Anne Frank was now a Cold War pawn.

The Diary of Anne Frank had been in print in Germany for nine years by the time the foundation stone was laid for the Anne Frank Village, but it was far from an immediate success. After a series of rejections by publishers, including from the respected Gottfried Bermann Fischer in the late 1940s, Otto turned down a further sequence of offers, including any from East Germany. The son of the diary's eventual German publisher recalled that Otto flatly rejected offers from the 'Eastern zone', because he strongly disapproved of communism.

Instead, Otto turned to the Heidelberg-based publisher Verlag Lambert Schneider, which had a long history of working with leading German Jewish figures and opposing Nazi rule. Otto visited owners Marion and Lambert Schneider in person, and the couple's son Lambert Schneider Junior recalled his visit: 'One day Otto Frank came to my parents with the manuscript. At first they were sceptical and reluctant, saying they weren't a children's publisher, after all; but they changed their minds once they'd read the diary.'

Lambert Schneider Senior described himself as a 'highly individualistic socialist with a religious bent' and had previously run a publishing house owned by Salman Schocken in Berlin, which had published both Franz Kafka and Walter Benjamin. (The publishing house was closed down by the Nazis and Schocken escaped to Palestine, where he later founded the *Haaretz* newspaper.) The first book published by Verlag Lambert Schneider – Martin Buber's and Franz Rosenzweig's new translation of the holy scriptures – was printed in 1925, but during the Nazi period the company released very few titles and existed in name only. Many Lambert Schneider authors were arrested, tortured or sent to concentration camps, and Schneider himself was interrogated by the Gestapo.

After the war, the company was granted a licence by the US occupying forces to resume publishing, and the Schneiders began rebuilding their business, bringing out works including *Die Wandlung* (*The Transformation*), one of the most important journals of the early post-war years in the Western-occupied zones; Karl Jaspers's *Die Schuldfrage* (*The Question of Guilt*); and Alexander Mitscherlich's and Fred Mielke's 1947 book documenting the trials of SS doctors and scientists at the American Military Court, *Das Diktat der Menschenverachtung* (published in English as *Doctors of Infamy: The Story of the Nazi Medical Crimes*). This latter book led to violent protests against the publisher.

The Diary of Anne Frank, called *Das Tagebuch der Anne Frank* in Germany, did not cause such a violent reaction when the first edition of 4,500 copies was published in late 1950. The book was elegantly designed and included photographs of the movable bookcase and the steps up to the hiding place, as well as the now iconic image of Anne sitting at a desk with an open book in front of her, her arms folded and her gaze directed upwards. Nonetheless, sales were slow. Publishing the diary in Germany had been an overriding priority for Otto since he first discovered Anne's pages, but he was hardly surprised by the deep ambivalence and denial with which his former fellow countrymen initially greeted its message about Nazi persecution. 'I thought they should read it,' Otto said. 'But in Germany in 1950 I had difficulty. It was a time when Germans didn't want to read about it.' Lambert Schneider agreed with Otto that it was an important book, but he didn't expect it to be a financial success.

Every foreign edition of the diary chose a different writer for the foreword, and the nature of each introduction always revealed much about the context of the country and who publishers expected to read it. Anne's words were never allowed to leap from the page unannounced but were always carefully set within a framework that positioned her as a victim in varying ways and allowed readers to understand the political connotations they were supposed to derive from her story. Invariably, although Anne was a young girl, the foreword was written by an 'elder statesperson' who would try to trammel her teenage exuberance and innocent outspokenness.

In Germany, the first foreword to the diary was written by Marie Baum, a 76-year-old former social activist, politician and distinguished university lecturer during the Weimar Republic, who had lost all her positions during Nazi rule due to her distant relationship to the Jewish Mendelssohn Bartholdy family. Baum praises Anne's capacity for description and self-reflection, and highlights her experience of adolescence in the 'monstrous, oppressive, fearful situation' of persecution. In her book *Anne Frank und die DDR*, Sylke Kirschnick comments, 'The bud metaphor used by the 76-year-old author of the foreword to describe Anne's development felt dated even in 1950. On the other hand, the empathy with these persecuted Jews that Marie Baum was signalling was by no means something that could be taken for granted at that time.' Baum did not talk about the historical context but used the foreword to make a direct connection between the Nazis' persecution of the Jews and the plight of the

Frank family and their friends hiding in the annexe. She did so in such a way that encouraged empathy for Anne without implicating current German readers or chastising them into believing they were responsible for her fate.

As ever, Otto had great hopes for the success of the diary and was not happy with what seemed like an initially poor reception. At first, he blamed the German translation made in Amsterdam by Anneliese Schütz. In working through the initial text, Schütz had chosen to remove phrases or references she believed would be meaningless to a German audience. She also struggled to translate some of a young girl's slang, turning what Anne had written in Dutch as 'the whole bag of tricks' into 'the whole rats' nest' in German. Sometimes, the meaning eluded her entirely, such as when she translated 'my telling replies' into 'my bewinged replies'. In some places in the text, Schütz added her own thoughts and suppositions too. Where Anne had written, 'He actually got Miep to bring him a banned book,' Schütz said, 'He got Miep – who of course had not the slightest suspicion – to bring him a banned book.'

Furthermore, Schütz had strong opinions about passages she believed the Germans would *not* want to read, stating, 'A book intended after all for sale in Germany cannot abuse the Germans.' As a result, Schütz cut Anne's description of what she had heard of the conditions in Westerbork and her comment that 'we must assume that most of them are murdered'. She also removed a comment that in the annexe they never listened to German radio stations apart from classical music. Anne's statement that the house rule was 'Only the language of civilised people may be spoken, thus no German!' was changed to, 'All civilised languages ... but only softly!' References to fascism and the war against Germany were also altered, entirely removing the word 'fascism' in one place and changing 'heroism in the war or when confronting the Germans' to 'heroism in the war and in the struggle against oppression' in another. The latter change reflects the repurposing of Anne's words by the socialist writers and translators who originally worked on the text. Their aim was to use the diary as a propaganda tool against fascism worldwide rather than a specific charge made against all Germans for their treatment of the Jews.

Initially, this shaping of Anne's story into a tale of a humanistic struggle against oppression was something Otto colluded with – and he wrote that he had purposely changed some of the text himself for this reason:

> Anne writes about the Germans, about what terrible people the Germans are. And I made it *these* Germans. Because there were other Germans too. And I'm sure I thought of discussing it with Anne. It is a matter of character, a matter of responsibility which I feel. We had friends in Germany. Anne had very good friends in Germany.

The Schütz translation of the diary would remain in print, as it was, for forty years, yet there's little evidence that her appeasements changed many hearts and minds. Opinion polls in the late 1940s and early 1950s showed that most Germans still believed Jews were a separate race, and as many as 40 per cent would support a return to Nazi rule. In December that year, Otto lamented that in Germany the book 'had sold very little, as the newspapers do not collaborate'. Publisher Marion Schneider reported that booksellers had returned copies of the book with

various excuses, while her husband later concluded in his alma-
nac: 'The time was not yet ripe for such a document.'

Anne's diary would not become a bestseller until six years
later, when it would owe its success to worldwide fame generated in another country – America. The Germans had ignored
their own story of Anne Frank and instead imported and championed an American interpretation of the Holocaust via the
Hollywood-style play. After Goodrich and Hackett's Broadway
premiere of *The Diary of Anne Frank* on 5 October 1955, Otto and
the producers immediately turned their attention to possible
European productions. At the European premiere in Sweden
in September 1956, Otto highlighted what he believed was the
universality of Anne's story: 'This is not a play for me, or even
for Jews or Germans – it is a play for all the world.'

In Germany, the play was launched on 1 October 1956, with
performances in multiple cities. This was highly unusual, as theatres normally competed for the exclusive rights to stage plays
first, but it signified a recognition that issues connected to the
Holocaust had a transcendent national importance. The same
practice was repeated in 1965 for the screening of Peter Weiss's
documentary play *Die Ermittlung* (*The Investigation*), about the
first Auschwitz trial in Frankfurt.

The German version of *The Diary of Anne Frank* premiered
in eight cities – West Berlin, Konstanz, Düsseldorf, Hamburg,
Karlsruhe, Vienna, Zurich and Dresden. Goodrich and Hackett
had carefully constructed the narrative of the play to end on the
final note of Otto Frank on stage alone, reading through Anne's
diary to find her quote, then spoken by the disembodied voice
of Anne, that she still believed in the goodness of humanity.
This universal sentiment removed Anne's story from the specific

Anne always wanted to be a famous writer. She began her diary at her desk at home in Merwedeplein.
© Anne Frank Fonds – Basel via Getty Images

Otto and Edith Frank on their honeymoon in Italy. © Anne Frank Fonds – Basel via Getty Images

Otto, Margot and Anne.
© Anne Frank Fonds
– Basel via Getty Images

A smiling Anne and Otto set off for Miep and Jan's wedding, Amsterdam, 16 July 1941. © Anne Frank Fonds – Basel via Getty Images

ABOVE LEFT Anne and Margot often bickered, but those who saw them in their final months in the camp at Bergen-Belsen remember their unbreakable bond. Seen here together in 1940. © Anne Frank Fonds – Basel via Getty Images

ABOVE RIGHT Otto and his staff from Opekta who would help him and his family in hiding. (*Top row from left to right*) Johannes Kleiman, Victor Kugler. (*Bottom row from left to right*) Miep Gies, Otto Frank and Bep Voskuijl. Amsterdam, 1935. © Anne Frank Fonds – Basel via Getty Images

RIGHT Otto, seen here in May 1936, was a distinguished, dapper gentleman and always 'very German'.
© Anne Frank Fonds – Basel via Getty Images

Otto's mother Alice Frank with Anneliese Schütz, who would later translate the German version of the diary, in Basel, Switzerland, 1936. A young Buddy Elias relaxes in the background. © Anne Frank Fonds – Basel via Getty Images

Otto's wedding to Fritzi Geiringer, 10 November 1953, Amsterdam. © Anne Frank Fonds – Basel via Getty Images

ABOVE After the initial publication of *Het Achterhuis*, Anne's diary swept the world and became one of the most influential books of the twentieth century.

RIGHT A seventeen-year-old Susan Strasberg took Broadway by storm in the first staging of *The Diary of Anne Frank* at the Cort Theatre, New York City, 1955.

Frances Goodrich and Albert Hackett won a Pulitzer Prize for their dramatisation of the diary in 1956 – but their work was the subject of a painful court case for Otto. © Bettmann/Getty Images

Hollywood director George Stevens built an exact replica of the Prinsengracht house to prepare for the filming of *The Diary of Anne Frank* in 1958.
© Keystone Features/Hulton Archive/Getty Images

Otto prepares to open the Anne Frank Village in Wuppertal, Germany, May 1959. © AP Photo/Horst Faas

Otto unveils a statue to his daughter in Amsterdam. Source: Bert Verhoeff/Anefo/Nationaal Archief via Wikimedia Commons

The Anne Frank rose is cultivated in Japan as a symbol of peace. Over the course of two weeks, it changes colour from orange to yellow to pink. © The Yomiuri Shimbun via AP Images

Otto spent his later years at his house in Birsfelden, Switzerland, dealing with voluminous correspondence about the diary. © Anne Frank Fonds – Basel via Getty Images

Otto's typewriter is now on display at the Holocaust Education Center in Fukuyama, Japan, a country where Anne retains an iconic status. © Kyodo via AP Images

Miep Gies and her husband Jan around the time she published her memoir about Anne in 1988.
Source: Rob Bogaerts/Anefo/Nationaal Archief via Wikimedia Commons

Anne's cousin Bernhard 'Buddy' Elias, who was a part of the Anne Frank Foundation in Switzerland for many years.
Source: Scott-Hendryk Dillan via Wikimedia Commons

After the war, Otto often showed people around the annexe. On what would have been Anne's fiftieth birthday, 12 June 1979, Otto demonstrated to Queen Juliana of the Netherlands how the bookcase concealed the entrance to their hiding place. © Bettmann/Getty Images

The front door of the house at 263 Prinsengracht, now the Anne Frank House, where millions of visitors have paid homage.

© Giovanni Mereghetti/Education Images/
Universal Images Group via Getty Images

circumstances of Nazi persecution and offered Germans the opportunity for redemption and reconciliation. While there had been ambivalence or indifference to the first edition of the book, the play unleashed a wave of emotion, propelling and cementing the success of further editions of the diary. Carol Ann Lee notes that a Berlin reviewer was stunned by the play: 'After the final curtain, the audience sat in stunned silence. There was no applause. Only the welling sound of deep sobs broke the absolute stillness. Then, still not speaking and seeming not to look at each other, the Berliners filed out of the theatre.' One West German newspaper called the play 'a present-day requiem', enabling the audience to engage in an act of contrition. Other articles appeared in West German publications with titles like: 'Are we guilty?' and 'The diary that shook the nation', while one audience member wrote to Ernst Deutsch, the actor playing Otto in Düsseldorf, to say, 'I was a "good Nazi". I never knew what it meant until the other night.'

In the following months, the play was performed in fifty-eight different locations across Germany and seen by more than 1 million people. Now, Germany seemed to want to remember Anne by rooting her firmly in her former homeland. To the bemusement of those who had known the family, a plaque was attached to the Franks' former home in Ganghoferstrasse in Frankfurt, and further plans sprang up to name streets and schools after her in both East and West Germany.

The play touched the young in particular. In 1957, the Hamburg Society for Christian–Jewish Cooperation organised for 2,000 teenagers to walk on a pilgrimage to Bergen-Belsen, where one of the youngsters, Erich Luth, said, 'We feel that Anne Frank died for all of us, for freedom and human dignity.'

In Mainz, hundreds of young people thronged to the theatre for an impromptu after-show discussion, and in Karlsruhe the *Hadassah Newsletter* observed that when Otto's brother Herbert attended a performance, Maria Magdalena Thising, the young actress playing Anne, refused to accept his compliments on her performance. She sobbed uncontrollably, saying, 'I won't take your hand – I am a German.'

Such was the intensity of the response, some German magazines and newspapers expressed fear that it was driving a wedge between the generations. 'The growing adulation of Anne Frank by young people gives cause for concern,' warned a Berlin journal. 'More and more often parents find themselves confronted with disturbing questions about wartime events, especially the persecution of religious minorities. Children no longer ask "What happened?" but "How could it have happened?" Their emotional intensity tends to create a sense of isolation between our generation and our youth.'

While some of the older generation fretted that the play was raising too many questions about their culpability in the Holocaust, other critics believed it did not go far enough. The influential Jewish writer and philosopher Hannah Arendt labelled the outpouring of emotion as Germany's 'cheap sentimentality at the expense of the great catastrophe', while Alvin Rosenfeld, the director of the Center for the Study of Contemporary Anti-semitism at the University of Indiana, later wrote that Germans named streets, schools and youth centres after Anne Frank out of sorrow and shame but still did not comprehend why, a generation ago, a significant number of their countrymen hunted down a fifteen-year-old Jewish girl, sending her off to suffer and die.

Similarly, writer Alex Sagan has argued that, unlike other works that dealt with the Holocaust, the play was 'precisely suited' to the German mood of the time and succeeded by 'accommodating German discomfort', keeping only the barest depiction of German criminality and featuring no Nazis on stage, even at the moment of Anne's arrest. 'But, if the Germans felt accused, the psychological discomfort of this situation was relieved by Anne's famous words, which could be deeply reassuring. Germans need not think the worst of themselves, for "people are really good at heart",' Sagan said. Even if Germans accused themselves, 'Anne Frank seemed to forgive them.'

In West Germany those words of absolution were printed across the cover of the first paperback edition of *Das Tagebuch der Anne Frank*. And unlike the hardback first edition, the paperback, published under licence by Fischer Bücherei, was an immediate success. By July 1956, the paperback was on its fourth print run and had sold 103,000 copies. A fifth print run followed in 1958 and then a sixth in 1959.

Otto had now struck a different commercial agreement, however: only half the licence income went to the publisher Lambert Schneider, with the other half going to the Anne Frank Foundation in Amsterdam and later to the Anne Frank Foundation in Basel. In addition, Marie Baum's foreword was replaced by a new introduction by the novelist and Protestant theologian Albrecht Goes.

Goes had been conscripted into the Wehrmacht in 1940 and had served as a radio operator and pastor during the war. After 1945 he had turned to writing and in 1954 published a novel, *Das Brandopfer* (*The Burnt Offering*), which tells the story of Frau Walker, a German butcher's wife, and her struggle to reconcile herself with Nazi persecution when her shop becomes the only place Jews can buy meat in the city for two hours every Friday evening. Goes's introduction to *Das Tagebuch der Anne Frank* mentions that the Franks were Jewish and that they were forced to emigrate, but not that they were specific victims of Nazi persecution. At the end he writes, 'In the world of 1955, which has not ceased to be a world of concentration camps and persecution, it is essential to make this voice heard.' Goes did not specify what he meant – but he did not have to. Readers understood the political reference; the Nazi era was over, but West Germany was now pitted against Soviet-controlled East Germany. Political oppression still existed, and thousands of innocent victims were still sent to suffer and die in Soviet gulags. The text did not discuss the differences between the two systems, or life and death in a Soviet gulag compared to a Nazi concentration camp, but instead it promoted one message: oppression by any undemocratic regime was essentially the same.

In East Germany, however, the context that framed the meaning of the story was very different. The people of the GDR first encountered *The Diary of Anne Frank* not through the book but through the 1956 staging of the play at the Dresden Theatre of the Young Generation, a youth theatre. The idea to stage the play in the GDR had come from theatre manager Rolf Buttner. Buttner took the role of Otto Frank, while 26-year-old Ruth Schröder was cast as Anne. Her husband Horst Westphal played Peter.

Ruth was significantly older than Anne and had red hair. For the first years of the production, directors usually demanded that actresses physically resembled Anne as closely as possible – so Ruth's hair was dyed black while she tried, with some difficulty, to work her way into the mind of a thirteen-year-old girl: 'I tried to let Anne come close to me, tried to identify with her. I had to get as close to her as possible, find a way back to my youth. I couldn't be twenty-six years old on the stage, after all.'

In his comments in the programme, guest director Helfried Schöbel wrote an unsparing and accusing message to the Dresden audience:

> Anne's diary is a document of the highest order, in both human and literary terms. It is one of those rare works of art that, like a burning mirror, reveals the fate of a whole era on the basis of a single example ... In 1933 we Germans allowed fascism to come over us, and, with the aid of our characteristic German thoroughness, made it the horror of Europe. We have every cause for reflection – for catharsis.

Schöbel's comments were surprisingly direct for either the West or East German state in the early 1950s. Ruth Schröder recalled that in East Germany at the time the most common response to the Holocaust was silence: 'I don't believe everyone in the GDR was always sincere about antifascism. If people were really committed to it, then that was good. But like so much else, it was often just for show in the worse sense.' While there was endless talk about particular well-known communist resistance fighters, there was, 'so far as I can recall, far less about the Nazis' persecution of the Jews. It was often as if nothing had happened. There was often silence.'

The audience reaction to the first stagings of the play in the GDR reflected the fact that most were school children who were usually unprepared for the serious nature of the story. Schröder remembered that if the children came on their own, they were frequently unruly: 'They often didn't have a clue what the play was actually about.' Sylke Kirschnick quotes the following letter from some children who saw a performance at the Theatre of the Young Guard in Halle:

Dear actors of the Theatre of the Young Guard,

We thank you for your performance of the play, *The Diary of Anne Frank.*

Unfortunately you were frequently disrupted by a few pupils from Year 8. The reprimand in the interval did not help much, unfortunately. We admire your courage in performing the play in front of young people. We wish you every success in your theatre work.

Form 7a, Goethe Schule, Brigitta R., Ursula K., Marianne K.

While West German reviews admitted some German culpability for Anne's fate, press in the GDR understood where they should firmly lay the blame: fascism. The magazine *Junge Welt* wrote,

It is good that we are reminded from time to time of those years in which the night of fascism fell over Germany and we became complicit in the suffering of many people. In 1933 these innocent people are driven out of Germany; are again hounded and persecuted. The Jews are dragged from their homes, crammed like cattle into railway carriages, and led straight to their destruction. Incomprehensible that we remained silent about it.

The *National-Zeitung* referred directly to 'Hitler's gas chambers', while *Die Union* attributed the mass murders directly to the Nazi leadership. The East German press could de-couple itself from the Nazis and point out that fascism was still alive and well across the border in the West German republic. One women's magazine wrote,

This was a conscious demonstration on the part of the theatrical artistes *with* their audience *against* the Bonn policy of granting the SS murderers rehabilitation for their past crimes so as to make them available once more for 'Greater German' tasks on behalf of Krupp and Adenauer, this time in the American-style uniforms of the Bundeswehr. It must be a very special kind of play to have given rise to this kind of statement across zonal and national borders.

Sometimes articles like this one were more nuanced – often they were just blunt propaganda. Anne's story was politically symbolic, in both the West and the East. In the GDR, Anne was a victim of fascism just like, according to one Dresden newspaper, victims of fascism everywhere: 'Her fate is not an isolated one, but represents the fate of all those persecuted by the Nazi regime and is consequently an indictment of all forms of discrimination and intolerance.'

The success of the first staging of the play had led to a wave of performances across the GDR. When the dramaturgs in Rostock wrote to Otto asking for more information about the motivation for the play, his response was included in the theatre programme and widely publicised in the East German press.

Such interest, coupled with the success of the play, led intellectuals and critics to question why the diary was not being supported more widely in the GDR. Theatre critic Henryk Keisch used the Communist Party organ *Neues Deutschland* to urge the GDR to make a stronger commitment to spreading Anne's story:

> It really wouldn't have hurt us to play a stronger part in this act of commitment to humanity – precisely because the idea came from West Germany, and all the more so because the stage play was written by two Americans. Right in the heart of the bastions of the new fascism, there are lively, fundamentally decent forces opposing it. Do we not have every possible reason to echo them?

Otto's initial opposition to an East German version of the diary was based on his fear that a state publisher would distort Anne's story to promote communist ideology. Although he had turned down an approach from one such company in 1949, copies of the text had still circulated amongst intellectuals and writers, prompting discussions about possible publication for years. Lin Brilleslijper – now known as Lin Jaldati – who had been in Bergen-Belsen with Anne and Margot and had given Otto the news of their deaths, had emigrated to the GDR and asked her husband – at Otto's request – to help find a German publisher. Jaldati's husband, Eberhard Rebling, made enquiries with an East German publishing company called Henschel, but they rejected the manuscript on the basis that Anne was not a resistance fighter. Writer and editor Gunther Lys, who had been incarcerated in Sachsenhausen, also claimed that he had seen and rejected the diary along with multiple other German editors, on the basis that it was 'adolescent, individualistic and sentimentalises the reader rather than changing his consciousness'. It's hard to know if this is true, but by the premiere of the play in 1956 Otto was reconsidering an East German edition.

The first edition of the diary to be published in the communist Eastern bloc had, in fact, been a great success. Publishing house Melantrich had sold more than 10,000 copies in Czechoslovakia within weeks of its release in the autumn of 1956 and was already planning a second edition. Otto noted this in a letter to Lambert Scheider on 16 November and suggested that interest in what he called the 'occupied countries' merited reconsidering publication in the GDR: 'I think it would be important for the population of East Germany to have the chance to read it, and it seems to me that the price of this edition should be such that wide sections of society are able to buy it.'

Otto's letter crossed in the post with a letter from Lambert Schneider suggesting the same thing. Several requests from Eastern zone publishers had been received, something they had always been loath to consider: 'I am intrinsically reluctant to grant a licence to the state-owned enterprises – the purely communist publishers, in other words – since we know that there are still plenty of concentration camps on the other side.'

One request, however, was from Union Verlag, a church publisher which Schneider could find 'nothing whatsoever to object to'. Union Verlag, the letter went on, 'reaches a predominantly bourgeois-minded public, and for that reason I am minded to think that we should agree to [their] request to publish an edition under licence'.

Union Verlag had been established by the East German Christian Democratic Party (CDU) in 1951 to publish predominantly religious books – but by 1956 this had expanded to philosophy, art and historical publications. Although their customers were largely middle-class, they would sell the diary to a larger readership that included teachers, young people, artists and blue-collar workers. Lambert Schneider and Union Verlag began discussions in the autumn of 1956, but the path to eventual publication in autumn 1957 involved torturous submissions to the East German 'Office for Literature and Publishing' at the 'Ministry of Culture' – which most people called the 'Censorship Office'.

Gerhard Desczyk, managing editor at Union Verlag, wrote a three-page 'expert assessment' of the book on 15 November 1956, commenting on its international success and quoting Henryk Keisch's review in *Neues Deutschland* querying why there had not been, as yet, a GDR edition. As was true in all aspects of public life in the GDR, Desczyk had to position the diary alongside the official ideology of the ruling SED Communist Party carefully, often couched in terms that were somewhat ambiguous and suggested the writer might have personally meant something quite different. He wrote, 'The publication of this book in the GDR will be especially welcomed by readers here, given that this diary is a document of humanity and of philanthropy – ideals with which the democratic forces in the GDR have always aligned themselves.'

Desczyk's assessment was submitted along with plans for a print run of 10,000 copies, a copy of the Lambert Schneider edition of the diary, a hard currency commitment of 7,000 DM and an exact calculation that 2,504 tons of paper would be required, dust jacket included. Within a few days the application was stamped: approved.

Publication was initially scheduled for the spring of 1957, but as the international success of the diary and play gathered momentum, the proposed print run of the GDR edition expanded to an initial 35,000 copies – which required Union Verlag to delay publication of two other titles so they could provide for the extra paper. In the summer of 1957, publicity for the East German edition began when the daily newspaper *BZ am Abend* printed its first instalment on 8 July. Extracts were also included in the 1957 edition of *Kindertruhe*, an annual for young girls, and in a school reader for Year 7 pupils. Otto agreed to a free audio recording of the diary with the German Central Library for the Blind in Leipzig.

The Diary of Anne Frank went on sale in East Germany in the autumn of 1957 at a price of 7 DM. Union Verlag agreed with Lambert Schneider and Otto that Albrecht Goes would write a new foreword for the edition, knowing full well that Goes's original introduction, which alluded to Soviet gulags, could never be published in the GDR. In addition, they asked Provost Heinrich Grüber, the official representative of the Evangelical Church of Germany in the GDR, to write an afterword.

Grüber had been incarcerated in Dachau by the Nazis for setting up an aid organisation that helped Jews married to non-Jews to emigrate to Palestine. After the war he had been a chairman of the powerful Victims of Fascism group in the Soviet zone and had written an account of a Christmas service at the former Nazi concentration camp Sachsenhausen, when it was being used by the Soviet forces as an internment camp for German prisoners. Grüber's was a favourable impression, stating, 'It is an unforgivable injustice to speak of this [Soviet] camp in the same breath as Hitler's concentration camps or to say it is the same as under the Nazis or worse. Camp life always entails

the loss of liberty, but under Hitler it was planned and system-
atically implemented cruelty.' Union Verlag believed the GDR
authorities would view *The Diary of Anne Frank* more favourably
with Grüber's support.

In the language of a 'fervent anti-fascist educator', Grüber
wrote:

> This book is an unforgettable experience, a stirring reminder to
> us all. We hope it has burned the old guilt into our consciences
> afresh … The more clearly we acknowledge the failings of the
> past, the greater is our duty, not just to make restitution for the
> injustice, but to take care and be on our guard so that we are never
> again complicit in the misery of so many people and peoples.

Grüber did not mention Anne's Jewishness in his afterword, but
his handwritten notes on the text include references to antisemitism, indicating that it was very much on his mind.

Union Verlag would publish six editions of the diary, with
print runs of between 5,000 and 40,000 copies. The first four
editions, two in hardback, two in paperback, remained on the
market in East Germany until 1961, and sold a total of 121,000
copies. In 1972, a planned reprint was shelved due to a shortage
of paper, and the fifth edition did not appear until 1980. The
Kinderbuchverlag (Children's Book Press) published a further
two editions of the diary in 1986 and 1988, and a final Union
Verlag edition was published in 1990, the year Germany was
reunified.

Provost Grüber's afterword appeared only in the first three
editions of the diary, however. His efforts to 'build bridges'

between East and West Germany by calling on young people in both sectors of Berlin to work together to repair Jewish cemeteries fell foul of ruling Communist Party thinking – and he resigned from the Victims of Fascism, as its original non-partisan nature was replaced by strict adherence to the party line. Grüber was banned from entering the GDR after 1964, and his afterword was struck from the diary thereafter.

Like Grüber, another well-known intellectual who would engage in tortured commentary on the diary was writer Arnold Zweig. Zweig became famous through his 1927 novel *The Case of Sergeant Grischa* before emigrating to Palestine in 1933 with his wife Beatrice. He returned to Europe in 1948 and settled in East Berlin, where he struggled to reconcile his Jewishness with the GDR's ongoing antisemitism and, latterly, its anti-Israeli agenda. Zweig wrote his first commentary on *The Diary of Anne Frank* for a CDU newspaper, *Neue Zeit*, on 6 October 1957. Without referring to Anne's Jewish background, he compared the unspoken persecution of the Jews to the persecution of religious minorities through history:

> Again and again reports are now surfacing that describe how, in the most inhumane era of modern history, individuals sought to escape the net of death created by the regrouping of our social structure. Thousands of people, everywhere, were caught up in it, the guilty, the semi-guilty, the innocent. When the Roman Empire was reaching its peak these people were called Christians. In the twentieth century they often bear a different name, but frequently belong to the same community, group, class, by virtue of their ancestry and religious faith.

He goes on to say it is not enough for a story like Anne Frank's to touch our hearts – it must engage 'the human intellect and [lead us to] the necessary active conclusions'.

In his second commentary, however, he takes on the diary from a very different angle. Writing again for *Neue Zeit*, six months later, on 21 March 1958, Zweig drew a direct comparison between Anne and the young girls he saw 'running or cycling through our streets'. Anne, though, 'as a Jewish child of Jewish parents', had to emigrate from Frankfurt to Amsterdam, where she remained as a result of her religious faith, 'number one on the extermination list of the Thousand Year Reich'. According to Zweig, there were only two courses of action open to the Jews: emigration and exile, or armed resistance against the Nazis.

How could Anne fight back, hidden away in the back rooms of a commercial building with 'all the difficulties and awfulness of that cave-like existence', and 'still you are unable to save your scrap of life?' Only the Red Army could 'exterminate' her persecutors, since 'the West lacks the strength to save you and yours'. Anne was a 'victim of fascism', and the contrast between East and West could not be clearer.

At an appearance at the East Berlin Press Centre in February 1959, Zweig used the metaphor of two bodies of water to describe the GDR and the Federal Republic and declared it the role of the writer to clear a channel between them, so they would one day form a single giant pool. He described the differences between them in stark terms, however: the GDR was like a fast-flowing river, a 'lovely and efficient river' that did an 'exceptionally good job' of watering a 'pure, clean, beautiful place'. His image of West Germany, meanwhile, was still 'the one I had in Birkenau some years ago ... there were ponds, and in the ponds the air bubbles rose to the surface, and these air bubbles were the bubbles from rotting corpses'. Zweig was introducing a radio broadcast to accompany the premiere of a feature-length documentary made by DEFA (the GDR state film company), named *Ein Tagebuch für Anne Frank*, or, in English, *A Diary for Anne Frank*. As Zweig's words suggest, although the name of the film shamelessly traded on the diary for publicity purposes, the result was a work of pure propaganda with no connection to Anne's original writing.

Director Joachim Hellweg's first name for his film was more fitting: 'Anne Frank and her Murderers'. Hellweg used actress Kati Székely, who was playing Anne on stage in East Berlin, to 'research' the Franks' background and fate. He used montages of concentration-camp footage to support her discovery that the victims of fascism had not only been persecuted and killed in the most heinous fashion, but also that those responsible were still holding high office across the border in West Germany. The highest offices of the East German state were involved in creating the film, allowing Hellweg to travel to the Netherlands to research archive material and make contact with Otto Frank through Lin Jaldati.

The GDR secretary general and then President Walter Ulbricht even requested further archive material from the Soviet Union, personally signing a three-page letter asking for relevant footage and pointing out the importance of the film:

Dear comrades,

The DEFA Studio for Newsreels and Documentary Films is currently working on a film about Anne Frank. The purpose of this film is to indict the SS murderers through the well-known fate of one individual, Anne Frank. It would therefore be of the greatest importance if certain materials currently held in the

Soviet Union could be made available to DEFA for the purposes of creating the film. The materials in question are as follows:

...

3. Footage showing the connections between industry and the SS leadership, e.g. Himmler's friends (industrialists) viewing the Dachau concentration camp, Himmler and [chemical company] IG Farben representatives viewing the Auschwitz concentration camp and the IG-Buna factory there (internal IG Farben footage in some cases).

4. Footage from the English film showing reports on the liberation of concentration camps in Germany by the English, e.g. SS guards being arrested by the English, Eisenhower's visit to the former Dachau concentration camp (with particular attention to Eisenhower standing next to corpses).

...

We would be extremely grateful if you could arrange for the materials required for the film to be made available to DEFA.

With communist greetings

W. Ulbricht

Ulbricht's letter showed that Anne had now achieved such a level of fame that he assumed the Soviet Union would automatically understand the benefit of becoming attached to her story. It also demonstrated that at the very highest level, the GDR had decided Anne's story was good propaganda in their campaign to show that fascists still lurked in the heart of West Germany.

The final film showed raids, deportations and murdered victims at concentration camps. It also named high-ranking West German officials and businessmen connected to the Nazi regime and the Holocaust, along with their photos and current home addresses. The East German press applauded the results. 'Anne's murderers living in West Germany', crowed the *Bauern Echo* on 13 March 1959. State newspaper *Neues Deutschland* was equally incendiary – 'DEFA documentary shows the fascist murderers of the Jews under the wing of the Adenauer regime' – while *Der Morgen* wrote simply: 'Anne Frank was their victim'.

Needless to say, in West Germany the reaction was outrage. The *Hamburger Echo* countered, 'Anne Frank working for the GDR', while *Der Tag* wrote, 'DEFA using Anne Frank for propaganda'. Tackling the allegation itself, the *Frankfurter Rundschau* responded by pointing out how many former Nazis were thriving under communist rule: 'SS in the service of the GDR. Forty-seven former National Socialists in the Volkskammer [GDR Parliament]'.

Otto hated the DEFA documentary and the accompanying book published in the GDR, which was also called *A Diary for Anne Frank*. No doubt he agreed with many of the comments outlined in an article in the Hamburg weekly publication *Die Zeit* on 3 April 1959, which described it as typical of the East German communist government 'to exploit the fate of Anne Frank for the polemical vilification of the political adversary'. The article referred to the way the film intercut harrowing scenes from the concentration camps with Anne's face, continuing, 'This is where the propaganda tricks begin … The film is another attempt to create the impression that the Federal Republic is the sole heir to Hitler and that Nazi Germany stopped at the River Elbe.' It conceded that there were some people in West Germany who had no business to be there but said, 'We have not tired of campaigning against them.' Meanwhile, it claimed that in the Soviet zone former Nazis sat in the East German Parliament and ran state enterprises, 'and we have heard nothing to suggest that there is any attempt over there to get rid of them'.

Otto detested the shameless manipulation of Anne and her diary for propaganda purposes, and it drove a wedge between him and Lin Jaldati. Lin had not only played a role in the making of the film and tried to co-opt Otto's support for it, but she continued to defend it. Although their friendship never broke down entirely, they argued about the DEFA documentary again in 1964 in an intense exchange of letters. Lin was angry that the Anne Frank House in Amsterdam had published a booklet of letters to Otto, including one from an East German young man which stated, 'Here in the GDR we are being taught to feel hatred again, and again there are Germans who do not hesitate to shoot at Germans risking their lives to cross barbed wire and minefields and walls in order to reach Germany – perhaps even just to reach their parents.'

Jaldati immediately wrote to Otto and without irony complained about the 'highly political' nature of the booklet, which 'misuses Anne's name for political purposes'. The letter was either a deliberate lie, she added, or had been mistranslated, as

> there are many things here that I do not approve of ... but one thing is certain: there are no old Nazis in the government. The Nazis were completely removed from schools and universities as early as 1946, and so children are not being taught to feel hatred against any people at all ... All opportunities here are open to everyone, and no one here asks whether this minister or that general is Jewish or not ... Everyone was appalled at the fact that Anne's name is being misused in this booklet for political purposes.

After a two-week pause, Otto replied – at length.

You say you have respected my wish that Margot and Anne should not be used for political purposes. If a film or a book is given the title, *Ein Tagebuch für Anne Frank*, its makers are firstly banking on its being confused with Anne's diary and secondly using her name to catch the eye and draw viewers or readers in for purely political purposes. In writing this, I want to stress that I wholly approve of the contents of the book, with the exception of its association with Anne.

Otto said that he did not want to become embroiled in a long political argument but that there was both a physical and a spiritual wall across East Germany. As he wrote the letter, he had a book in front of him naming more than 300 former Nazis who were now allegedly avowed communists holding high office in East Germany, 'but people don't change their inner attitudes so easily'. The Anne Frank Foundation welcomed young people from Eastern Europe to all their conferences and events, but so far 'this has hardly been possible'.

Otto had no wish to fall out with Lin Jaldati completely, and subsequently he asked the Anne Frank House to reprint the booklet without the letter from the GDR. As he told the *Haagse Post*, he had spent a great deal of time reflecting on antisemitism in his former homeland and on the former Nazis still in high positions:

Neo-fascism arises because we still have too many old Nazis. And because the West German government is too weak when it comes to this. As much as I'm against the countries of the Eastern bloc in general, because I disapprove of any dictatorship, whether it is fascist or communist, I have to say that in the East many more Nazis have been removed than in the West. Under Adenauer they have not removed them, on the basis that 'if we get rid of all these people, we will have no teachers left, we will have no lawyers left, there will be nobody left'. They left many of them in charge.

Germany weighed on his mind. In 1960, Otto wrote an article for an American magazine, *Coronet*, titled: 'Has Germany forgotten Anne Frank?'

The older generation of Germans cannot yet face up to past history and communicate its lessons to the future. I believe that unless it does, unless the questions of German youth are answered fully and frankly, the fragile growth of democracy in Germany may come to an end ... I am intensely interested in Germany, its future and its youth. My concern is that never again should Germany experience the madness of racial prejudice and that Anne's life should not have been empty and without meaning. Of all the letters inspired by a reading of *The Diary*, I have been most diligent about answering the ones from German youth. For their education – in democratic ideals and ways of life – is of paramount importance to me.

Otto went on to say that although he was born and raised in Germany, he remained as baffled by the country as other Europeans and Americans: 'Germany is a busy, busy land. But when it comes to the education of its youth towards democratic values, the clocks of Germany are running all too slowly.' The rest of Europe was repelled by Germany's past and worried about the future, and while Europeans understood that they could not live without Germany, they also could not quite work out how to live with it. Otto concluded, 'In that respect I am a typical European, for those are my reactions too.'

As Otto's article suggested, young Germans from both West Germany and the GDR wrote impassioned, sometimes anguished, letters to him about their feelings for Anne and their reactions to the diary. In February 1957, a eighteen-year-old schoolgirl from Rostock wrote to Otto:

Last night I came home totally shaken and churned up after a performance of *The Diary* in Rostock, and now I just have to write to you. I want to thank you a hundred, no, a thousand times for giving your permission for the dramatisation of Anne's diary. I knew it all before, they'd told us about it in school – and yet I didn't know it, hadn't ever responded to it the way I do now that I have seen it. Perhaps it will be some consolation to you if I tell you: I will never, ever, forget your Anne, and nor will I forget her murderers. But I won't forget, either, that she believed in the goodness of people right to the very end, and I will dedicate my whole life to pure, true humanity.

A female Jewish survivor of the Holocaust also wrote to Otto, in April 1958, to tell him that the play meant so much to her as someone returning to live in post-war Germany:

I want to thank you for publishing the diary, since there are still very many people who don't want to believe the wrong done to the Jews, or who have already forgotten it. I myself am a Jew and was in the Theresienstadt concentration camp, I'm the only Jew in my whole district and unfortunately I never meet any other members of my faith. Many thanks again for what you have given me through the book.

Others engaged directly with Anne's comments about Germans. A 37-year-old male teacher from Tessin wrote to Otto in February 1959:

> I can understand your daughter only too well when she writes that there was nothing she hated more than *these* Germans, even though she herself had had German citizenship. Who *could* love *these* Germans? – Hounding, persecution and concentration camps speak a clear language … I don't want to lose myself in accusations against my own people, but I do have to acknowledge on the basis of what happened that we have a huge amount – a *huge* amount – to atone for.

Readers from the GDR often wrote to Otto to differentiate not only between present-day Germans and the Nazis but also between socialist Germans living in the GDR and *these* Germans who they believed were still active in the West. An eighteen-year-old schoolboy from Weissensee, Thuringia, wrote that he had seen the play, read the diary and studied it in school:

> I have to admit to you that I cried. It made such a deep impression on me that I was ashamed to be German. Believe me, what was done to you and your family under fascism was done by Germans who do not deserve to be Germans. If there

are anti-Semitic riots in West Germany again today, these are caused by a few incorrigibles who will, in time, end up where they belong. We young people in the GDR will always honour the memory of Anne and those who shared her suffering.

As newspapers and journals had feared, however, some young people thought *these* Germans were not Western fascists but their own parents, as a letter from a boy from Dessau shows:

Forgive our parents for making themselves complicit in the death of your daughter Anne and in all the victims of the war that Germany stirred up. My thoughts are often with you, in the house where your daughter Anne wrote her diary – a diary that shows what Anne suffered because of us Germans.

The war had been over for twenty years, but young Germans still remembered Anne Frank. Sometimes that was prompted by school namings, youth groups and projects like the refugee village. And sometimes youthful idealism mixed uneasily with state-sponsored ideology that did not resonate with Otto's desire for the diary to reflect Anne's 'democratic ideals and way of life'.

Shortly after the heated debate about the DEFA documentary, Otto engaged directly with an advertising designer from Leipzig, Kurt Friedrich, over his design for a proposed GDR Anne Frank postage stamp and 'news wall' tribute – something that was quite common in East Germany, usually displayed in a case on the street for pedestrians to read. Otto did not object to the picture of Anne on the stamp but disagreed with the text:

I do however object to the text you have used: 'Day of Remembrance for the Victims of Fascism'. Through her diary, ANNE has become the symbol in thirty-three countries of all those innocents persecuted, both then and now, on the basis of their race, religion or beliefs ... Which means that the focus is on the purely human. I am therefore opposed as a matter of principle to Anne's being used in any way at all for the purposes of political propaganda.

Friedrich changed the wall display in accordance with Otto's wishes, but a short newspaper article accompanying the display concluded with the words: 'Let us also remember that the spectre of militarism and the seeds of racial hatred are again on the rise in the West of our Fatherland!' No doubt Friedrich had to get the text approved by the East German government, just as schools, kindergartens, youth groups and workers' associations had to jump through many state-sanctioned hoops to pay tribute to Anne.

Anne Frank ranked as the second most popular 'foreign' figure for naming requests for schools and youth groups in the GDR, after Georgi Dimitrov, the first communist leader of Bulgaria. Each request was instigated by the young people themselves, but only six youth groups in the GDR were actually named after Anne, in comparison to thirty-three each for Nazi resistance fighters Hans and Sophie Scholl. Most people who suggested an Anne Frank naming did so because her personal story meant something to young people, but they knew they would have to 'put up with the ideological language and official phrases' to be able to teach her story and get the naming approved. One pioneer youth group wrote, 'The name of Anne Frank was chosen because, both on a rational and an emotional level, the life and sufferings of this girl have the potential to serve as a means of communist education.' Building on the mission set for the FDJ and the Pioneers, the campaign programme of the FDJ and the Pioneer Organisation was given the slogan, 'We are fighting for the name of Anne Frank'. It was an extremely clunky explanation, but it got the job done.

After suggesting the name, schools and youth groups had to get formal state agreement at a national and local level, as well as from the Anne Frank House in Amsterdam. Then they had to prove that they had studied Anne's story, read her diary, seen the play and would assume a responsibility for her 'legacy'. If approved, the name change was recognised at a formal ceremony with an official certificate.

One of the first schools to request a name change was the Polytechnische Oberschule in the Thuringian town of Themar. Its school newspaper dated 13 January 1960 read: 'In response to the wave of antisemitic hatred emanating from West Germany, our school has requested official permission to change its name to "Anne-Frank-Oberschule".' Many teachers would have remembered the war years, but the application only mentioned antisemitism in present-day West Germany.

For the next three decades the Anne Frank Secondary School of Themar commemorated Anne Frank in a variety of official ways. An Anne Frank memorial bearing her image and a reproduction of her signature was installed in the school, and students laid flowers before it every year on Anne's birthday on 12 June. The school also celebrated with military-style flag ceremonies in front of the memorial, and students would stand saluting the GDR flag and singing the Anne Frank song, written in 1963 by teacher Eric Wrogner:

Anne Frank is the name of our school,
In which we learn and are joyful.
Anne Frank is our role-model!
The wind declares it clearly!

With book, with hammer and protractor,
With work and joyful games,
We will soon be masters of the new age.
That is our highest goal of all!
Anne Frank...
Anne Frank...

Although the impetus for renaming schools and youth groups came from young people themselves, as time passed Anne was becoming an intangible idea – a topic discussed in one lesson per year. A political goal, not a real girl. Many students said Anne Frank had inspired them to join the East German Army, while one explained how awful it must have been for Anne not to be able to express herself freely: 'You'd be constantly afraid they'd be standing outside your door and listening to what you were saying, since you wouldn't be able to just hide yourself away in a corner where you could just voice your thoughts, just for yourself.' As Anne was a slightly uncomfortable icon for the GDR, those who supported her *were* monitored by the state. Children who had campaigned to rename their schools or youth groups after Anne were surprised to find that their well-meaning attempts had been investigated and recorded in full by the Stasi – particularly if they had written to Otto or to the Anne Frank House in Amsterdam.

Still, it was not only young people who requested permission to commemorate Anne. The GDR workforce was divided up into labour brigades that often named themselves after well-known communist figures. Occasionally, however, some women's brigades asked to name themselves after Anne, and they continued to read and discuss the diary for many years. The packaging brigade at VEB Porzellankombinat Kahla, for example, had adopted the name 'Anne Frank' in 1962 and then commissioned a sculpture of Anne in 1977, by artist Albert Borstel. Borstel wrote an extremely thoughtful entry in the brigade diary, explaining how he had conceived and created the piece:

> I condensed the subject I was given – 'Anne Frank' – into a situation that typified her. Anne is sitting on a chair, engrossed in her diary, as she so often was. Suddenly there are unfamiliar noises. She sits up and listens in their direction. What was it? Every detail in the sculpture as a whole has a specific meaning. The rectangular base symbolises her confinement within the hiding place; her sitting on a chair her restricted movement. Her posture, emphasised through static verticals, shows her strength of will and her courage. The position of her head reveals cleverness and reflectiveness – but also alertness to an unknown danger. Her legs, poised to jump up, emphasise her determination to overcome fear and anxiety. The diary of Anne Frank is at the centre. She is clutching it tightly. For it is her innermost self.

The Diary of Anne Frank was out of print for several years in the 1970s, when anti-Zionism in the Eastern bloc was at its height, yet Anne remained a potent figure for many ordinary

East Germans, and the 1980s saw a resurgence of interest in her work. Union Verlag brought out a new hardback edition of the diary, and a children's publisher brought out an edition for young people that was serialised in an East German youth magazine. A second wave of productions of the play swept East German theatres, and radio and TV broadcasts discussed Anne and her story. Young Germans of the 1980s reacted very differently from the older generation, who had first seen the play or read the book decades earlier. This time they did not burst into tears but reacted thoughtfully to the persecution of the Jews. One student wrote, 'The play shows how bad life was for the Jews in around 1940. They were persecuted and tormented in every possible way … The play was an insight into the cruelty of the fascists.' Another commented, 'In 1942, under Hitler's leadership, the Nazis mounted a storm against the Jews. Hitler wanted to have a Germany of pure race. All Jews were first marked with a star, then later arrested and mostly murdered.'

Now, young people often directly referred to the Holocaust as a crime and stated that differentiating the Jews as a separate race was wrong: 'The Frank family are Jews and are persecuted by Hitler … Hitler's persecution of the Jews was a huge crime. Jews are people, just the same as us,' said one. Most had grown up with a copy of the diary in their home and saw school performances of the play where discussion revolved around questions like, 'How did Anne's experience compare to struggles such as opposition to apartheid in South Africa?'

The diary was also used by church youth groups, which appealed to large numbers of young people who wanted to think and discuss things more freely. Increasingly, such groups became the place where dissent towards the regime could quietly be fostered, and Rudi Pahnke, a pastor from Prenzlauer Berg in East Berlin, used the diary to start discussions about individual responsibility under a dictatorship, broadening out Anne's experience as a Jew to talk about other persecuted groups under the Nazis, including the Roma and gay men.

The 1980s also saw the first large-scale, state-sanctioned commemorations for Anne in the GDR – including a visit by Miep Gies and the first Anne Frank exhibit staged in conjunction with the Anne Frank House. The period also brought about the re-emergence of Lin Jaldati. Like many prominent Jewish citizens, Jaldati had been banished from public life in the GDR in the 1970s – but towards the end of the decade she returned, presenting *An Evening for Anne Frank* in commemoration of what would have been Anne's fiftieth birthday. Her daughter remembered, 'Lin suddenly had a vision of Anne as a child and thought, "My God, she'd be a grown woman of fifty now" ... And she had the feeling she just had to do something for Anne. That's how the idea came about.'

First performed on stage and then for state television, the programme included witness accounts from Westerbork, Auschwitz and Bergen-Belsen, with extracts from the diary and Jewish folk songs. In October 1979, *An Evening with Anne Frank* was included in the Berlin Festival, and it went on to tour with enormous success in New York, Zurich, Basel and at the Yad Vashem Holocaust Remembrance Center in Jerusalem, culminating in a performance in Amsterdam attended by Queen Beatrix of the Netherlands.

Jaldati reported that the discussions that took place after the performance were more stimulating than the event itself. She had little time for apportioning guilt for crimes that had been committed by earlier generations. According to her friend Jalda Rebling, the real question was: 'What are you doing now? ... Where do you draw the line? Where are you in danger of running after some Führer just because he sounds so good?'

Anne was so relatable to teenagers, Lin maintained, because it was easy for them to grasp that it could have happened to them. 'Lin and [her sister] Janny were always clear that it was all about the search for humanity,' says Rebling. 'The two women were incredibly committed and motivated to do everything possible to ensure that what they had lived through could never happen again. That was the driving force of their lives.'

Lin Jaldati's memories of Anne now featured prominently in newspaper stories commemorating Anne's fiftieth birthday. In the early years after the publication of the diary and the play, almost all media stories about Anne were propaganda pieces condemning 'fascist' West Germany and the US. Now, they had a different flavour – a newspaper article about the sculpture commissioned by the Anne Frank packaging brigade; a radio documentary about a school that bore her name; or a piece about the Anne Frank House in Amsterdam. As the 1980s progressed, these stories were complemented by articles and programmes with a new hook: the rise of neo-Nazis in West Germany.

The truth was, neo-Nazism, xenophobia and antisemitism were rising in Europe during the 1980s, and not just in democracies. Dr Peter Kirchner, president of the Jewish Community in East Berlin, highlighted that this was something the GDR could no longer ignore when he spoke at the opening of 'Die Welt der Anne Frank' ('Anne Frank in the World') – the hugely popular international touring exhibition organised by the Anne Frank House in Amsterdam. Making his opening remarks at the TV tower in

East Berlin on 7 July 1989, Kirchner said, 'Almost forty-five years after the Liberation, old and unfortunately also new Nazis are raising their heads again, and we are again hearing about xenophobia and antisemitic activities. Let us not be lulled into believing such things are only possible outside the borders of our country.'

Kirchner had wanted to host the exhibit in the GDR since he had seen it in West Berlin three years earlier. The exhibition showed the history of the Frank family, from their origins in Frankfurt, through to the Nazi period and including family photos that had never been seen before by the public. It also showed life in everyday Nazi Germany, focusing on youth, leisure and culture, as well as the creation of concentration camps and life in the occupied Netherlands. Kirchner was impressed and wrote to Cor Suijk, then at the Anne Frank House, on 14 July 1986:

> The government of the GDR is planning to rebuild the former synagogue in Oranienburger Strasse in the course of the next few years, with a view to using it as a museum. And it occurred to me that – even though it would not be for some years – this would be a fitting place to present the Anne Frank exhibition to a wider public in our part of the city too.

By now an economic crisis meant that the GDR was desperate for foreign currency, and it jettisoned its anti-Zionism in favour of better relations with Israel. Lin Jaldati was now allowed to perform in Israel, and East Germany planned a number of events to mark the fiftieth anniversary of Kristallnacht. Kirchner's proposal to bring the Anne Frank exhibit to East Berlin was also approved, and preparations began to stage the exhibit in July 1989.

Despite a supposed change in the government mindset, predictably there were immediate problems over what the exhibit could show and say. One panel referred not only to the 'liberation' of Germany by the Allies but also to its 'conquest'. In East Berlin, the word 'conquest' was removed. Other objections related to references to the Berlin Wall, which was known in the GDR as the 'anti-fascist protection barrier', and to a depiction of a Soviet poster that featured an antisemitic caricature.

Preparations for an official press conference created more headaches. The East Berlin city council contended that xenophobia, right-wing extremism and antisemitism did not exist in the GDR and were Western problems caused by the inequalities of capitalism. The Anne Frank House rejected this, however, and insisted that wording remain, stating that such discrimination should be opposed 'everywhere'. Author Sylke Kirschnick notes that one visitor to the exhibition later wrote in the comment book: 'Neo-Nazis not just in West Germany – in the GDR too.'

Another disagreement was about the extent to which Germans should accept individual responsibility for what had happened – something the GDR had always insisted was irrelevant, as it claimed the state had taken all responsibility and had created a socialist, fascist-free future. When the exhibit opened on 19 June 1989, East German media followed the official line, stating, 'It also clearly shows the resurgence of fascism, racism and antisemitism in Western Europe.' Meanwhile the Mayor of East Berlin Erhard Krack said that the GDR had always made sure 'Jewish fellow-citizens ... have found a true home here'.

Peter Kirchner spoke from the heart when he said,

As Jews ... we remember and we will always remember. But this exhibition is only partly aimed at us. It is not the surviving victims and their descendants who need to come to these rooms over the next few weeks. What is shown here is addressed primarily to the generation of perpetrators and their descendants. Whatever form a German state took after 1945, every German must be encouraged to reflect on the events described here, so that they reconsider their own behaviour, both then and now, and feel called upon to do everything in their power to ensure that nothing like it ever happens again.

The Anne Frank commemorated in school ceremonies and official statues was unreal and remote, but the exhibit awakened new interest in her story, and soon someone who had known her and protected her and her diary was to bring her to life: Miep Gies.

Miep's visit in September 1989 was in aid of promoting her own memoir, *Anne Frank Remembered*, and her appearances at East Berlin bookstores and speaking events led newspapers to reprint extracts from the diary, drawing crowds of fascinated fans. Miep and her husband Jan were visiting in the dying days of communist rule, but the East German state still exercised an iron grip over arrangements, making sure she rarely spoke to any ordinary citizens.

A radio reporter dived into the queue at one event to ask people why they were there. An eleven year old girl said she had come on her own, without her parents, because she was so keen to meet Miep. 'I'm on my own, because I've got the Anne Frank book at home too. I wrote to [Miep] too ... and told her I'm very glad she helped Anne Frank and her family, that I respect her and think it's great that she's come to the GDR.' Another woman had come from one of the Anne Frank work brigades and said,

> We have a teaching group named after Anne Frank. New train-ees have been joining it ever since 1970. We have a folder with everything that gets published about Anne Frank. We also have a copy of [Miep's book]. Anne Frank was young too, and also wanted to live in peace and freedom. That wasn't granted to her. And young people, especially, can be happy and joyful that they have such a good future ahead of them.

Neither Miep nor her husband encountered any of the democ-ratisation and human rights movements that were sweeping East Germany in the autumn of 1989. As the FDJ newspaper *Junge Welt* bid them farewell with the headline 'See you again in the GDR!', the Berlin Wall tumbled only days later – taking Germany's commemoration of Anne Frank into a new era. Only time would tell whether *The Diary of Anne Frank* would still be relevant when Anne was no longer a pawn of the Cold War.

In West Germany, Anne Frank was still of interest when something newsworthy transpired, like the publication of the *Critical Edition* of the diary which proved that the text was au-thentic, or news that a group of young people wanted to set up an 'Anne Frank meeting place' in Frankfurt. Unlike in East Ger-many, in the West comments could also be crass and offensive, and in the summer of 1998 a DJ on a late-night radio show was sacked after calling 'shitty Anne Frank' a 'depressed girl with shitty diaries'.

Without the Cold War backdrop, Anne was becoming more
of a figurehead for victims of Jewish persecution and the Holocaust. At a ceremony to commemorate the fiftieth anniversary
of the liberation of Bergen-Belsen, German President Roman
Herzog said the name 'Anne Frank' stood for all the Jewish
victims:

> One of the many who suffered and died in this place was a girl
> whose story is known to many and whose name almost stands for
> all those who fell victim to barbarity: Anne Frank. On 11 April
> 1944 she wrote in her diary: 'One day this terrible war will be
> over, one day we will be people again and not just Jews!' In this
> one sentence we clearly see what lay at the root of the barbarity:
> selection. Selection was not just a word of terror in the camps. It
> was the underlying principle of National Socialism itself.
>
> People lost their human faces. They were divided up, reject-
> ed on the basis of their characteristics. Instead of 'not just Jews',
> Anne Frank could also have written, 'not just Sinti or Roma,
> not just Russians, not just Christians, not just trade unionists, not
> just socialists, not just the disabled, not just this or that minority'.
>
> It is our responsibility to never again allow such selections. To
> never again allow recognition of humanity to be dependent on
> race or origin, conviction or belief, health or ability. To never again
> allow a distinction to be made between life that is worthwhile
> and life that is not worthwhile. The lesson of Bergen-Belsen is
> this: human dignity is inviolable.

It was an important piece of political theatre, but after years of
grandiose state propaganda on both sides, the 2000s ushered in
an era in which grassroots groups would explore Anne's legacy

in ways that were more meaningful for a new generation of Germans. Amongst them, prisoners. 'I'd never have thought I still knew so much about that time,' said Anne, a 64-year-old former nurse addressing a group of fellow prisoners in Berlin Lichtenberg women's prison in 2017. Anne was serving a sentence for drug crimes after struggling for years with depression and addiction to painkillers, cannabis and heroin. She was now taking part in a project organised by the Anne Frank Centre in Berlin, to learn about Anne and the Holocaust. Through seminars and group work, the project encouraged prisoners to reflect on tolerance, antisemitism and what *The Diary of Anne Frank* meant to them. Thinking about her own life and the anti-semitism of her parents' generation, Anne told a reporter from *Jüdische Allgemeine*, 'It keeps happening: the Jews have always been the scapegoats, throughout history.'

Although the Anne Frank Centre in Berlin was originally set up to support the touring Anne Frank exhibit, the popularity of its work gave it a wider remit to reach young people and prisoners. Today about 40,000 people visit the centre every year, and director Veronika Nahm says its mission is to make sure all young people know about Anne and her story: 'Some of the young visitors to the centre come from troubled backgrounds and have experienced very difficult circumstances. Sometimes they just don't have the emotional resources to deal with suffering from the past too – but on the whole, there is still a strong resonance. Visitors seem deeply interested and moved.'

Nahm says that today one of their challenges is that there is only a small Jewish community in Germany, and many young people do not know any Jews. She explains,

For many non-Jewish children, antisemitism is a problem that belongs to the past. The sheer extremity of the Nazi atrocities against the Jews can make modern-day antisemitism pale into insignificance by comparison. Very often, they don't really connect the story of Anne Frank with antisemitism, or with any other aspect of life today. The centre often has to focus on simply conveying the history first.

Nonetheless, the centre does emphasise antisemitism as much as it can and also explores the concept of identity in general. Nahm says, 'Sometimes we impose an identity or label on others that isn't necessarily all that relevant to the way they identify themselves. We address all forms of discrimination.'

Since 2004, the centre has taken the Anne Frank exhibition into forty-three prisons and young offenders' institutions across Germany, where prisoners spend two days learning about Anne and her story, and then present that information to other prisoners and prison visitors.

'Young prisoners are a much-neglected group,' Nahm says.

There are very few programmes for them. They often have little experience of education and have been the victims of discrimination themselves. They often also hold anti-democratic attitudes – they have, after all, fallen through the cracks in the system. So the centre adapts its materials to them. Feedback suggests it makes a very strong impression. It's not about the centre telling them what happened; but more about enabling them to tell others.

Marcel, a twenty-year-old with 'dark, dreamy eyes', is a guide at the Anne Frank exhibit in Hamelin Prison. Serving three and a half years for burglary and theft, he says he knew virtually nothing about Anne Frank or the Nazis. He told reporter Sandra Löhr: 'The seminar itself has made me more confident too. But it also made me desperately sad. I've seen how sick humans can be. That we can do things like that! Us humans! It's totally sick.'

The ongoing work of the Anne Frank Centre in prisons, and plans by the Anne Frank Foundation to open the Frank Family Center in Frankfurt, show that Anne Frank has a role in modern Germany – but perhaps it is a more personal role. Only a few miles from the gleaming new Frank family archive, the Anne Frank Village in Wuppertal lies in forgotten ruins. After the official opening, and the attention of the world's media turned elsewhere, construction ground to a halt over a dispute about money. Builders dug up the original foundation stone laid by Otto and relaid it at a new site in nearby Hilgershöhe, where twenty houses were eventually completed. Machine operator Hieronym Orlowski, his wife Verenia and their young son Jerome became the first family to move in in July 1961. Although French President Charles de Gaulle was the family's official patron, the opening was a strangely quiet affair, with no flags, speeches or VIPs.

Shortly afterwards, all twenty houses were occupied and welfare groups started the thankless task of trying to integrate the new arrivals into the local community. Local aid units took the new residents to job interviews, schools and language lessons, while church associations organised summer fetes and Christmas parties. Poles, Czechoslovakians, Yugoslavs, Latvians and Hungarians rubbed along next to each other, not really communicating or forming new friendships, while Germans showed a distinct lack of interest in the new village, situated in an area of Wuppertal they called the 'ghetto of misery'.

A community started with such fanfare and publicity had died a quiet death, leaving only a couple of old signs behind. Like all top-down impositions, the Anne Frank Village had vanished, along with its Cold War manifesto for integrating migrants and for freedom. But across the world the spirit of the diary lived on – and grew, blossoming in the cracks.

CHAPTER 6

BLOOMING IN THE CRACKS: ANNE FRANK AROUND THE WORLD

'I have seen many Anne Franks in Cambodia.'
YOUK CHHANG, CAMBODIA'S LEADING RESEARCHER ON
GENOCIDE, JEWISH TELEGRAPHIC AGENCY, 6 OCTOBER 2008

Fourteen-year-old Youk Chhang was alone at home when he heard that Phnom Penh had fallen to the Khmer Rouge. It was 17 April 1975 and Cambodia had been engaged in a ferocious civil war for five years, culminating in the Marxist group, under the leadership of Pol Pot, seizing the capital and the nation as a whole.

Chhang, the youngest of nine children and the son of a gem merchant, was waiting at home that day when the young Khmer soldiers arrived. Chhang's mother had gone to see his sister, who was about to give birth. He wanted to wait for her, but the soldiers ordered him at gunpoint to leave immediately, and Chhang joined millions of other residents making their way out of Phnom Penh on foot. Although Chhang could not remember the name of his mother's home village, he vaguely remembered that it was about 45 miles south of the capital, in Takeo Province. He headed in that direction. 'When I was separated from my family, I felt numb and I kept thinking of my mother,' he says. 'I did not have any food; only two novels, a pair of shoes, some T-shirts, jeans and a bicycle.'

Once he had reached the village the local people sheltered him and kept his presence a secret from the Khmer authorities until his mother arrived. Within four months of his escape from Phnom Penh, however, the family was sent to one of Pol Pot's notorious work camps, where Chhang remained for four years until Vietnamese soldiers invaded the country in 1979 and overthrew the Khmer government. 'Innocence itself was a crime,' Chhang told *The Diplomat*. Caught sneaking into a rice field to pick watergrass and mushrooms for his starving sister, he was tortured in front of the work camp by the Khmer Rouge for hours. 'I will never forget this, they tortured me in front of my mother and she was too afraid to cry because even crying was a crime.'

Chhang was sent to a Khmer Rouge prison, where he languished for months until one day an older prisoner spoke up on his behalf. Soon after, Chhang was surprised to be released, but he learned later that the man who defended him had been murdered – 'In exchange for me, they killed him.'

Soon life got even worse. When Chhang's pregnant sister was also accused of stealing rice, the Khmer Rouge 'cut her open with a knife to see if the rice was in her stomach'. To survive, Chhang says, people had to 'steal, cheat, lie and point the finger at others'. More than 1.5 million Cambodians died in the work camps and prisons of the Khmer Rouge during the four years when the communist group tried to turn the country into an 'agrarian utopia'. After declaring that the nation would start again at 'Year Zero', Pol Pot had emptied the cities, abolished money, private property and religion, and killed anyone suspected of being an intellectual. Often that meant people who wore glasses or spoke a foreign language. Educated, middle-class families were executed in the hundreds of thousands. Hundreds of thousands more died of starvation, exhaustion and disease in the work camps in the countryside. The sites where Pol Pot and the Khmer Rouge had committed genocide became known as 'The Killing Fields'.

Chhang lost his father and most of his siblings to the brutal Khmer regime. After the end of Pol Pot's rule, he set off again on foot for Phnom Penh with his mother and a home-made wooden cart. It took them eighteen months to reach the capital, but at his mother's urging Chhang then embarked on a dangerous escape over the border to Thailand, where he lived in a refugee camp until he was chosen for resettlement in the United States in 1985.

In the US, Chhang led a human rights and democracy training programme for Cambodia, becoming a senior research fellow at the Center for the Study of Genocide, Conflict Resolution and Human Rights at Rutgers University and a member of the founding group of the Institute for International Criminal Investigations in The Hague. In 1995, he returned to Cambodia as the director of the Documentation Center of Cambodia (DC-Cam), which was founded as a field office of

Yale University's Cambodia Genocide Program. The centre now works with Asian countries on genocide education, including Thailand, Indonesia, Malaysia, the Philippines and Myanmar, and is currently conducting studies to see whether or not those countries teach the history of Khmer Rouge in their school curriculum, as well as whether or not they teach their own histories after the Second World War. 'In the Cambodian genocide we lost about 2 million people,' Chhang told me.

> So, my objective is about justice. I fought for justice, I want justice. I'm one of the survivors myself. But justice is very difficult to achieve after so many years. I also want to remember, because for me, memory is a form of justice. Justice and memory is a foundation for reconciliation.

One of the key tools Chhang uses to encourage young Cambodians to understand genocide is *The Diary of Anne Frank*. Chhang was sitting in a coffee shop one day with the Dutch ambassador, when they started discussing the diary – a book Chhang had barely heard of. They jotted down the idea of using it for educational purposes on the back of a napkin. In passing, the ambassador said, 'I'm sure there's a lot of Anne Franks in Cambodia.'

Chhang was determined to read the diary, but at first, he admits, he found it hard to relate to:

> The initial problem was the location. Europe seemed so distant. I had to buy a map, and then I tried to visualise it. Secondly, Anne Frank is not me. She's a girl. It took me about six months

of reading the diary several times, and looking at photographs, to really understand it.

Sovicheth Meta, who translated the diary into the Khmer language, points out that there are strong similarities to the Cambodian experience: 'The family and living conditions are very similar. Anne Frank had a father, we also have a father. The police came and took away their belongings, the police did that to us. It's very humanistic which makes it easy to relate to.'

Chhang got the agreement of the Anne Frank Foundation in Basel to use the book in Cambodia and to translate it. But surprisingly the Dutch embassy in Cambodia refused to give financial support for the project – although the ambassador did offer to pay for it personally. Chhang refused the offer, saying, 'I want your government's support not your pocket money.' After the text was translated and published alongside an English version, Chhang told the Cambodian government that they were free to distribute it to students, who were desperate to learn foreign languages. It was a useful tool, as, Chhang observed, they learned English at the same time as understanding more about the Holocaust. 'Since then, we've been successfully giving out thousands and thousands of copies of the book in high schools,' Chhang says. 'Then we broadcast it as a radio programme so that everyone could hear it.'

Chhang's next aim was to create a textbook beginning with extracts from the diary and followed by excerpts from another book he had published, *First They Killed My Father*, about the genocide in Cambodia. The textbook ended with writings by Holocaust survivor Hédi Fried. 'In Cambodia there's no history, and there's no difference between propaganda and history,' Chhang says.

> Textbooks stop in 1975 and jump to 1980. The 'plot', so to speak, is empty. It's not education. I proposed a new textbook with a different approach. In Cambodia we knew about Hitler, we knew about Germany, and we knew Jewish people. I started to get to think about what Cambodia could take from the Holocaust.

The DC-Cam centre has produced the Cambodia genocide textbook since 2009, and it is used in schools from ages seven to twelve, as well as in the foundation year of every Cambodian university.

While girls identify with Anne, Chhang says boys identify with the war story soldiers – and with the story of Otto Frank. 'Language is very important,' Meta, the translator, explains. 'In the Khmer language we don't have some English expressions. The first thing that I tried to do was to understand the meaning and the message behind the sentence before I could try [to] explain it.' Meta has translated the word 'Holocaust' as '*bochea phleung*' in Khmer, which means 'sacrifice by fire'. Chhang points out that language is key for another reason:

> Language is the cause of genocide; the use of language to describe people, how you communicate that, and how you translate it. It's the key. We published *The Diary of Anne Frank* as a bilingual book in English and Khmer, and that helped start the discussion. The first question readers confront is – who is Anne Frank? So, lesson one is looking at who Anne Frank is ... Then

you have started the conversation. First you read the book. Then you do role play, and the students start to learn the story.

In the students' imaginations, Europe is a place of cleanliness, mountains, snow and flowers – but they become more curious when they learn that it is also the site of the Holocaust. Chhang says the invisible power of *The Diary of Anne Frank* is that it encompasses both the beauty and the horror:

> It's scary when you find the beauty in such a story. You don't have to talk about torture to explain the Holocaust, or horror. A lot of people expect victims of genocide to be old, to be vulnerable, to be sad, to be suffering. You don't have to be in those positions to be a victim of the Holocaust or genocide at all. That is the perception of the outsider, but we who survive don't want others to experience what we have experienced. We are happy to have hope. We are hoping to dream.

Chhang is now expanding his work across Asia and to other countries with a shared experience of genocide. One such nation where the diary has also played a role is Rwanda – a country coming to terms with its own terrible genocide when the Hutu-led government murdered between 500,000 and 1 million of the Tutsi minority population.

Teacher Aimable Mpayimana encountered *The Diary of Anne Frank* for the first time when he was attending a one-week Freedom Writers Foundation course in Long Beach, California. The foundation was established by Erin Gruwell, who developed a methodology to help 'unteachable' students reach their potential, after her own experiences as a young teacher at Wilson High School. She began teaching students about the Holocaust after she saw a picture one student had drawn, depicting another black student with large lips. It was these kinds of drawings, she told them, that led to genocide. The key text that resonated with her students was *The Diary of Anne Frank*.

'I didn't know about Anne Frank,' Aimable Mpayimana says. 'We hadn't heard of her in Rwanda. I had to get the group to stop and tell me about her life and experiences in the annexe. I felt like everyone was looking at me and thinking – how can you not know about Anne Frank?' That week in Long Beach, Aimable also met Jan Erik Dubbelman, who led the international department at the Anne Frank House in Amsterdam, and visited the Holocaust Museum in Los Angeles. He began to think about how the Holocaust could inform the teaching of Rwanda's own history. After his return, he started working with *The Diary of Anne Frank* in one village where the students were orphans who had lost their parents in the genocide. As copies of the diary were not available in Rwanda and the students struggled with both French and English, Aimable developed multi-media resources to help them. 'I was worried the students would find Anne Frank exotic and not relatable,' he says. 'But to my surprise they made very powerful connections between Anne's experiences and their own lives.' One teenage girl, Chantal, described how her own parents had been taken away, and so she could directly understand how hate could lead to genocide and how important it was to uphold human rights.

'We can't compare pain, but we can understand,' Aimable says. Written by a teenage girl, and speaking to Rwandan teenagers, the diary 'sets out the clear steps that progressively led to the Holocaust. Those steps are very similar to the steps that led to the genocide in Rwanda, and elsewhere. It's a wake-up call.'

If *The Diary of Anne Frank* has helped people in societies recovering from genocide, it has been used and abused by tyrants too. In 2004, the Anne Frank Foundation in Switzerland granted permission for the diary to be translated and distributed in North Korea for a peppercorn payment of less than $2,000. Once published, it was enthusiastically promoted by dictator Kim Jong-il, who ruled that it would be taught in all schools as an example of how 'Nazis' such as the US regime would destroy the world through their war-like behaviour. When a Dutch documentary crew interviewed North Korean children about why they read the diary, they replied, 'According to our respected leader Kim Jong-il, *The Diary of Anne Frank* is one of the greatest classics of the world. That is why we read the diary – out of great respect for our leader Kim Jong-il.'

Some believed that concentration camps still existed – in the United States. 'As long as there are American Nazis, there will be secret places where innocent people are murdered … The prisons in America are comparable to concentration camps.' Another commented that they would never go into hiding like Anne and her family: 'I would go and fight instead of living like a beggar as Anne did.' Reading the diary had taught them that 'America will have to be destroyed … only then will Anne's wonderful dream of peace come true'.

The misuse of the diary in North Korea is perhaps the most egregious example of Anne's story being employed as twisted propaganda. But as the history of the diary in East Germany has shown, there have been many other examples of Anne's unique status as both a personal icon to millions and a political pawn.

Over the course of more than seven decades, the diary has outlasted many regimes and ideologies – and it has not blossomed through tin-eared political propaganda but instead through individuals in countries as disparate as Chile, South Africa and Russia finding meaning, truth and identification in Anne's words and in Otto's determination to spread her legacy throughout the world. Often, ordinary people have understood its essence, even in countries with the harshest political oppression. 'The diary is a litmus test for whether a society is totally totalitarian, or if there are cracks,' says Jan Erik Dubbelman, who has recently retired after thirty-seven years of taking the Anne Frank exhibit around the world.

Dubbelman first read the diary at age thirteen but found it hard to identify with Anne. It was only once he became a father himself that he began to relate to Otto and think about how it must have felt to want to protect your children but be unable to do so – and then to have to rebuild a life laid to ruin. After he started working for the Anne Frank House in 1982, Dubbelman encountered many stories of how the diary had spread in unlikely countries.

In Russia, the first edition of the diary was published in 1960 after considerable effort by writer Ilya Ehrenburg, who was a towering but hotly contested literary figure increasingly arguing for reform in the post-Stalin years. Ehrenburg was born into a Jewish family in Kyiv in 1891 but soon moved to Moscow with his family, later spending months in a Tsarist jail for being part of the Bolshevik underground. When he was released, Ehrenburg headed to Paris, where he soon became bored and disillusioned with politics and devoted himself to art and literature, becoming friends with André Gide, Malraux and Picasso, and even writing a satirical chapter in a novel ridiculing Lenin.

In the 1930s, Ehrenburg 'walked a tightrope', acting as a bridge between Western and Russian culture at the same time as working as a journalist and a highly effective representative of the Soviet regime. Critics called him a 'stooge of Stalin'; Ehrenburg called himself 'an acrobat'. During the Second World War he distinguished himself as a great Soviet patriot, writing more than 2,000 articles from the front lines for *Red Star* and *Pravda*. Since the 1930s he had consistently drawn attention to Hitler's antisemitism, and he declared in 1944 that Hitler's greatest crime was the destruction of 6 million Jews. Biographer Joshua Rubenstein says,

> There's no question he was the most important Soviet journalist during the war. And many people feel he was the most important journalist of any front during World War Two, because it is fair to say he influenced the course of the war. Hitler himself blamed Ehrenburg for reverses on the Eastern Front. Stalin said that Ehrenburg was worth a division.

Through his writing, Rubenstein says, Ehrenburg taught the Red Army 'how to hate' and changed the perception that the German enemies were the same ones faced in the First World War: 'They weren't, they were Nazis.'

In 1943, Ehrenburg began to compile the Soviet Union's most significant contribution to documenting the Holocaust, working with Vasily Grossman and more than two dozen other journalists to compile front-line documents and testimony outlining the true scale of Nazi massacres and atrocities committed in Soviet territory during the war. 'The Black Book', as it was known, was banned under Stalin and attained almost mythical status until it was finally published in 1980.

Ehrenburg survived Stalin's post-war crackdown and systematic campaign against Jews. While hundreds of other writers were arrested, executed or sent to labour camps, Ehrenburg continued to publish novels and became a member of the Supreme Soviet, the highest governing body of the USSR. Yet despite the suspicions of fellow writers and activists, there is no record that he ever betrayed other authors or collaborated in their persecution. In the final months of Stalin's life, Ehrenburg refused to sign a collective appeal condemning the 'doctors' plot', which was a supposed conspiracy of largely Jewish doctors to poison Stalin, and he wrote to Stalin to explain his actions.

After Stalin's death in 1953, Ehrenburg became a key liberal figure in the Soviet firmament, pushing for reform and opposing censorship. During the 'ambiguous, back and forth, pro-conservative, pro-liberal' Khrushchev era, Ehrenburg tried to negotiate an opening up on Soviet culture, arranging the first Picasso exhibit in Soviet history and writing his great work *The Thaw*. One of his other significant efforts was the publication of Anne's diary. 'Ehrenburg was responsible for the Russian translation of *The Diary of Anne Frank*,' Joshua Rubenstein says. 'Without his intervention that book would not have been made available in the Soviet Union.'

Stories about Holocaust atrocities committed outside Soviet

territory usually found it easier to pass state censorship, and the first articles about Anne Frank had appeared in the mid-1950s in connection with the Goodrich and Hackett play. In March 1956, journalist and literary translator Boris Izakov saw the play on Broadway in New York and wrote a review for the Soviet Ministry of Culture's weekly journal. He referred to Anne, incorrectly, as 'a girl who was hiding in Holland during the Hitlerite occupation and who perished in Buchenwald'. Two months later, the Moscow magazine *Spark* also featured a review of the play. Neither mentioned that the Franks were Jewish. This was not uncommon; Russian scholar Gennady Estraikh points out that at the time the Soviets even wrote about the Warsaw Ghetto without mentioning that its inhabitants were Jewish.

Two more articles referencing Anne followed, including one in the main weekly newsletter of the Soviet writers' union. In 1959, the British Foreign Office commented that the *Soviet Woman Journal* had written a review of the diary, 'without mentioning that she was a Jewess'.

As interest reached a peak, the Moscow publishing house Iskusstvo (Art) published a Russian translation of the play with a print run of 15,000 – and in the summer of 1958, Goodrich and Hackett visited the Soviet Union to assess the chances of the play being performed. As Gennady Estraikh notes, the play fell into a strange category, one that only existed in communist countries: neither banned nor officially allowed to be performed, the play existed in a loophole, with some theatres taking it upon themselves to stage productions. In the early 1960s at least four theatre companies took the risk: the State Theatre for Young Spectators in Riga; the Theatre for Drama and Comedy in

Leningrad; the Russian Drama Theatre in Tbilisi, Georgia; and most prominently the student theatre at Moscow State University, which performed the play more than sixty times in 1960 and 1961.

In August 1959, the film version of *The Diary of Anne Frank* was entered into the Moscow Film Festival by the US State Department but was screened only once at 11 p.m. due to Cold War tensions. The US government had initially decided to boycott the festival, believing it was organised to divert attention from the American National Exhibition in Moscow. At the last moment, however, the State Department changed its mind and sent *The Diary of Anne Frank* as the sole American entry. It was a pointed choice, driven by the fact that Jewish life in the Soviet Union was now receiving a lot of negative attention in the West, with rumours that the Soviets wanted to resettle Jews in far eastern parts of the country. Moscow responded through a series of press reviews of the film that compared Anne to Russian heroes of the war who had 'fought on', showing more bravery and 'spiritual resistance'. The Soviets then struck back further by also screening *Ein Tagebuch für Anne Frank*, the East German propaganda documentary so hated by Otto Frank.

At the same time, preparation began to produce a Russian translation of the diary, which was published on 13 October 1960 by Moscow publishing house Inostrannaia Literatura (Foreign Literature). Russian scholars noted that unlike other Soviet books, *The Diary of Anne Frank* did not list its print run on the back page. This was highly unusual and prevented people from easily understanding whether this was a state-sanctioned book that could expect to sell large numbers of copies. The print run was informally estimated to be about 10,000 copies and sold out within days. As the Soviet Union had a large Jewish population and Anne Frank was now a familiar figure in the press, the disguised small print run might signify that the Soviet authorities wanted to avoid turning Anne into too much of a national heroine.

The book was translated by the highly influential Rita Rait-Kovaleva, who also translated *The Catcher in the Rye* and shaped a generation of Russian reading of foreign literature. Her work shows that she consulted the German edition of the diary, and it bore some signs of Soviet censorship. A reference to Jesus was replaced with 'the legend of Jesus', and a comment about the problems faced by the Franks was supplemented with the words, 'like all other people', which fitted Soviet thinking that everyone had suffered in the war, not just the Jews.

'The fate of this book is extraordinary,' Ilya Ehrenburg wrote in the introduction. 'It appeared in Holland ten years ago, was translated into seventeen languages and bought in millions of copies.' Yet, he noted, this is not a novel by a celebrated writer: 'It is the diary of a thirteen-year-old girl, but it shakes the reader more than any masterfully written book could do.' The end of the book is all too clear, Ehrenburg writes, going on to describe how he attended the Nuremberg trials but had subsequently watched former Nazis and members of the Third Reich take up prominent positions in West German business and government and 'enjoy life'.

Anne Frank admitted she was little in politics. She did not play tribunal or parliament. She wanted to live. She dreamed of love.

She would have made a fine mother. She was killed. Her diary reminds everybody of the crime that was perpetrated. It must not be allowed to happen again!

Even without a large print run, the diary and the play made a big impact on Soviet culture. In 1961, Yevgeny Yevtushenko referred to Anne Frank in his well-known poem 'Babi Yar', while war veteran and Yiddish poet Moshe Teif wrote 'A Ballad about Anne Frank', which was only read by a tiny audience at the time but was later set to music. Anne's 'lack of resistance' was mentioned less in the press, and a newspaper article stated that the diary was one of the most heroic and important documents from the Second World War.

'The thaw', however, was not to last, and a new period of anti-semitism and anti-Zionism meant that *The Diary of Anne Frank* once again slipped into official obscurity in the Soviet Union. For decades Anne's voice was silent – but possessing a rare copy of *The Diary of Anne Frank* was a sign between owners that they had met a like-minded person who stood for reform and freedom and opposed the system.

The years of the post-Stalin thaw in the Eastern bloc also saw the first Polish publication of the diary, in 1957. Academic Iwona Guść traced the story of the diary in Poland in her article 'Ania's Diary: The Polish Translation of the Diary of Anne Frank', noting that writer and translator Jan Parandowski first began discussing a possible Polish translation of the diary after he read the French edition and met Otto at the PEN International conference in Amsterdam in 1954. Only a few weeks after that meeting, Parandowski told Otto he had spoken to an editor about a Polish edition of Anne's 'deeply human book' and suggested that his wife, who was Jewish, could translate. Parandowski suggested a new introduction, claiming that the French version was too superficial and would not resonate with Poles, who had their own experiences of Nazi occupation and knew of hundreds of 'Annes' who had hidden in Polish houses.

Parandowski's efforts, however, did not come to immediate fruition – once again it was the success of the play, and in particular its staging in East and West Germany, that raised interest in Poland. Within a month a Polish weekly newspaper, *Od A do Z*, had published three extracts from the diary translated into Polish, arguing the case for a Polish production of the play on the basis of its 'anti-fascist' message, which had been the subject of so much press coverage in the GDR. Other newspapers followed suit, and by the autumn of 1956 three Polish publishing houses, including the state publishing house known as PIW, had written to Otto asking for permission to publish a Polish edition. Otto consulted Jan Parandowski and Kurt Harrer, a translator he knew in Dresden, who urged him to accept an offer from Silesia Publishing House. But before he could do this, Otto received a letter from Silesia on 22 January 1957 to say PIW would be going ahead with publication – something they had discussed and begun work on months before.

While Otto was annoyed by the process and remained unsure about publishing in communist countries, Parandowski assured him that PIW was the largest and most highly thought of publisher in Poland, and they published his own books. When Otto finally signed the contract on 3 August 1957, the Polish edition was already translated and awaiting approval to be printed. One month later, 10,000 copies of the diary went on sale in Poland, and the book was so popular a second print run was ordered in 1959 for a further 20,000 copies.

The haste of the publishers was not only motivated by the success of the play in East Germany but also by 'Polish October' – or 'Polish Thaw' – which marked political reform and liberalisation after a period of workers' protests. A new government with First Secretary Władysław Gomułka meant an easing in political censorship and a greater freedom to publish foreign literature. Seeing a window of opportunity, publishers had hurriedly pressed ahead even without Otto's consent, understanding that no one knew how long such periods would last.

Taking advantage of the new political circumstances, producers had already staged the Goodrich and Hackett play to packed houses in Warsaw for six months by the time of publication, and state radio broadcasters played a shorter version to coincide with its release. Another radio broadcast by one of the country's most famous actresses and resistance fighters, Danuta Mancewicz, only highlighted how popular and important the diary had become.

Between 1957 and 1961 the diary was staged widely in theatres across Poland, and it became the most popular play ever staged by a foreign author. In her research, Iwona Guść found an estimated 60,000 people saw the play in the first year, with a further 50,000 attending between 1960 and 1961. In the beginning the play was performed in the evenings and catered to an adult audience, but as its wider appeal and message became clear, it was also staged by the Youth State Theatre in Kraków and adapted for a youth radio programme. Teachers were encouraged to take their students to performances, with the Communist Party newspaper *Trybuna Ludu* exhorting,

> The didactic impact of this piece is unquestionable; its internationalist spirit and its role in combating persistent manifestations of nationalism, chauvinism [and] antisemitism are clear and obvious. The youth gathered in the theatre ... will not only be moved by this play but will also be filled with just and noble ideas.

The call to anti-fascism was similar to much of the commentary in East Germany, but the unusual reference to antisemitism reflected that this issue was – briefly – important in Polish politics in the mid-1950s. In the political upheavals of the time, one faction had invoked antisemitic rhetoric, and the monument to the fighters of the Warsaw Ghetto was vandalised. The suicide of a Jewish girl who was being bullied at school made newspaper headlines, and Jewish intellectuals and critics supported the stance of Polish Prime Minister Józef Cyrankiewicz when he spoke out against antisemitism in February 1957.

Journalists and critics took great pains to write about an 'Anne Frank' they believed Poles would identify with, claiming that the essence of Anne could be seen in the children lost in the Warsaw Ghetto uprising. Meanwhile the Polish writer and Auschwitz survivor Seweryna Szmaglewska said, 'Those who helped to hide and take care of the persecuted will recognise their own determination in the behaviour of Miep.'

Similarly, although Adam Lyfell, the chief editor at PIW, had gone to enormous efforts to produce an accurate translation of the diary – asking Otto to supply the original Dutch English and German editions – names and expressions were 'domesticated' into Polish. Anne was changed to Ania, Peter to Piotr and Anne's cat Moortje to Murzynek.

Critics and writers attempted to align Jewish suffering with Polish suffering in order to make Anne's story more relatable – but by the mid-1960s all attempts to address antisemitism were outlawed again. A more nationalist faction of the Communist Party had taken control, and attempts to tackle antisemitism were now associated with 'Zionism' and 'Western anti-Polish propaganda'. Across the Soviet sphere the political agenda took 'an increasingly anti-Jewish turn', and even acknowledging that the vast majority of the victims in Nazi extermination camps were Jewish was severely criticised.

As early as 1961 Otto heard that despite their initial interest, PIW would not be going ahead with plans to publish Anne's short stories. And in April 1963, Otto was officially informed that the diary would no longer be available in Polish bookshops. The window of opportunity had closed. But Jan Erik Dubbelman states that it is no coincidence that most of the critics who supported the diary were later part of the Solidarity movement to oppose and overthrow communism in Poland, just as the success of the first Anne Frank exhibition in East Berlin captured the public imagination only weeks before the fall of the Berlin Wall. Iwona Guść writes that *The Diary of Anne Frank* returned to a newly democratic Poland in 1993, 'in a new translation, and an entirely new political context'.

Once again, the diary had taken seed in the cracks. But in the rest of the world, where it was freely available, it was by no means obvious that this phenomenon of the 1950s would have a second life and continue to resonate as an important text throughout the rest of the twentieth century. By the 1980s Penguin considered the diary to be a 'dead title' unworthy of investment or promotion, and while the first Anne Frank exhibition in Amsterdam was opened with great fanfare by the Queen of the Netherlands, its sister exhibit in New York was considered an extremely expensive failure – probably not to be repeated.

At the Anne Frank House, Jan Erik Dubbelman persisted, taking a long period of unpaid leave to move to London and try to stage the exhibition in the UK. For six months he lived in a dingy squat in Islington, riding around on his bike and raising funds to pay off the large debt the previous exhibition had incurred. Travelling on National Express buses and staying in 'fleapit' hotels, he took the Anne Frank in the World exhibit to twenty towns and cities across the country between 1986 and 1990. The Jewish community was at first wary, concerned that staging the exhibit could in fact exacerbate antisemitism, but their fears were unfounded. Dubbelman noted that while in the past interest in the diary might have been generated by parents with memories of the war, it was now children visiting on school trips who would engage most with Anne, and then return bringing their parents with them.

Life in the UK in the mid-1980s mirrored Dubbelman's notion that the exhibition resonated most in societies on the cusp of undergoing huge transformation. The country was experiencing immense political and social upheaval, with a bombastic Conservative government led by Margaret Thatcher laying waste to swathes of traditional industries and consigning a generation, particularly in the north, Scotland and Wales, to mass unemployment. Those involved in the Anne Frank exhibition noticed that while they could sometimes get the sympathetic ear of a Conservative minister or politician, strong practical support usually came from the embattled left, like the soon-to-be-abolished Greater London Council, and in northern heartlands like Manchester, Barnsley and Bradford.

The truth was that Dubbelman had taken huge risks to stage the UK exhibition – the financial investment was massive, and he had 'no money, and no support from the leadership at the Anne Frank House', which was scarred by the previous exhibition having taken them to the brink of bankruptcy. Yet the UK exhibition was a success, attracting huge visitor numbers and media attention. One visitor was Gillian Walnes Perry, who as a result co-founded the Anne Frank Trust in the UK in 1990 with Eva Schloss. The Anne Frank Trust UK has now run educational programmes for more than thirty years, and along with the work of other organisations like the Holocaust Educational Trust it restarted a conversation about the Holocaust that had become dormant.

Holocaust historian Tony Kushner became involved with the Anne Frank exhibition after it visited Manchester, and he recalled that when he had studied the Second World War at both O-Level and A-Level, there had been no mention of Jews or the Holocaust on the curriculum. Kushner told Gillian Walnes Perry:

> If you had said to me in 1989 that Holocaust education would become part of the school curriculum, there would be war crimes legislation in two years, that the Imperial War Museum would have a Holocaust exhibition larger than the World War Two exhibition, and that there would be a national Holocaust Memorial Day, I would have laughed at you at the improbability of it all.

Since the 1980s the Anne Frank in the World touring exhibit has visited more than 6,500 communities in ninety countries. Often, the exhibit draws crowds where the themes of dictatorship, oppression and liberation resonate with a population's own experiences of a transition to democracy. When the exhibit arrived in a newly democratic Chile, Dubbelman worried that a story about a Jewish family in a long-ago European war would generate little interest. So, he conducted thirty-four press interviews in a week, and more than 5,000 people visited. In Colombia and Sri Lanka, the exhibit often visited communities still ravaged by violence and played a role in peace-building activities between different groups.

Nowhere was that link to a fragile democracy more apparent than in South Africa, where *The Diary of Anne Frank* was inexorably linked to President Nelson Mandela and the African National Congress (ANC). Shortly after his release from prison, Mandela spoke about the role the book had played in his life, saying that although he had read it before his arrest, reading it again while incarcerated meant that 'the lessons sunk more deeply in our souls, and for everyone in our situation'. Mandela said that non-white South Africans had suffered under an apartheid regime that had imitated the Nazis by imposing a cruel and murderous white-minority rule, keeping the majority of the population in bondage. He and his comrades had been imprisoned on Robben Island, a small, barren piece of land off the coast of Cape Town – but Anne's diary was unique in demonstrating the 'invincibility of the human spirit' as they undertook backbreaking labour in the quarry by day, and at night watched the lights of the city twinkling tantalisingly close, but always out of reach. Mandela shared the diary – at great risk – with other prisoners on the island, so they too could understand that they were 'following in the footsteps of great fighters for human rights – including Anne Frank'.

Sharing and talking about such material was strictly forbidden, but the prisoners often read and learned together in the quarry. At one point the diary fell apart from constant use, and at night in their cells the prisoners painstakingly copied out the pages in tiny handwriting, to reconstruct the book. Such a strong connection between the diary and the ANC meant that the idea of taking the touring exhibit to the newly democratic South Africa of the 1990s was met with initial ambivalence by some white South Africans. (The ANC supported both the Palestine Liberation Organization's leader Yasser Arafat and Muammar Gaddafi of Libya, both of whom were sworn enemies of Israel.) Despite this, one prominent member of the Jewish community in Cape Town, Myra Osrin, was visiting London in 1991 when Gillian Walnes Perry, who was by then running the UK exhibition, asked if she would be interested in taking the exhibit to South Africa. Most of those involved with the exhibition and the Anne Frank House were staunchly anti-apartheid and would never have considered taking it to a country that promoted racial discrimination and human rights abuses – but the release of Nelson Mandela and the advent of democratic elections now made it possible. Osrin agreed that she was interested and travelled to Amsterdam to meet Jan Erik Dubbelman at the Anne Frank House. There, they discussed her experience organising an exhibition and book for Holocaust survivors in South Africa and forming the Holocaust Education Council – which would eventually lead to the establishment of the Cape Town Holocaust and Genocide Centre. The team was particularly impressed by her commitment to setting up a multi-faith leadership council, working with people from all racial groups to ensure an Anne Frank exhibition would be diverse and accessible for everyone.

Before the launch of the exhibition in Cape Town three years later, Osrin organised a workshop for teachers from white, 'coloured' and black schools to meet, discuss the project and create teaching materials. Education had been used as a deliberate tool by the apartheid government to keep the different races apart, and non-white children were deliberately denied a good education. Not only were schools still segregated, there was no central government department for the education of all children. As the teachers began an animated conversation – that only eventually turned to the topic of Anne Frank – Osrin realised that it was the first time such a mixed group had sat down together. They had literally never met, but the workshop about Anne had brought them together. Osrin says,

> I don't say the Anne Frank exhibition was the only thing to help with the transition of the country, but I do believe it was one of them. The project had two primary intentions. First, to educate people about the history of the Holocaust; second to use the Holocaust story to teach people about the evils of discrimination and the importance of human rights.

Another key part of its success, Osrin believes, is that she worked with the University of the Western Cape's Mayibuye Centre to create an ancillary exhibition, 'Apartheid and Resistance', to be staged alongside Anne Frank in the World. Most of the children who visited 'didn't even know how to spell Holocaust', Osrin says, but equally, nor did they not know the details about their own history of 'pass laws', segregation and discrimination.

The Anne Frank in the World exhibition was opened at the National Gallery in Cape Town by Archbishop Desmond Tutu; in Port Elizabeth by leading ANC figure Govan Mbeki; and in Johannesburg at the Museum of Africa by President Nelson Mandela. Speaking at the opening, Mandela reaffirmed the inspiration he had drawn from the diary and its message about the 'invincibility of the cause of freedom and justice'. There were strong parallels between the liberation of Europe from the Nazis and the liberation of South Africa. Apartheid rulers and the Nazis had shared an 'inherently evil belief' in the superiority of some races over others. They had both derived pleasure from the suffering of other human beings – 'but because these beliefs are patently false, and because they were, and will always be, challenged by the likes of Anne Frank, they are bound to fail'. Anne Frank was particularly relevant to a South Africa emerging from apartheid, Mandela concluded, as it enabled them to explore the past 'in order to heal, to reconcile and to build the future'.

In the second week of the exhibit in Cape Town, Myra Osrin realised why the story of Anne Frank resonated with so many South Africans. A school bus had arrived unexpectedly from a township school, and the teacher stopped to speak to her on the way out. 'You have no idea how important this exhibition has been for my students' self-esteem,' the teacher said. Osrin was perplexed, but he explained, 'This is the first time they can see a person can be discriminated against, even if he or she doesn't have black skin.'

For eighteen months the Anne Frank exhibition drew thousands of visitors in Cape Town, Port Elizabeth, Durban, Johannesburg, Bloemfontein and Pretoria. When it closed in 1995, Jan Erik Dubbelman continued to work in South Africa for many years, partnering with other organisations to make sure they were reaching a diverse range of South African communities. In some cases that meant working jointly with the Hector Pieterson Museum in Soweto, named after the twelve-year-old boy who was famously photographed dying in his friend's arms after the Soweto school uprising in 1976. In other cases, it meant working in townships where teenagers were so deprived the Anne Frank team sent them home with food after discovering they were sucking their thumbs due to hunger.

After the Cape Town Holocaust and Genocide Centre was established in 1999, a smaller centre opened in Durban in 2007, complete with a replica of Anne Frank's room in the annexe. That year, the Holocaust became an official part of the school curriculum in South Africa, ensuring all high-school students would learn about that period of history and emphasising the personal responsibility everyone has to challenge discrimination.

Rather than questioning the role Anne Frank could play in their lives in modern South Africa, young people flocked to the exhibition and workshops, starved for knowledge and full of attention and interest, Jan Erik Dubbelman remembers. Buses of young people would arrive in Cape Town from the outlying winelands, where their families lived in extreme rural poverty. Blind people took part, representing a group not even previously acknowledged in apartheid South Africa. Teachers came, desperate to explore the topics with their students but having no tools or material to do so. Surveying the impact of their work,

Jan Erik Dubbelman says, 'In an arid landscape, Anne Frank flourished.'

Dubbelman believes *The Diary of Anne Frank* will always be meaningful in countries directly affected by genocide and oppression – as well as those directly affected by the consequences of the Second World War, including Germany, the former Soviet Union and Japan. After the small, almost clandestine, publication of the diary in the 1960s, Anne Frank only reappeared in the Soviet Union in 1990. For decades it was impossible to talk about the Holocaust; the extermination was absent from official Soviet histories of the Second World War and Jews were discriminated against in all aspects of public life. By the end of the 1980s, however, Soviet President Mikhail Gorbachev's glasnost reforms led to the collapse of communist rule in the Eastern bloc countries of Europe, the withdrawal of Soviet troops from war in Afghanistan and independence movements in the Baltic states of Lithuania, Estonia and Latvia. As the Anne Frank House prepared for the first ever visit of the Anne Frank in the World exhibit to Moscow, the cracks in the systems had never been wider – nor the premise for the exhibit more fragile.

The Moscow exhibit had been organised through the personal connection of the liberal rabbi of The Hague Awraham Soetendorp and a member of the Russian Academy of Sciences. Yet Dubbelman worried about the success of the exhibit when there was no grassroots support, no community groups, to create the right context for talking about Anne.

He need not have worried. In reality, the hosting of the exhibition opened the floodgates for talking about antisemitism, the experience of Jewish Russians and what had happened during the war. Dubbelman told Gillian Walnes Perry that he could still picture 'the dramatic scene of elderly Jewish attendees at the exhibition launch event openly and unashamedly shedding tears'. It was their first experience of a public event about the Holocaust, but their tears weren't only about that but also about 'the very fact that it could happen here at all'.

Walnes Perry remembers that young people in Russia often argued that antisemitism didn't exist in the new Russia, even though restrictions were still in place preventing Jews from attending university or getting jobs. Not everyone supported the project, and sometimes the warnings could be chilling. After one debate at the Moscow House of Writers, Dubbelman discovered that a target had been drawn on the back of the coat worn by Elena Yacovitz, the young journalist who helped him organise the exhibit.

After Moscow, the exhibit travelled to Ukraine, a country with direct experience of Nazi occupation and where many atrocities of the Holocaust and the Second World War had been committed. On the opening night at the Museum of Lenin in Kyiv, Dubbelman found himself speaking to dozens of middle-aged survivors of Nazi horrors, who had come to the exhibit and felt they could share their experiences for the first time. One lady was Clara Vinakur, who told Dubbelman she had been shot alongside her family by the Nazi execution squads, and had lain in a mass grave with hundreds of others, pretending to be dead until the soldiers had left. She had waited more than forty years to tell her story.

The exhibit opened the door for those who visited to talk about antisemitism, human rights abuses and the Holocaust in

their own countries. From Ukraine, one survivor sent a manuscript to the Anne Frank House about a concentration camp in
Moldova that was unknown in the West. And from Moscow,
one of the exhibition's key volunteers, historian Ilya Altman,
visited the Anne Frank House in Amsterdam and went on to
found the Russian Research and Educational Holocaust Center
as a result.

When the exhibit visited the now independent Baltic states
in the late 1990s, the exhibit and its volunteers found themselves
facing some of the most challenging antisemitism and a resurgence of ethnic nationalism. In Lithuania, where a staggering
96 per cent of the Jewish population had been murdered by the
Nazis and local collaborators, the exhibit was organised in partnership with the Jewish Museum in Vilnius and then toured
nine more cities. So little was known about Anne Frank or
spoken about the Holocaust that Gillian Walnes Perry received
a letter from one partner museum to the Anne Frank House
that started, 'Dear Anne Frank, We would very much like to
show your exhibition.' On that first tour, however, more than
12,000 people visited the exhibit and took part in drama workshops with young people from the Jewish and non-Jewish population. In Latvia, those same drama workshops not only asked
young people to think about antisemitism but also brought
together Latvians and ethnic Russians to discuss the country's
more recent nationalist laws, such as the citizenship law that
disenfranchised the sizeable Russian population.

Otto's stepdaughter Eva Schloss remembered her visit to
Latvia with the Anne Frank exhibit, where young people also
took part in a play written about her own life. 'It was tough,' she

wrote. People were very unwilling to think about antisemitism, and one teenage boy was so ashamed of being Jewish he could scarcely admit it, even to her. The drama workshops proved to be the most difficult but also the most rewarding in all her travels relating to Anne.

A number of children and young people in the Baltic states had written their own diaries of life under Nazi occupation, including Yitskhok Rudashevski, who was murdered aged fifteen in the Ponary Woods in Lithuania; Gabik Heller from the Vilna Ghetto in Vilnius; Ilya Gerber and Tamara Lazerson from the ghetto in Kaunas, Lithuania; and Gertrude Schneider, who was incarcerated in the ghetto in Riga, Latvia. Inevitably, many of those would be labelled as Baltic 'Anne Franks'. As Anne's iconic status grew, teenage 'Anne Franks' appeared in every war zone from Vietnam to Bosnia. One country, however, adopted her name as much more than a lazy shorthand for a teenage diarist. In Japan, Anne represented a national era, women's development and all the guilt, sorrow, loss and horror of the war. Anne Frank was a state of mind.

Otto Frank had begun corresponding with publishers about the possibility of a Japanese edition of the diary as early as 1952. In his letters, he wrote that he was 'near to a nervous breakdown' and 'must keep quiet a little'. His expectations were low. Yet much to everyone's surprise, Japan was not only one of the first countries to publish the diary but also one with good publishing terms and strong sales.

On 23 January 1953, the director of publisher Bungei Shunju Shinsha, Mr Y. Washio, wrote to Otto to tell him they were delighted to publish the diary and wanted to introduce it to

Japanese readers of all ages and classes. Washio told Otto that the translator would be Kaito Kozo, from a distinguished company, and that the publishers had written to well-known people to ask for their quotes. 'It is our profound desire, to make this book a bridge between our countries,' Washio concludes.

After publication, Washio wrote again to thank Otto for writing a magazine article to accompany the book, and reported that the diary was being read 'by a remarkable number of Japanese'. As of 20 March, they had published more than 101,000 copies and started a thirteenth printing. As hoped, the book was being read by Japanese men and women from all backgrounds, and many of them had written in with comments that would be made into a separate publication. Of those readers, many asked for Otto's address and would strike up correspondences with him. Washio ended his letter with the news that after one bookstore wrote and asked for a portrait of Anne, nearly sixty others followed and portraits of Anne were now staring out of shop windows across Japan.

There was no doubt that Anne Frank was an immediate sensation in Japan – but many remained puzzled about why. Although Otto never visited, he received thousands of letters from Japanese readers who had been moved by the diary. Many talked about Anne's intimate writing about her family, falling in love with Peter and the emotional and sexual development that was a revelation to young Japanese people in the 1950s and 1960s. Girls began to refer to having their 'Anne Frank' as a euphemism for having a period – still a taboo in Japan. In the late 1960s, one consumer brand started marketing 'Anne Frank tampons' until Otto asked them to stop.

After a chance meeting with Otto, Makoto Otsuka set up the Holocaust Education Center in Fukuyama City in 1971. Something between a museum and a memorial shrine, the centre remains the only Holocaust site in Japan with a collection of artefacts that tell the story of Europe's Jewish population in the twentieth century. Otsuka told Deutsche Welle: 'Although there are no historical facts to prove it, there are opinions that the Jewish people and the Japanese people have the same ancestors. Some people have found common points in Judaism and the Shinto religion, as well as in pronunciations in Hebrew and Japanese.' Otsuka speaks Hebrew and welcomes school visits, adding that the aim of his centre is to promote peace.

Although French journalist Alain Lewkowicz says young Japanese people are 'shockingly ignorant' of history, they all read Anne Frank at school and have the diary passed down to them from older generations. 'They might not know about the Holocaust, or exactly who Hitler was, but they know Anne Frank.' As he discovered when he was developing an iPad app about Anne Frank in Japan, Anne is now a topic of at least four Manga comic books and three animated films. More than 30,000 Japanese tourists visit the Anne Frank House in Amsterdam every year – 5,000 more than Israelis.

However, critics claim that without setting the diary within the correct historical context, right-wing groups in Japan have been able to appropriate Anne as an excuse for a regime that committed war crimes. Yuko Tojo was the granddaughter of General Hideki Tojo, the Second World War Japanese premier who ordered the 1941 attack on Pearl Harbor and was executed for Class-A war crimes. She told Lewkowicz: 'I am like Anne

Frank.' Before her death in 2013, Tojo ran for parliamentary office, aiming to restore the reputation of her grandfather and the 'pride' of the Japanese people. She compared her experience to Anne Frank, describing how her family was forced to flee and hide on the day Japan surrendered to the Allies: 'August 15, 1945, was the day that everyone else became free,' Yuko told Reuters. 'But that was the day our post-war life of fleeing and hiding began … My grandfather was certainly responsible for the nation, but having responsibility and doing bad things are different. He was not a criminal.' The Allies had tampered with post-war history, she added. 'Japan's culture and the Japanese spirit, right down to the bottom of our hearts, were all dyed with this version of history. And it's been that way for the past sixty years.'

Alain Lewkowicz says, 'Anne Frank was the ultimate victim' in a nation that also thought of itself that way. For Yoko Takagi, who has organised the Anne Frank exhibition in more than eighty venues in Japan, the picture is a little more complicated. Takagi says she believes the diary remains a popular way for the Japanese people to connect the suffering of one child – Anne – to the suffering of their own children at the end of the Second World War. Although they may not understand the Holocaust or the wider context of the Second World War, she thinks that 'through looking at the genocide of the Holocaust, educators can see an important doorway into a very difficult time in Japanese history for young people to learn about – that of the cruelty of the Japanese occupying army'. Although they understand that the atomic bombs dropped on Hiroshima and Nagasaki were 'immensely cruel', she hopes they will also understand that 'once wars start, human beings, and in our case, the Japanese Army, are capable of very cruel things'. Gillian Walnes Perry reports that today Anne Frank is taught in schools alongside the history of Chiune Sugihara, the Japanese diplomat who saved the lives of 6,000 Lithuanian Jews by issuing ten-day transit visas to those fleeing the Soviet Union in the direction of the United States.

One beautiful legacy of Anne Frank in Japan is the Anne Frank rose, the 'Souvenir d'Anne Frank', which was cultivated by Belgian horticulturalist Hippolyte Delforge and sent by Otto to Japanese schoolgirl Michiko Otsuki in the early 1970s. Of the dozen bushes Otto sent, only one survived – and was grafted onto a Japanese rose by Michiko's uncle Ryuichi Yamamuro, and planted at the Peace Gardens of Hiroshima and Nagasaki. After it prospered, Yamamuro sent roses and copies of *The Diary of Anne Frank* to schools across Japan – work that his son continues today.

In the text that accompanies the Anne Frank rose is a haiku by Tsuda Kiyoka that reads: 'In the rose garden, unless you retrace your steps, you'll find no way out.'

CHAPTER 7

FAKE NEWS: ANNE FRANK ON TRIAL

'At the moment there are four court cases in West Germany, two in Hamburg, and two in Frankfurt, concerning accusations that the diary is a forgery. I fought against this in 1961 and won, but the same accusations are still being expressed, and I have to fight against them over and over again.'

OTTO FRANK, 1979

Within a few short years, Anne's intimate teenage hopes, dreams and frustrations had propelled *The Diary of Anne Frank* to astonishing heights of popularity around the world. But, as Otto was discovering, such fame also brought the iconic book he had shaped under attack.

The first crack was the painful and unpleasant battle waged by Meyer Levin. Levin undoubtedly believed that Otto had watered down the uniquely terrible fate the Jews had suffered during the Holocaust. Yet surely, even in the grips of his utter obsession, he could not have realised that by challenging the play's credibility and message he was opening the door for

Holocaust deniers and Nazi sympathisers to go further? As time went by, claims surfaced that *The Diary of Anne Frank* was edited, altered or fabricated in such a way as to spread 'fake news' about the persecution of the Jews and the murder of 6 million people.

Otto Frank was well aware that antisemitism was still rife in Europe and Germany. Teenagers disrupted the opening of the play in Linz in Austria in 1957, in what was described as a 'full-blown Nazi riot'. One year later, in Wuppertal, a poster for the play was daubed with the words: 'Death to the Jewish swine. Too few Jews went up in smoke. Anne Frank was a Jewish swine too.'

In November 1957, the first articles appeared in Swedish newspaper *Fria Ord* suggesting that the diary was not really written by Anne. *Fria Ord*, meaning 'free words', was a traditionally anti-communist publication that had supported the Nazi idea of an Aryan super-race. After the war, it was one of the few public outlets for Swedes who still held those views. In two articles titled, 'Jewish Psyche – A Study Around Anne Frank and Meyer Levin', Danish critic Harald Nielsen used the furore over the play to claim that the diary had been partly written by Meyer Levin himself. As evidence, Nielsen studied Levin's work and claimed that the names Anne and Peter were not traditional Jewish names.

Bizarre as this seemed, a similar article appeared in a Norwegian newspaper in March 1958. The newspaper *Folk og Land* was the mouthpiece of the far-right Norwegian Nasjonal Samling Party, which had been the only legal party during the German occupation in the Second World War and was active in Nazi historical revisionism. This article went further, claiming the diary was a forgery. Levin's lawsuit was 'proof', surely, 'that the two men had conspired and collaborated to forge a young girl's diary. Why else would two Jews sue each other in a New York court for breach of contract and plagiarism?' The article went on:

The most recent addition to the field of political autobiographical literature is 'The Diary of Anne Frank'. It has advanced triumphantly around the world in millions of copies – the book about the horrors, the suffering and the death of the poor Jewish teenager, written by the hand of a gentle innocent child. One could weep tears of blood in sympathy, and clench one's fists against those damned beasts, the trampling Nazi Germans.

Anne's father narrowly escaped with his life, we are told. He only consented highly unwillingly to the publication of the diary, so the advert tells us.

What a press the book has received! What advertising on TV and radio! It has been filmed. Like a plague, it has swept through the meeting halls of all countries. Discussed in the pulpits. Read aloud in schools, even in the lower classes. Good little Anne has become the whole world's cosseted child, so to speak. Advertising without equal in world literature.

But just pinch yourself and it becomes clear that this book, too, just like Eva Braun's, is a forgery and that the book was written by a canny Jew. A Jewish lawyer over in New York is demanding between 4 and 5 million krona from the publisher for his work, the rewriting of the manuscript for this purpose.

We eagerly await the verdict. The Danish academic Hans Nielsen, who has undertaken thorough research in order to uncover the truth about the book, has written that it must be a fake … The truth is from God, the lie from Satan.

Although the circulation of *Folk og Land* was never more than a few thousand copies, over the years it would have a significant impact. The article was translated into German and published in Austria in *Europa Korrespondenz*, and then in *Reichsruf, Wochenzeitung für das Nationale Deutschland*, the weekly newspaper for the neo-Nazi political party Deutsche Reichspartei. *Europa Korrespondenz* also published an article claiming that Dr Louis de Jong, the director of the Netherlands State Institute for War Documentation, was the true author of the diary – based upon the fact he had written an article about Anne and the diary for *Reader's Digest*.

Otto Frank may not have known about these articles, but even if he did, he decided to ignore them. It was only when Lothar Stielau, a member of the far-right Deutsche Reichspartei, wrote an article about the 'pent-up demand' amongst Germans to catch up with the rest of the world – this time through what he considered the misguided staging of a student production of *The Adventures of Tom Sawyer* – that Otto was spurred into action. Stielau was a fifty-year-old former Nazi stormtrooper who had become a high-school English teacher at the prestigious Cathedral School in Lübeck. After the war, he joined Deutsche Reichspartei and rose to become the district chairman for the city. His article was printed in the school alumni magazine:

Tom Sawyer's Big Adventure
Shortly after our acting group's June production, some upper sixth form students with an interest in the subject asked me, too, for my views on it; I gave them to understand the following:

In 1945 we Germans undoubtedly needed to catch up with ideas from around the world. Since then, this need has been met, to the extent that the pendulum is now swinging back and there is a noticeable need to catch up with things that have emerged from our own culture. For this and other reasons, Tom Sawyer is somewhat irrelevant to the people of our country in 1958. We see the intention behind the 're-education work' in the newly polished play and are disgruntled: among a whole bunch of warped characters there is only one morally dazzling 'white' angel – a n***o, and the only n***o among all the whites, white deadbeats and children, at that!

And it's not even about arousing sympathy with this endangered n***o, nor is it the usual spiel with or without brotherhood in the sense of the fatherlandless cosmopolitanism of yesteryear. Rather, it is about the kindling of *hatred*: anyone who does not share the author's attitude must be hated. Again and again it strikes in this direction to ensure that the hatred takes root. There certainly are ideologies whose bearers often act in this way, must act in this way, even. But is that our way? Not everyone can be expected to have the attitude of Sophocles: 'I was not born to share hate, but to share love.'

Only one short paragraph in Stielau's rambling, turgid article refers to Anne Frank – yet its meaning is stark. Stielau compared the diary to other well-known faked diaries (including that of Hitler's wife) and accused its publishers of doing so to make money from a defeated Germany: 'The forged diaries of Eva Braun, the Queen of England and the not much more genuine one of Anne Frank may have earned the beneficiaries of the German defeat a few million, but they have also made us extremely sensitive.'

Previous articles had slipped under the radar, but on this

occasion the Central Council of Jews in Germany read Stielau's ramblings and passed on the piece to publisher Fischer Verlag – who discussed it with Otto when he visited a week later. While Otto considered his response, the Ministry of Culture for Schleswig-Holstein (the state in which Lübeck is based) stated that Stielau had 'caused offence' and began an investigation into whether he had breached his professional obligation to remain politically neutral. At an interview to discuss the situation, Stielau said that while he was not challenging the fact that Anne Frank had kept a diary, none of the published versions beared any resemblance to her original text. Rather than use the German word *fälschen* (meaning fake) to describe the diary, he should have chosen the word *verfälschen* (meaning significantly altered).

As the investigation got underway, Heinrich Buddeberg, chairman of the Deutsche Reichspartei in Schleswig-Holstein, came to Stielau's defence. He wrote a letter to Lübeck newspaper the *Lübecker Nachrichten*, claiming that Stielau was being politically persecuted by the Social Democrats and repeating the story that Meyer Levin was part-author of the diary. On the day Buddeberg's letter was published, the Ministry of Culture ordered that Stielau be temporarily suspended from teaching, as he had generated political propaganda in conflict with his job in education and was unworthy of the respect and confidence his profession should command.

Later that month, through his Frankfurt attorney Dr A. Flesch, Otto took action. 'Anne Frank's father sues German teacher for smearing diary', newspaper headlines announced.

Otto Frank, father of Anne Frank, has filed a libel suit against a former Lübeck high school teacher who asserted that the famous

'Diary' was forged. The suit charges Lothar Stielau with libel, defamation of the memory of the dead, making false accusations and antisemitism. The Schleswig-Holstein Ministry of Culture has suspended Stielau, despite the teacher's assertion that he was not motivated by discrimination in writing the article.

In filing the charges, Flesch stated that Anne's manuscripts were in Amsterdam, where they could be read and verified. He also outlined the difference between the book and the play and reiterated that Stielau had questioned the authenticity of the diary itself.

The prospect of a looming court case set off immediate ripples of concern across the higher echelons of German government and society. Stielau had written an article of no more than two pages for a tiny school magazine and had mentioned Anne Frank only once – yet its ramifications for West Germany's standing as a new post-war democracy were huge. Almost immediately after the complaint was filed, the public prosecutor's office contacted Otto to ask when he had read the article. Soon after, the Federal Minister for Justice in Bonn asked his counterpart in Schleswig-Holstein to keep him fully updated about the case, stressing its sensitivity:

Letter from Federal Justice Minister to Justice Minister of State of Schleswig-Holstein, 29.1.1959

Ref. criminal complaint by the businessman Otto Frank against the teacher Lothar Stielau of Lübeck ref. defamation and libel against the memory of a deceased person.

According to a press report, the businessman Otto Frank, father of Anne Frank, who died in the Neuengamme concentration camp [*sic*], has lodged a criminal complaint at the Lübeck state prosecutor's office against the Lübeck teacher Lothar Stielau for defamation and libel of the memory of a deceased person. Since any criminal proceedings could be expected to arouse considerable public interest, I would be grateful to receive more details about the facts of the case and any further developments.

pp. Dr von der Linden

On 16 January, *Die Zeit*, the broadsheet newspaper of record in Hamburg, devoted 2,000 words to Stielau's case and what it meant for Germany as a whole. Stielau was, they stated, a 'Germanist', and thoroughly 'Teutonic' in outlook. It was this point of view that had led him to write the article in the first place. In his article he had, however, included the damning sentence comparing *The Diary of Anne Frank* with the already discredited and fraudulent diaries of Eva Braun and the Queen of England. Stielau's first act of 'wicked deviousness' was placing Anne, 'the Jewish girl who ended up in Bergen-Belsen', next to Eva Braun. Associating Otto with the 'money-hungry buccaneers' of those fraudulent books was his second great wrongdoing, the newspaper argued.

Lothar Stielau had turned up years earlier for a job at Lübeck's Cathedral School with a 'de-Nazification' certificate in his pocket, but the real question was less about him and more about how Germany tackled its past. Should Stielau have been turned away from the job because of his past? Should Germans be suspicious of their new partners and friends, who may have been Nazis in the Third Reich? And how would the country reconcile everything that occurred in the Nazi era with anti-semitism? This was the 'heart of the matter'.

'It is well known that there are anti-Semites. Thank God that there is this too: the majority of Germans are not anti-Semitic.' The Nazis were skilled, just like the communists, in allaying moral concerns through 'vague' and 'never exactly formulated' ideology, *Die Zeit* continued.

> Among these 'retired Nazis' are many who are upright democrats today: not as products of any re-education, but as people of our time. Foreign countries, if they are interested in these things, may take note that not even the majority of the 'ideal Nazis' of the time were anti-Semites. On the other hand: there was once in Germany – just like in other countries today – anti-Semitism that was religious or at the same time cultural.

Before the Nazi era, antisemites could claim that they were 'ranting' about Jews in the same way that Protestants ranted about Catholics – 'since the gassings, however, we know what "anti-Semitism" can mean in Germany. And because that is the case, there can no longer be an unbiased anti-Semite with us.' The state could take official action, *Die Zeit* concluded, but Lübeck was once part of the Hanseatic League and a 'haven of democracy'. As such, the burden also fell on ordinary citizens, who had a joint responsibility for open discussion and law and order.

In April, the public prosecutor explained that the authenticity of the diary would be determined by the court, writing, 'Given the delicate nature of the attitude of foreign countries towards Germany and her people due to their National Socialist past, a judicial inquiry is the only way of arriving at a satisfactory conclusion.'

A conviction would have to take several complicated matters into consideration. Firstly, the 'inner attitude' of Stielau towards Jews, their persecution by the Nazis and Anne Frank, as well as Stielau's behaviour as a teacher. Secondly, the court would have to authenticate the diary itself, which might prove complicated given the changes various editors had made over the years leading up to publication. To illustrate this, the prosecutor referred to an article in *Der Spiegel* that quoted one of the original Dutch writers who had helped Otto with the publication of the diary, Ab Cauvern, saying, 'At the beginning I made a good many changes,' as well as to the inconsistencies caused by the translations into different languages and censorship by various publishers who were worried about some of the sexual content.

Stielau made his first appearance before the court three months later, on 18 June, in a hearing that was entirely devoted to his background and political opinions. Stielau admitted that his fear of communism had meant he turned first to the Nazis and then to the 'unreservedly pro-German' Deutsche Reichspartei, but he denied that he was antisemitic:

My criticism, and here one can look at the draft and the final publication in the same way, is directed at the fact that authors are connecting certain people's experiences – be they of the saddest kind (Anne Frank), or of a representative nature (the Queen of England), or of an erotic nature (Eva Braun) – with the German defeat and exploiting them, with the result that they are making millions of marks from them – especially from dramatisations and film adaptations.

Before 1945 I was neither an antisemite, nor did I take any position against the Jews. At that time I took the view that, while the races are different, they are not different in value. After 1945 I have never – especially in public or in my school lessons – described a Jew or a n***o as being 'other', or attacked one in any other way. Quite the reverse: on a school trip to Clausthal-Zellerfeld in June 1958, I immediately publicly boxed the ears of a sixth form secondary school pupil ... for shouting the word 'n****r' at a coloured mining student.

With respect to the wording of the note in the article where the diaries of Eva Braun, the Queen of England, Anne Frank are mentioned in sequence, I would like to say the following: my comment was intended to point out that we are nowadays playing fast and loose with important things that have anything at all to do with war and post-war conditions. Above all, they are being exploited for economic purposes. I have never set myself against the memory of the ill-fated Anne Frank with a single thought, much less a single word. She can't have ever done anything wrong with her diary. If I am challenged that deliberately conflating the terms superstition and religion can also carry a value judgement, I reply that my mention of very different diaries by very different individuals is solely about the effects of such representations on those individuals, who have been used by others without their consent, in some cases after their death, for economic gain, and always in connection with German adversity.

One week later, Stielau appeared again, this time with a substantially changed defence, claiming that his article referred only to the play written by Goodrich and Hackett, rather than to the diary itself.

This was a dramatic about-face, but perhaps a cleverly advised one given the tremendous press interest in the court battle between Otto and Meyer Levin. Under questioning, Stielau was queried by the magistrate as to why he had not mentioned this seemingly crucial detail before – especially as Stielau admitted that he had neither read the play nor seen any performance of it. Instead, Stielau said, he had read many newspaper articles discussing the play that made him doubt its authenticity.

The case did not resume in court for a year, and when Stielau appeared again on 25 April 1960, he reiterated that he had only been referring to the play. In the intervening twelve months, Otto, Bep Voskuijl, Miep and Jan Gies, a handwriting expert and an historian had given evidence about the authenticity of the diary. Otto explained the events that led up to publication, from Miep handing him the original pages to Cauvern's edits, which Otto claimed involved only correcting Germanisms and grammatical errors. Bep and Miep and Jan Gies testified separately that they had known Anne was writing a diary, and confirmed Otto's account of Miep returning it to him after the war.

Finding appropriate historical confirmation was trickier, especially as the court seemed not to know what kind of verification it needed. A historical institute in Munich turned down a request to verify the diary, saying the matter related to handwriting and not to history – and also because no one could read Dutch. In the end, Dr Annemarie Hübner of Hamburg University agreed to assess what was labelled 'Typescript II' and compare it to the German book to see if it was a 'true' and 'faithful' translation. A Hamburg handwriting expert, Minna Becker, and another expert, Dorothea Ockelmann, were also asked to report on whether the handwritten diary and the loose sheets kept by Otto in Basel were written by the same person who had sent a letter in 1940 and two postcards in 1941 and 1942, signed 'Anne'.

The three women travelled to Basel in October 1959, to conduct their investigations in person. Five months later, Becker and Ockelmann submitted a 130-page assessment, stating that the handwriting was identical to the specimen submitted as 'Anne Frank'. They were also asked to consider the timing of the writing on the loose sheets and agreed that, given how Anne's handwriting matured as she got older, the loose sheets were not written before the other parts of the diary. The following month Dr Hübner submitted her report, in which she wrote, 'The text of the printed manuscript [Typescript II] must be considered authentic by virtue of its substance, the ideas expressed in it and its form.' The German book had some 'mistakes in translation' but these were minor faults, and 'immaterial to an understanding of the total context'.

Stielau's lawyers, Noack and Noack, immediately challenged the expert evidence, claiming that Dr Hübner's opinion was 'worthless' because she was unqualified to consider handwriting, and that it was unclear what her report was supposed to prove. They did, however, use Hübner's report to point out what they called 'inconsistencies' in the translation and claimed that the diary could not be considered 'a document' in the legal sense unless it was translated word for word.

Noack and Noack also argued that the complaint had started on the wrong premise, as Stielau was referring to the play not the diary. It was only natural that Stielau had never seen the play, because Goodrich and Hackett had been investigated by the California Un-American Activities Committee and had been communist sympathisers since the 1930s. They digressed to add that it was shocking that adaptations were not faithful to the original text and sought to make money from the diary. One edition of the book even included a photo of the actress playing Anne in the play, rather than Anne herself. In a letter to the magistrate, Noack and Noack said,

> It must be stressed again and again that the article in question concerns the *amateur play* put on by school pupils and therefore for any unbiased reader can only have been aimed at the stage play by Goodrich and Hackett, something that was immediately clear to the editor of the school newspaper when he read the article in question, since he added the headings 'Amateur play' and 'Commentary on the play'.
>
> The accused's [Stielau] attack is precisely to the effect that no money should be made from serious biographical texts by means of theatrical representations that are no longer accurate to the text. Can it be right to do business by putting the image of an actress on the American edition of the book, and not one of Anne Frank? It is this kind of shameless advertising that damages the memory and reputation of Anne Frank, not the accused's battle against representations that do not accurately reproduce a diary that has a huge amount to say to the world when conveyed in full and without any alterations...

After considering their complaint specifically relating to Hübner's report, the public prosecutor appointed another 'senior assessor', Dr Friedrich Sieburg. But this also proved a difficult role, as it was unclear what problem Sieburg was supposed to get to the bottom of. Sieburg, a publicist and reporter for *Frankfurter Allgemeine Zeitung*, focused on the content and importance of the diary but did not review the manuscripts of the translations, not the least because he didn't understand Dutch.

In October 1960, Sieberg submitted his report, which stated that it would be very unlikely for someone to forge a diary of a completely unknown person. In addition, Anne often wrote about outside events that could be easily verified. Noack and Noack said this report was 'worthless' too, adding, 'It is impossible to tell from the opinion which question the expert is actually trying to answer, nor is it known which question he should have answered.'

Whether or not they were to the point, the submissions by the expert witnesses were also not entirely correct. Becker and Ockelmann had concluded that everything had been written by Anne, but in fact their material had included a postcard, a pasted-in letter and a birthday card that were not written by her. Some of Hübner's report was also open to interpretation, depending upon how much importance was placed upon inconsistencies between the Dutch and the German. The German translation had changed some of Anne's more youthful phrasing for words that sounded more mature, and had of course removed some of her more explicit thoughts.

Following Noack and Noack's final objections, the public prosecutor set forth the full details of the case against Stielau. Totalling more than thirty-seven pages, the file included a summary of the entire case, including Stielau's original article, the newspaper articles he had quoted (all of which referred to both the diary and the play) and the fact that he had never seen or read the play. The prosecution asserted that Stielau and his fascist comrade Buddeberg were guilty of libel under German Penal Code Article 186, for denying the authenticity of the diary, and of defamation under Article 185, for using the term 'profiteers from Germany's defeat'.

In June 1961, the Third Criminal Division of the court in Lübeck found that Stielau and Buddeberg had a case to answer. If found guilty, they faced either a fine or up to two years in prison. But before the case could come to trial, Otto's and Stielau's lawyers dramatically announced that they had reached a settlement. As part of the settlement, Stielau and Buddeberg declared that the investigation had proved to them there were no grounds for claiming the diary was a forgery. They had meant no offence to Otto Frank and had not meant to sully the memory of Anne. Stielau withdrew his phrase 'profiteers from Germany's defeat'.

For their part, Otto and the German publishers stated that the investigation had not revealed any antisemitic tendencies on Stielau's or Buddeberg's part. Otto agreed to drop the criminal charges, and Stielau contributed 1,000 DM to his legal costs. Buddeberg refused to pay any costs at all. The court ruling on 9 November 1961 records,

> The accused Buddeberg was not prepared to cover any of the costs, the accused Stielau wanted to cover 1,000 DM of the very much higher court costs. This was what the chamber had to assume with regard to the accused. At the same time it seemed unreasonable to impose even part of the costs on the plaintiffs. They had not filed their criminal complaints frivolously, but with clear justification. The preliminary investigation found that their presentation of the facts was correct in all material respects, and that that of the accused was not correct. The chamber also does not view the fact that, by withdrawing their criminal complaints, the plaintiffs have caused the proceedings to end before reaching a conclusion in the expectation that costs would be imposed on

the accused, as grounds to impose them on the plaintiffs. If an insulted person is satisfied with a formal apology by the offender without a judicial punishment, this is to be welcomed since it is a better means of restoring the legal peace than a criminal sentence...

The withdrawal of the criminal complaints in the present case is particularly to be welcomed since the various foreign and domestic political interests on the margins of the case, either real or apparent, could have led to disagreeable disputes in public and consequently impaired the public peace had the full trial gone ahead.

Accordingly, it would have been unreasonable to require the plaintiffs to pay the court costs.

Stielau and Buddeberg appeared to have been let off very lightly, and the question on everyone's mind was – why?

Otto later revealed that he had felt pressured to reach a settlement by the judge, who told him that the case was causing unpleasant 'foreign' repercussions – hinted at in the ruling above. Even if he found Stielau guilty, the judge told Otto, he would only have been able to hand down a very lenient sentence. Newspapers took the judgment as proof that the diary was genuine, with the *Hamburger Echo* reporting, 'Following thorough examinations by experts and the statements of witnesses, the authenticity of the diary was beyond doubt. The two accused regretted their claims, which they said had been made "without any attempt at factual verification".' Yet the punishment seemed unsatisfactory, with *Bildzeitung* stating, 'High school teacher libels Anne Frank... but judge lets him off'.

Speaking after the judgment, Otto's lawyer told the press:

The memory of Anne Frank was too precious to her father for him to insist on a punishment that, even if not merely a fine, would only have involved a short term of imprisonment plus a probation period ... On the other hand, he has been given full satisfaction in the case, since the authenticity of the diary had been established beyond doubt.

If only that had been the case. Rather than putting to bed the question of authenticity once and for all, Otto's settlement gave future Holocaust deniers the opportunity to claim the case had not been proven. Later Otto lamented, 'Had I but known that there would be people who would consider a settlement in this case as insufficient proof, I certainly should not have dropped the case.'

Articles claiming the diary was a fraud, based on the lies and dissemination from other articles, now spread across a global network of fascists and Holocaust deniers in Germany, France, the US and the UK. In 1967, Teressa Hendry summarised in English the main arguments from *Fria Ord*, in an article for *American Mercury* under the headline: 'Was Anne Frank's diary a hoax?' Hendry claimed the real author of the diary was Meyer Levin.

Although *American Mercury* began in the 1920s as a publication that featured important American writers like William Faulkner and F. Scott Fitzgerald, a takeover in the 1950s by financier Russell Maguire turned it into an extreme right-wing magazine, and steered it 'toward the fever swamps of antisemitism'. Maguire hired a writer who went on to found the American Nazi Party, and the magazine was eventually sold on to a series of neo-Nazi owners and funders, becoming a quarterly publication with a circulation of about 7,000 copies by the late 1960s.

Hendry's article was typical of many of the pieces that claimed to question the 'truth' of the Holocaust, appearing to pose legitimate questions and sowing doubt through quoting the distortions and lies used in articles by other Holocaust deniers. The Western world had been aware of Anne Frank for some years, Hendry wrote, 'through the medium of what purports to be her personally written story', although any 'informed literary inspection would have shown that it was impossible to have been the work of a teenager'. Hendry then stated that this was confirmed by the New York Supreme Court, when it awarded Meyer Levin damages as an 'honorarium for Levin's work on the "Anne Frank Diary"'. She said, 'Mr Frank in Switzerland, has promised to pay his race-kin, Meyer Levin, not less than $50,000 because he had used the dialogue of Author Levin just as it was and "implanted" it in the diary as being his daughter's intellectual work.'

These untruths were repeated again, as fact, by Richard Harwood (a pseudonym of Richard Verrall from the British National Front) in his pamphlet *Did Six Million Really Die? The Truth at Last*, which was published in English, German and Dutch in 1975 and 1976. The diary was, according to Harwood, 'just one more fraud, in a whole series of frauds in support of the "Holocaust" legend and the saga of the Six Million'. Harwood's pamphlet was the subject of a criminal case in Canada and was found by that country's Supreme Court to have 'misrepresented the work of historians, misquoted witnesses, fabricated evidence, and cited non-existent authorities' – yet it was still available on Amazon until it was removed in 2017.

Notorious Holocaust denier David Irving again repeated the claim that the diary had been written by Meyer Levin and Otto

Frank in his 1977 book *Hitler's War*, stating that many forgeries were on record, including 'The "Diary of Anne Frank" (in this case a civil lawsuit brought by a New York scriptwriter has proved that he wrote it in collaboration with the girl's father)'.

Otto managed to get the publishers to remove the sentence from further copies of the book and pay damages due to the large number of copies that were already in circulation. But this did little to deter Holocaust deniers from continuing to use untruths about the diary in support of their despicable cause.

Three years later, in 1978, Ditlieb Felderer, an Austrian who took Swedish citizenship, published an entire book, titled *Anne Frank's Diary – A Hoax*, which included bizarre chapters devoted to Anne's 'drug addiction', based upon the fact she took one valerian pill a day, and her 'sexual extravaganza', about her relationship with Peter.

Later that year, Teressa Hendry's *American Mercury* articles were reprinted in a Washington weekly magazine, *The Spotlight*, which had a much larger circulation of more than 300,000 readers and supported the campaign of, amongst others, Louisiana politician and former Grand Wizard of the Ku Klux Klan David Duke. The re-emergence of these articles and their use by other writers to quote and seed further untruths were not isolated incidents; they were part of a determined effort by a network of so-called revisionist historians during the 1970s to deny that the Nazis had murdered 6 million Jews, and even that gas chambers and concentration camps had existed. In 1978, Willis Carto, a man involved in both *The Spotlight* and *American Mercury*, founded the Institute for Historical Review, which organised an annual conference and the quarterly *Journal of Historical*

Review, to provide Holocaust deniers with the smokescreen of legitimacy to spread their views.

Otto Frank was now in the last years of his life, and he might have hoped to spend them promoting Anne's legacy and enjoying time with his wife Fritzi and their family. Instead, he was at the heart of a battle over the legitimacy of the diary – with the truth about the Holocaust and the murder of his children at stake.

Otto's next clash would be with Heinz Roth, an architect from Odenhausen, near Frankfurt. Roth ran his own neo-Nazi publishing house and began publishing pamphlets with titles like *Anne Frank's Diary – A Forgery* and *Anne Frank's Diary – The Big Fraud*. In December 1975, a quote from one of these pamphlets appeared in the letters column of Austrian publication *Neue Ordnung*, repeating the claim that Meyer Levin and Otto had written the diary themselves. Otto read the story and wrote a letter to *Neue Ordnung* explaining that these claims had already been disproven in court and withdrawn from David Irving's book. He also sent a copy of the letter to Heinz Roth himself, who refused to respond to any of Otto's detailed points, claiming he only wanted to get to the 'pure historical truth'.

At first, Otto told the German Department of Justice, he was reluctant to take legal action against Roth because of his age and health. But Roth proved 'stubborn and intractable', and copies of his pamphlet were distributed after a performance of the play in Hamburg in February 1976. When Roth published a new pamphlet – *The Diary of Anne Frank – Truth or Forgery?* – a few months later, Otto intervened and asked the Frankfurt Court to issue an injunction to stop Roth from using certain phrases in future. These included:

1. 'Anne Frank's diary – a forgery.'
2. 'This world-famous bestseller is a forgery.'
3. 'Millions of schoolchildren have been forced and are still being forced to read this fake ... and now it turns out that it is the product of a New York scriptwriter in collaboration with the girl's father!'
4. 'This fraud was exposed for the first time not just recently but over a decade ago!'

As with the Stielau case, the Roth case also came to an unsatisfactory conclusion. Heinz Roth died in November 1978, and Otto Frank passed away in August 1980. When the court returned on 6 December 1980, both men were dead, and in their absence the court recorded that the claim that Meyer Levin and Otto Frank had written the diary was false – but that Roth had not been given enough opportunity to prove that the diary was a forgery. This was a strange ruling, given that Roth had died two years earlier.

And unfortunately, the evidence presented in the Roth case had opened up another avenue for Holocaust deniers – this time through a report commissioned by his defence lawyers and written by British-born French academic Robert Faurisson.

Faurisson worked at the Department of Literature at the University of Lyon and would become a well-known fixture on the 'historical revisionism' circuit. In 1974, he wrote a lengthy letter to Yad Vashem, the Holocaust memorial in Israel, to state that, based upon his own study of archive material, there had been no Nazi genocide against the Jews. Four years later, he turned his attention to Anne Frank.

Faurisson read the diary in French, Dutch and German and

travelled to Basel, where Otto agreed to take part in a long interview with him to go over each question point by point. Otto found the experience gruelling and upsetting and later said that many of the words Faurisson had put in his mouth were twisted and untrue. Faurisson's written analysis quoted extracts from the diary in a highly misleading and selective way, purposefully distorting the circumstances surrounding what had been written. His study, *The Diary of Anne Frank – Is It Authentic?* (later published in other countries as *The Diary of Anne Frank – A Forgery*), plucks out certain details described by Anne, like the noise of a vacuum cleaner, the ringing of an alarm clock and the racket caused by a bag of beans breaking open, to prove that no family could really have gone unnoticed in hiding in a building where other people were working and doing business. 'Vacuum cleaners at that time were exceptionally noisy. I must ask: is this credible?' Faurisson writes. 'The use of an alarm clock, for instance, needs explanation. The noisy carpentry must be explained.'

In the diary itself, of course, Anne explains only a few words later how each of these things occurred. The vacuum cleaner was only used at 12.30, after 'the warehousemen have gone home'. After Anne wrote that the breaking bag of beans was loud enough to wake the dead, she went on to write, 'Thank God there were no strangers in the house.' Yet Faurisson's report was submitted as an 'expert' opinion to the court in the Roth trial, and his allegations continued to circulate alongside the many other discredited articles and books.

As the long list of court cases shows, Holocaust deniers found it incredibly easy to produce articles filled with lies and deliberately misleading quotes – but proving their guilt and deciding the appropriate punishment in a court of law was a long and seemingly difficult process.

Two other cases in the late 1970s ended in acquittals. E. Schönborn, the chairman of the extreme right-wing Combat League of German Soldiers, was prosecuted for distributing leaflets outside the Anne Frank schools in Frankfurt and Nuremberg, claiming that the diary was a forgery and the product of a Jewish anti-German propaganda campaign 'intended to support the lie about the six million gassed Jews and to finance the state of Israel'. Yet the judge found that he had the right to free speech and had not denied human rights to any Jews.

Former Hitler Youth leader Werner Kuhnt was also brought before a Stuttgart court in 1979, for writing an article regurgitating the claim that the diary was a forgery written by Meyer Levin and Otto – but the court found that there was no evidence of antisemitism, nor that Kuhnt had insulted human dignity.

Two other noteworthy cases in the 1970s were brought against Ernst Römer and Edgar Geiss. Römer had been distributing the last two pages of Harwood's pamphlet *Did Six Million Really Die?* outside a performance of the play in Hamburg in 1976, using the title 'Best-Seller – A Lie'. One year later, Römer was fined 1,500 DM for defamation, but he appealed the decision. During the appeal hearing in August 1978, journalist Edgar Geiss appeared in the courtroom and started handing out leaflets alleging the diary was a fraud. He too was taken to court and was handed a more severe sentence of months in prison, due to his previous convictions. He also appealed against his conviction.

The court decided to hear the appeals of Römer and Geiss together and asked the German Federal Criminal Police Office to prepare an expert opinion on the diary 'by an examination of paper and writing material to establish that the writings attributed to Anne Frank were produced during the years 1941–44'. The office conducted a short investigation in the spring of 1980 and produced a four-page report that found the paper and ink used in the diaries were all manufactured before 1951. It noted, however, that some of the corrections written in the margins of the diary were written in ballpoint ink, only available after 1951. This was consistent with the fact the pages had been edited and translated in the 1950s as it was prepared for publication – but in the most damaging blow yet, *Der Speigel* seized on the detail and used it to introduce a long article about the debate over the diary. On 6 October 1980, two months after Otto's death, the magazine wrote, 'Proved by a Bundeskriminalamt report: *The Diary of Anne Frank* was edited at a later date. Further doubt is therefore cast on the authenticity of the document.'

Of course, the diary had been edited at a later date – as any book would be. Otto had confirmed that his former friend and colleague in Amsterdam Johannes Kleiman had made corrections to the text itself for clarification. Yet *Der Spiegel* conflated the 'corrections' with the earlier handwriting report by Minna Becker, which stated that all the text had been written by the same person. Although the magazine admitted that handwriting was no longer considered credible evidence in court, it concluded, 'If the handwriting of the original entries matches that of the editions, then there must have been an imposter at work.'

The article caused a furore and was a devastating blow. Until its publication, only those on the extreme-right fringe had challenged the authenticity of the diary and their articles had only been read by a small number of people. But now, one of

Germany's biggest mainstream magazines had weighed in. Those who had worked on and supported the diary for years agonised about what to do, deciding in the end that the only way to counter the claims was to ask the Netherlands Forensic Institute and the National Institute for War Documentation (NIOD) to launch a comprehensive investigation into the diary, producing detailed handwriting analysis and a forensic examination of the materials used. When it was completed, the report weighed in at 150 pages and demolished any idea that the diary was a forgery. It concluded, 'The report of the Netherlands Forensic Institute has convincingly demonstrated that both versions of the diary of Anne Frank were written by her in the years 1942 to 1944. The allegations that the diary was the work of someone else … are thus conclusively refuted.'

The report and all three versions of the diary, as Anne worked on them and they were edited, were published in a special edition of the diary, *The Diary of Anne Frank, The Critical Edition*, in 1986, from which many of the sources for this chapter are drawn. The NIOD report and the publication of the *Critical Edition* had conclusively authenticated the origin of the diary and Anne's authorship – but there were still some surprises in store. The most notable of these was the sensational emergence of the 'five missing pages' – the revelation by the former director of the Anne Frank House Cor Suijk that he had been keeping secret five loose pages from Anne's diary at the request of Otto.

Suijk's story was that during the German Bureau investigation of the 1970s, Otto had been asked to produce all of Anne's writing for analysis. He had done this – except for five pages of the diary he did not want anyone to read. Those five pages contained some of Anne's most explosive comments about how she perceived, amongst other things, her parents' marriage. Otto asked Suijk to take the pages for safekeeping and keep them out of the public eye for Otto's lifetime and the lifetime of his second wife Fritzi. Suijk kept the pages secret for decades, and after Fritzi's death in 1998 he made them available to writer Melissa Müller. The revelation that there were unpublished extracts from Anne's diary caused a sensation.

Not everyone was convinced by Suijk's story, with some at the Anne Frank House and the Anne Frank Foundation in Basel pointing out that Anne's comments were included in her first, unrevised, diary but had been removed from the publication at the request of the Frank family because they were unkind to her mother Edith. Once again, the NIOD and the Netherlands Forensic Institute studied the sheets and concluded that they were written in the same hand as the rest of the diary. They were Anne's authentic words; now the only question remained: who owned them?

Otto had asked the NIOD to keep and look after the original diary after his death (although the Anne Frank Foundation in Basel received the royalties from the publication). When the extra fives pages came to light, the NIOD asked Suijk to return them to be included in the new *Critical Edition* of the diary. Suijk refused, claiming Otto had given them to him – and he wanted to auction them to raise money for a new Anne Frank Center in New York.

In the eyes of the world's media, here the *Chicago Tribune*, Suijk was 'holding hostage five pages of Anne Frank's diary' as a form of 'academic blackmail'. And while Suijk claimed that he was the legal owner, those who knew Otto said that while he might have asked Suijk to hold on to the pages for safekeeping, he would never have gifted Anne's work to someone else.

The courts decided otherwise, and Suijk was declared the legal owner of the pages, free to sell them to whomever he chose. Rather than lose them to the highest bidder, the Dutch nation then took the unusual step of buying the pages for $300,000, donating them to the NIOD so they could be included in future editions of the diary.

Otto had spent the last years of his life battling 'fake news' about Anne and the diary. For more than thirty years he had guarded and fought for her legacy. Yet his death had not diminished interest in her work; instead, the emergence of the 'five missing pages' had raised the spectre of a new, ugly battle: without Otto, who owned Anne Frank?

CHAPTER 8

WHO OWNS
ANNE FRANK?

*'We have to, myself included, see Anne as a symbol, as one of
thousands. When I speak to people, I need to turn off that she
is one of my daughters. Otherwise you can't keep doing it.'*
Otto Frank, interview with the *Haagse Post*,
3 August 1968

Otto Frank spent the last few years of his life in a neat Swiss
house in Basel, working in his study with his wife Fritzi at
his side. Together they discussed the thousands of letters they
received from around the world, considered legal matters relating to the diary and planned all aspects of Anne's legacy. Fritzi's
daughter Eva Schloss remembered,

> He would pace up and down the floor of their work room, read-
> ing out a letter from a seventeen-year-old girl in California who
> had written to say her parents didn't understand her. 'Now, how
> do you think we should respond to this?' he'd ask my mother.

She would sit, fingers poised over the typewriter, and give such matters a more womanly sense of consideration.

'I have a lot of correspondence, which no longer is about Anne or the diary, but did find its base there,' Otto told the *Haagse Post*.

> For instance, I have been corresponding with a Japanese girl, for ten or twelve years now. That girl doesn't have her father any-more. She was so taken by the diary, that she started writing to me, for years now – from school until the end of her engagement, a few weeks ago.

The couple had lived in the attic rooms of the Elias house on Herbstgasse for eight years before finally buying a home of their own in the suburb of Birsfelden in 1961. They decided to live on the ground floor and rent out the floor above. In the study, Otto had some of the mementos associated with the diary – a lithograph of Anne by Marc Chagall from a French edition of the book and a photo of the statue of Anne that was erected in Utrecht. Outside, in the large garden, he tended the 'Anne Frank' rose.

Eva Schloss remembered that Otto was a wonderful step-father to her and grandfather to her three daughters, even though the loss of her own father and brother meant 'it still hurt me a little to see how much Mutti and Otto loved each other'. Fritzi explained to her that she had loved both her hus-bands, and they both had been right for her time of life. When Fritzi was young, Eva's father had been dashing, exciting and adventurous. With Otto, she had a more equal relationship. 'We discuss everything and we share everything together and make decisions. Your father was the right husband for me when I was a young woman, and Otto is the right husband for me now that I am older.' Quietly she added, 'We both have suffered so much, and we understand each other perfectly.'

Otto carried his granddaughters' photos with him in his wallet and would often show them to people. The family spent summer holidays together – visiting the beach in Cornwall and then Tuscany, where photos show Otto clowning on the sand – and the winter skiing in Switzerland. Early in the morning, Otto would arrive in Eva and her husband Zvi's bedroom and beat on their bed with a walking stick, booming, 'Time to get up! Everybody up!' True to his background in the German Army, he never liked anyone lying in bed or being messy, and he would sometimes put on overalls and clean out the garage or tidy up in the garden when he visited their house in London.

Marriage to Fritzi had brought Otto happiness and love and the family life he craved. He could enjoy teaching his granddaughters to ice-skate or ride a bike and delight in telling them his imaginative made-up stories. He expressed his feelings to one young woman who wrote to him after the war:

All you know about me has happened twenty-six years ago and, though this period was an important part of my life leaving unforgettable marks on my soul, I had to go on, living a new life ... think of me not only as Anne's father as you know me from the book and play, but also as a man enjoying a new family life and loving his grandchildren.

Nonetheless, Eva writes in her book *After Auschwitz*, the full truth was rather more complicated. 'Our new lives always included the ghosts of the people from our original families, and the success of *The Diary of Anne Frank* meant that Anne in particular was to play an important, and sometimes all-consuming, role in our lives,' she says.

Otto and Fritzi both felt a tremendous responsibility to the diary and to Anne, not only answering every piece of correspondence but also living frugally, never taking taxis and eating simple meals. 'The money we make is Anne's money,' Otto would tell people. The idea of benefiting from her death was grotesque. 'There was one issue, however, where Otto admitted he was unfair,' Eva writes.

Reading through Otto's appointment books and correspondence before the diary was published he talks frequently about both of his children, making no distinction between Anne and Margot. Perhaps he favoured one over the other, as many parents do, but there is no evidence of it, and he often writes about Margot, and her interests and personality. After the discovery of the diary, however, his thoughts turned almost exclusively to Anne – and he rarely mentioned Margot, or his first wife Edith except in relation to Anne.

The diary and Anne's legacy had become his life, and 'although he was pleasant to everyone – he had little interest in people who were not interested in "Anne Frank"'. At home, Otto often used Anne's example when talking to his granddaughters, telling them 'Anne would not have done that' if he thought they had done something wrong, something Eva reported they sometimes found unnerving. 'Occasionally he would even call one of the girls "Anne", and our youngest daughter Sylvia always wanted me to sleep in bed with her when we visited Mutti and Otto's apartment because she felt that it was haunted with a "spooky" presence,' she says.

Otto's granddaughter Sylvia called Basel a 'ghost town' and said that while she remembered fondly how he took part in all their activities and had taught them to ride bikes and ice-skate,

> I felt that there was a barrier between us. We always knew that somehow our lives took second place to Mutti and Otto's life with Anne Frank. Maybe I was the one who put up that barrier, but I felt that we always had to live up to his expectations of Anne.

Eva herself sometimes felt frustrated with her mother Fritzi when she put her relationship with Otto first, delaying plans they'd made for the day so she could help Otto answer more letters about the diary. Eva would gently remind her that they needed to get going, 'but she'd look across the table at Otto, and he'd gesture helplessly at the pile of unanswered letters – and another trip would be cancelled'.

Despite the enormous physical and psychological strain of surviving two world wars and Auschwitz, Otto remained remarkably healthy, celebrating his ninetieth birthday in London. By 1980, however, there were signs that something was wrong. 'I'm not ill,' he told people, 'I'm just tired.' He did not know that a doctor had already told Fritzi several months earlier that he was suffering from lung cancer and had little time left.

By the summer of that year, Otto still enjoyed company but

was now very weak and only wanted to see one person at a time. Eva recalled, 'He looked almost hollowed out, with his skin turning a ghastly shade of grey.' Fritzi insisted on looking after him at home for as long as she could and virtually carried him around the flat, but in the end he was admitted to hospital. On 19 August 1980, Otto died. In the last decades of his life he had become a father figure to thousands of people around the world, many of whom had sensed his deep humanity and integrity and had written to him, forming what for some became a lifelong bond. His death brought a flood of condolences, and the Anne Frank Stichting in Holland chartered a plane to fly down the many mourners who wanted to attend the funeral – including Anne's friend Jacqueline van Maarsen.

Otto wanted to be cremated in a simple service, which was not Jewish tradition. Afterwards his friends convened for a memorial at the house in Birsfelden, where they listened to some of Otto's own words that had been recorded in an interview. Eva Schloss wrote, 'His calm words echoed throughout their small home like an otherworldly presence who already knew the role he would play in history.'

Otto had tried to preserve the legacy of the past but also to live in the present, telling one young Anne Frank fan as he marched her to the tram stop in Basel: 'I never retrace my steps.' His death was a moment to stop and reflect on the remarkable life he had led: a once privileged young man who had been forced to rebuild his life several times and had endured unimaginable loss and heartbreak, but who had always found a way to move forward with immense dignity, resilience and courage. His unwavering desire in the second part of his life was to ensure the success of *The Diary of Anne Frank*. Part of that was a relentless drive to spread Anne's legacy and message of human understanding. Part of it must also have been that in the diary Otto could live with his children again in a world where they would always be in the annexe, arguing, laughing, talking – and alive. For thirty-five years Otto had been completely convinced of the importance of the diary, just as he had stuck by his convictions about what Anne's legacy should be, even if others did not agree with his vision. Now, Otto was gone, and without his unwavering judgement and moral authority, the future of *The Diary of Anne Frank* would only become more complicated and contested.

Otto's last journey was taken against doctors' orders when he was already extremely weak and unwell. Fittingly, it was to Amsterdam, where, on 12 June, Otto and Fritzi attended a commemoration to Anne on her birthday, at Westerkerk church. Afterwards, Queen Beatrix presented him with one of the country's highest honours – the Orde van Oranje-Nassau – and accompanied him to look around the annexe. Otto was pleased that she was 'most interested and asked many questions'.

The annexe was now situated within what is known as the 'Anne Frank House' and had already become a shrine for thousands of visitors from around the world. The purchase and preservation of the house at 263 Prinsengracht was one of the most concrete and enduring parts of Anne's legacy, but Otto's role in its founding and development was fraught and emotional – and would be further complicated by an institution he set up in Basel, the Anne Frank Foundation, which would hold the copyright to the diary after his death.

The fate of the house was determined back in the mid-1950s, when so many other momentous events connected to the diary were also in motion. Otto's life had been going through a huge transformation in the spring of 1953. He was fully immersed in the US and the international publications of the diary, and already embroiled in the first stages of the dispute with Meyer Levin. While he teetered on the edge of a nervous breakdown, he had also fallen in love with Fritzi and was building a new life with her. Now that the diary occupied his time and gave him some income, he could retire from his role at Opekta – but there was still the question of what would happen to the building at 263 Prinsengracht. Otto still visited the annexe often, even for brief moments, and it was now also taking on a meaning for many of the readers of the book. Joseph Marks at Doubleday had first suggested to Otto that perhaps all the publishers could club together to buy the house and turn it into a library for young people. A few months later, in March 1953, Otto discovered the building was up for sale, and he wanted to buy it even though the asking price had gone up from fl. 20,000 to fl. 30,000 – and was far beyond his means at the time.

Otto discussed the matter with Barbara Zimmerman, who talked about it to Frank Price at Doubleday, and they suggested that perhaps the Dutch government could contribute to such a project. The idea was then raised at a meeting of Opekta shareholders, who recognised that the property was important to Otto and agreed to buy it and establish a foundation there.

A larger problem, however, was that the building was literally falling down and would be very expensive to repair. A few months later, Otto discovered that textile and clothing company Berghaus had bought the house next door and planned to demolish it – a process that would probably also cause the already weak house at 263 to collapse.

Otto despaired: without the income from a play or film he could not yet afford the cost of rebuilding the house, and Opekta told him they could not pay the extra amount, which they anticipated would, in reality, be much higher than projected. The secret annexe should be so much more than a 'dead monument', Otto told Barbara Zimmerman; it was his dream to turn the house into a youth centre for young people from around the world. Even so, Otto admitted, he had to be reasonable – and the dream seemed even more impossible when Berghaus announced that they planned to buy a large part of the street and demolish it. Opekta accepted the Berghaus offer for 263 Prinsengracht on the condition that they could do business there for one more year. It seemed like the Franks' last residence and the symbolic home of the diary would be no more.

For the next three years Otto was consumed with the enormous success of the diary, the twists and turns of the play and the prospect of a film. He was now firmly settled in Switzerland and had retired from his remaining businesses. Despite this, Otto admitted to friends that he found the eventual office move from Prinsengracht to a new building in Amsterdam West very difficult and emotional. It was almost impossible to let go.

In early 1956, however, there was wonderful news – a concerted campaign in the Dutch press, led by Otto's friends and longstanding business partner Johannes Kleiman, had raised awareness about the possible demolition of 263 Prinsengracht and championed its unique historical role. 'Anne Frank's secret annexe awaits the wrecker's ball,' warned *Het Vrije Volk*, who said that the Franks' hiding place was a 'monument to a time of oppression and man-hunts, terror and darkness'. The Netherlands would be the subject of a 'national scandal' if it was pulled down.

Amsterdam's local historical society added that there could be no better way of honouring Anne's memory and remembering the city's darkest years of occupation than by saving the house.

Kleiman told reporters that although they had received donations from abroad, they needed to raise the substantial sum of fl. 350,000 to save the row from demolition – and he believed that the Dutch also had a responsibility to help. Otto reinforced this when he spoke to the Mayor of Amsterdam, saying that while he would like to buy the house himself, he did not think that was the right course of action because he wanted to set up a charitable organisation and youth centre. Protests grew, and at one stage a group of leading artists staged a permanent vigil outside the house to stop demolition crews.

In January 1957, Amsterdam City Council finally capitulated and offered Berghaus an alternative site for their office, claiming their plans for Prinsengracht were 'out of harmony' with the neighbourhood. A few months later Berghaus handed back 263 Prinsengracht to the newly formed Anne Frank Stichting – a society dedicated to the restoration and preservation of the house and annexe, as well as to the 'propagation of the ideals left as legacy to the world in the diary of Anne Frank'. Board members included a former resistance worker, a concentration camp survivor, a publisher, a lawyer and a director of KLM. Otto was represented on the board by Johannes Kleiman.

The news that the annexe was suddenly saved shot around the world, with the *New York Times Magazine* writing a lengthy feature on the new society: 'Mr Frank sat alone in a coffee house the other day while reporters were shown through the Prinsengracht building by the executives of the newly formed Anne Frank Foundation...' The tour coincided with Meyer Levin's looming New York court case, so the make-up of the new board was remarkable given that, as the magazine remarked, none of the other founders were Jewish. This could be explained, they noted, by the fact that although the Jews were the victims of Nazism everywhere, the story was a 'Dutch tragedy that happened to take place in Amsterdam', in a country where 'the pain was felt by people of all conscience regardless of faith'.

The house would become a focal point for international tourists, but its site also had an added meaning for the Dutch. Prinsengracht is situated in a neighbourhood that was well known as a home for political refugees through the centuries, and French philosopher in exile René Descartes had probably watched the original construction of the house and annexe from the back window of his own residence at 6 Westermarkt in 1634.

While the front of the house would be renovated to accommodate exhibitions about Anne and the war, Otto decreed that the annexe itself must remain as it was. According to Carol Ann Lee, when Otto was asked if furniture should be added, he replied vehemently: 'No! During the war everything was taken away and I want to leave it like that.' If visitors remarked that the empty rooms seemed spacious, Otto told them that far from being empty they had been filled with an 'unbearable tension'.

In the lead-up to the opening, Otto took an active role in fundraising but clashed with the other trustees and Kleiman, who wrote to tell him that the atmosphere in the stichting was 'not very good' and that Otto made his life more difficult by communicating through him rather than passing on news and information directly. Otto had planned to spend a considerable amount of the royalties from the play and special screenings of the film on the renovation, and he even proposed a collection in the streets of Amsterdam (Kleiman told him this would be inappropriate since they were not fundraising for a natural disaster). In addition, Otto organised scores of fundraising letters to go out to wealthy American friends and supporters, establishing the American Anne Frank Foundation, whose founding committee included Eleanor Roosevelt and John F. Kennedy. Hundreds of private donors contributed, and Otto himself gave a large amount, as did the West German government and the city of Frankfurt.

The Anne Frank House at 263 Prinsengracht officially opened on 3 May 1960, on the eve of Dutch Memorial Day. After chairing a meeting of the Anne Frank Stichting, Otto visited the house and spent some time inside with Miep, her husband Jan, Bep and the Mayor of Amsterdam. Johannes Kleiman had died the previous year, but his wife joined the small group. It was a momentous and solemn day, and amidst all the fanfare an almost unbearably poignant and personal moment for Otto. While people gathered to celebrate the opening, upstairs, where Anne had slept, her photos of Greta Garbo, Rudy Vallée and Queen Elizabeth and Princess Margaret were still taped to the wall, staring down into the empty room. Later, speaking at the opening ceremony, Otto was overcome with emotion and could not continue. He apologised for not being able to speak longer, but explained, 'The thought of what happened here is too much for me.'

For several years individuals had been able to organise private tours of the house and annexe, but now it was open to the world. The ground floors of 263 and 265 Prinsengracht had been converted into a lecture hall, with the second and third floors made into spaces for exhibitions. On the same day, the Mayor of

Amsterdam laid the foundation post for the Anne Frank Sticht-ing Youth Centre, which would be built next door on the plot where the old canal houses had been demolished. There would be accommodation for students during the academic year, with summer conferences that would bring together young people from around the world to discuss topics like discrimination, war and the differences between Christianity and Judaism. It was this connection to young people that Otto felt most passionate about, telling journalists that the house was neither a museum nor a place of pilgrimage; it was an earnest warning from the past and a mission of hope for the future.

'My duty is not the past,' Otto told the *Haagse Post*.

My duty is the future, the youth. What can we do? How can we do better? The Anne Frank Stichting's duty is to preserve the house and to spread Anne's ideas. To me, the house is less im-portant as a memory than as a base to work from. Humankind must know the past to build the future. That's our guideline. We do not want to show the past to only focus on what has hap-pened and to breed hatred towards the Germans. But you cannot avoid it: you have to know about the past and you need to draw lessons from it. That is the whole intention of the Anne Frank Stichting and myself.

The house at 263 Prinsengracht would become, as Holocaust ac-ademic and writer James E. Young described it, Holland's 'shrine of the book'. A place where the 'nearly holy testament of her diary is to be taught and studied'. Otto had steered every aspect of the publication of the diary in every country and had also attempted to influence the play and the film. Acres of archived letters are testament to his determination, thoroughness and involvement, but as the letters batted back and forth between the Hacketts and their agent over the play showed, his interventions were not always welcomed. As a new generation of young people found their voices in the 1960s, it would be far harder for Otto to control the Anne Frank House and Youth Centre.

Cor Suijk, who ran the house in the 1970s, observed that Otto was a good listener but his calm and open demeanour was deceptive: 'He would seldom overlook mistakes the Anne Frank Stichting staff and I, as their director, had made.' Suijk told Carol Ann Lee that staff feared his regular visits and usually scattered rather than hear his unhappiness about the upkeep of the house or how the archives and artefacts were cared for. 'Not many of these workers were eager to meet him … His ability to notice shoddy work and sloppy thinking in our publications was distinctly feared. He could be very unrelenting, speaking insistently, but would never shout.' His criticisms, Suijk noted, were 'absolutely right'.

Only six months after the official opening, Otto returned from a visit to the youth centre and said that while overall it had been a success, 'not everything had been organised as I would have wished'. A year later, in February 1962, Otto complained that his relationship with the board of the stichting was now so bad he was refusing to take part in meetings, and it was 'working very badly on my nerves'. The problem, as he saw it, was the relationship between the house and the youth centre, with the board favouring the former. It was 'against everything Anne stands for', Otto wrote, and if it weren't for the encouragement he found in letters from young people from around the world, he would retire from the board altogether. For the remainder of the year Otto engaged in a difficult struggle to replace some of the existing board members with others who were more inclined to his way of thinking. After asking the Mayor of Amsterdam to mediate, Otto succeeded, but by then he had already decided that he did not want the Anne Frank Stichting to be the inheritor of Anne's legacy.

In January 1963, Otto established the Anne Frank Foundation in Basel, which would inherit and manage the copyright of *The Diary of Anne Frank* and all her other writings upon his death. Otto conceived the foundation as a small organisation that would be run by his family and close friends to 'promote charitable work and play a social and cultural role in the spirit of Anne Frank'.

In the meantime, the political and cultural upheavals of the 1960s were challenging the meaning of Anne's legacy far more than Otto could have imagined. In 1961, President John F. Kennedy asked his visiting Secretary of Labor Arthur Goldberg to lay a wreath at the Anne Frank House. Kennedy described this as 'an expression of the American people's enduring sympathy and support for all those who support freedom ... [Anne's] words written as they were in the face of a monstrous tyranny, have significant meaning today as millions who read them live in the shadow of another such tyranny.' Kennedy was praising Anne Frank but 'warning of another Nazi-like peril', wrote the *New York Times*, but not everyone at the Anne Frank House, or in Amsterdam, supported America's Cold War aims. By the end of the decade, the Anne Frank House had become a focal point for those who wanted to protest the Vietnam War and 'sought to expose visitors on the Prinsengracht to vivid denunciations of the United States as a successor to Nazi Germany'. Otto was deeply disturbed that decisions taken by the Anne Frank House and Youth Centre were moving away from what he believed was Anne's universalist message of peace. The leadership of the house was even denounced by the Dutch Secretary of Agriculture as 'crypto-communist' for running an exhibit comparing Nazis to apartheid South Africa, exposing leading South African politicians who had supported the Nazi cause in the Second World War and highlighting that Israel had shot down a Libyan spy plane.

Otto was painfully aware of the house's ambivalent attitude towards Israel. In 1976, debate had raged over plans by the Reformed Church Youth Council to hold a meeting at the Anne Frank House for the Dutch Palestine Committee, which excluded the Israel Work Group. Although the founding statutes of the Anne Frank House supported the Jewish desire for their own state 'as realised historically in the state of Israel', this sentiment was often not reflected in practice during the 1960s and 1970s – leading the *Jerusalem Post* to concur that the house was in the grips of what it called the 'ultra-left'.

Young people had taken Anne's legacy as an entry point into the political struggles of that tumultuous time, but Otto was now an old man who was not part of that zeitgeist. However universal Otto wanted Anne's legacy to be, the Franks' experience was rooted in the persecution and murder of the Jews. Now, young people were occupying the Anne Frank House to argue about whether Israel was the oppressor. Otto could hardly have been more alienated from the political direction the Anne Frank House had taken – but the 1980s saw this reverse course. Incoming director Hans Westra eschewed the more political campaigns of earlier decades and placed a renewed focus on

Anne and the diary itself. The work of Jan Erik Dubbelman and the international department took the touring exhibit around the world and played a large role in invigorating Anne's legacy and demonstrating the resonance her story still had.

Dubbelman's struggle to fund the exhibit also exposed the precarious financial state of the house. The organisation was in deep financial trouble within a few years of opening, and the sheer number of visitors meant that by 1970 it required serious structural rebuilding. The Mayor of Amsterdam made various pleas for public donations, and the house continued to receive money from international donors, including Volkswagen, who donated the proceeds from their 10,000th and 10,001st cars imported into the Netherlands (somewhat controversially, as historian David Barnouw points out; Dutch memories of the occupation were long and bitter, and many refused even to ride in a German car). A previous request had been denied, but the stichting applied again for a Dutch government grant and introduced an admission fee to stay open. The house was saved but the youth centre, which had been such a central part of Otto's dream, closed.

In the face of political disagreements and precarious finances, Otto was not confident that the house had the correct physical environment or skills to preserve archive material. Upon his death, he gave copyright for all Anne's works to the Anne Frank Foundation in Switzerland and passed the original physical diary over to be cared for by the NIOD. Anne's legacy was now split between three organisations that would sometimes closely collaborate but also bitterly disagree over the years.

The fallout from Otto's death was felt in a more personal way too, when his will exposed a rift with one of his closest friends,

Miep Gies. Miep had been exceptionally attached to Otto since they had first worked together before the war, and she had played a crucial role in helping to hide and sustain the family before their betrayal. Her actions had saved the diary, and after the war Miep had welcomed a destitute Otto into her home, where he lived with Miep and her husband Jan for years. Miep loved Otto.

After his death, however, Miep claimed to be surprised and upset by the terms of Otto's will, which he had drawn up in December 1978, claiming she had been expecting to receive a larger amount of money. Otto's main beneficiary was his wife Fritzi, to whom he left 220,000 Swiss francs, followed by a smaller amount for his sister and brother. They also received an annual amount from royalties, to be administered by the Anne Frank Foundation for the rest of their lifetimes. Otto bequeathed the remainder of the money to the foundation itself and gave Miep Gies and Bep Voskuijl Dutch fl. 10,000 each.

According to Cor Suijk, Miep had been expecting to receive more and felt that Fritzi had persuaded Otto to change his mind. In her biography of Otto, Carol Ann Lee quotes Suijk as saying, 'Otto wanted to leave her more money, and originally he had, but Fritzi insisted that he change his will, out of jealousy.' Miep had also complained, according to Suijk, that she and her husband had always had to stay in a hotel when they visited Otto in Switzerland and 'that they had to pay for the hotel themselves'.

Fritzi's daughter Eva replied to the allegations, pointing out that Otto was perfectly capable of making up his own mind about what to spend his money on, and if he had wanted to leave Miep more, he would have done so. His first thoughts had been to provide for his wife, and moreover he never felt that the money belonged to him. It remained, in Otto's mind, Anne's money. Eva's husband Zvi added that Otto was utterly correct in all his dealings. Otto's apartment in Basel was very small and would have been extremely uncomfortable for visitors, who would not have had their own bedroom. Friends and family were often put up in nearby hotels and, Eva added, 'I am sure he paid their bill. Sure of it. It's wicked to say otherwise.'

Miep later wrote her own book and received the recognition she deserved for her bravery in protecting the family and preserving Anne's legacy. Nevertheless, it was an ugly argument, and one that foreshadowed future disputes.

In 2011, a dispute between the Anne Frank House and the Anne Frank Foundation boiled over into a court case about a portion of the archives which were on long-term loan to the house but which the foundation wanted to relocate to the new Frank Family Center in Frankfurt. The Anne Frank House wanted to keep them, but two years later an Amsterdam court ruled that the archives should be returned to the foundation, the rightful owners.

Although the two organisations had collaborated for many years, the legal dispute led to harsh words, with Yves Kugelmann, a board member of the Anne Frank Foundation, accusing the house of appropriating Jewish belongings and then refusing to give them back in much the same way as the Nazis. In return, opponents of the foundation claimed that it was unaccountable and that president Buddy Elias and his wife had struck up strange friendships, including one with a middle-aged Scandinavian woman who claimed to embody the diarist. 'She regards herself as a reincarnation of Anne Frank,' Buddy Elias told me when I interviewed him in 2014. 'We know her very well. There's nothing I can say to [her assertion]. It's her story.' Elias added that he did not personally accept the claim but 'there are things in life that we do not know. It could be, it could not be, I don't know.'

The broader context, of course, was who could lay claim to the wishes and intentions of Otto Frank, which both sides claimed the other had misinterpreted. Anne Frank biographer Melissa Müller told the *New York Times*: 'Both organisations want to own Anne Frank … Both want to impose a way for the world to see Anne Frank.'

The disagreement continued in 2015, when the Anne Frank Foundation took the Anne Frank House to court for taking a copy of Anne's complete writing and making it available for scholarly research. That same year, the foundation successfully extended the copyright on *The Diary of Anne Frank* for a further thirty-five years by petitioning to add Otto Frank as the official co-author. Otto had fought bitter court cases to deny that he was the 'author' of the diary – a point the legal ruling undid at a stroke. Foundation officials 'should think very carefully about the consequences', French lawyer Agnès Tricoire told the *New York Times*. 'If you follow their arguments, it means that they have lied for years about the fact that it was only written by Anne Frank.'

Sitting beneath a giant black-and-white photo of Anne in his office, the current director of the Anne Frank House, Ronald Leopold, said he was saddened by the court case but convinced of the unique nature of the house he oversees:

The main feature of this house is its emptiness. And I think it's the feature that makes this place stand out amidst all those hundreds or maybe even thousands of places in Europe that remind us of the Holocaust and the Second World War, because I think it's probably one of the few places where you connect to that history in a very emotional, personal way.

As Otto Frank insisted, the house and the secret annexe remain unfurnished. History did not stand still in 1945, Leopold says, but you can find, amidst the canals and beautiful buildings of Amsterdam, one house that is still empty. 'It's the emptiness of those 60,000 people who were deported and murdered from this city between 1941 and 1945,' he says. 'It's the emptiness in Otto Frank's soul having lost his whole family. It's an emptiness that symbolises and represents the absence of Anne Frank.'

Many of those who knew Otto and remembered Anne have now passed away. Fritzi Frank died in London in 1998. Miep Gies died in 2010, aged 100. And Buddy Elias, who played such a significant role in the Anne Frank Foundation, passed away in March 2015. Elias had hoped that a new generation of projects, like the Frank Family Center, would put Anne and her legacy in their proper context – something that Yves Kugelmann of the Anne Frank Foundation supports. He claims that the foundation has urged the Anne Frank House to better acknowledge historical context, including Anne's Jewish heritage. Kugelmann dislikes the term 'icon' and evocatively describes Anne as a young girl who perished, only for her legacy to be picked over by a series of scavengers who plucked relevant nuggets and reused them for the purposes of their own beliefs and causes. 'The bottom line is that the broad public's knowledge about her is inaccurate, decontextualized and therefore easy to distort,' Kugelmann told the *Times of Israel* in 2017. 'She's become an iconized saint instead of a real Jewish girl who was in hiding from the Nazis and their Dutch collaborators.' Anne had been 'transformed into a kind of kitsch, and everybody uses her for anything'.

Sometimes her fame is uncomfortable. Anne's friend Jacqueline van Maarsen says that to this day most of her Jewish friends don't want to discuss Anne Frank with her. Their reluctance signifies an unspoken resentment over the attention received by one girl, when almost every Jewish family lost members in the Holocaust. 'There were so many Anne Franks,' van Maarsen says, 'only they did not write diaries.'

As the people of the Netherlands are acutely aware, Anne's story did not reflect the situation for the vast majority of Dutch Jews, who often had neither the wherewithal nor the money to go into hiding – and were deported to their deaths. 'Anne Frank was never my preferred story to tell, because it's not a good example for the Holocaust,' says Kugelmann. 'It's the wrong example for a very important topic, and partly what I've learned in the foundation is that people like to take the wrong example of the Holocaust because it's easier to deal with it.'

In the twenty-first century, Ronald Leopold says he believes there will be only two enduring entrance points into understanding the Holocaust. One will be through *The Diary of Anne Frank*, 'showing us the many aspects of being human that we are fighting for. The other will be Auschwitz where there is only "the abyss".'

At the US Holocaust Memorial Museum in Washington DC, Anne is already there representing both facets. Speaking on a cold, blustery day at its opening on 22 April 1993, Holocaust survivor and Nobel laureate Elie Wiesel said he had first been entrusted with the vision to create the memorial by President Jimmy Carter in 1978. His words are now engraved in stone at the entrance to the museum: 'For the dead and the living, we must bear witness.' That meant, Wiesel said, 'not only are we responsible for the memories of the dead, we are also responsible for what we are doing with those memories'. A museum should be a place to bring people together, not to separate them in memory.

Inside, visitors meet Anne Frank twice. First, they see her face, a symbol of both the Final Solution in Western Europe and the 'fate of hundreds of thousands of Jewish children who died in the Holocaust'. Then, on the second floor, before visitors embark on a journey to the Final Solution, they read perhaps the most famous words from *The Diary of Anne Frank*: 'I still believe that people are really good at heart.'

In his book *Selling the Holocaust: From Auschwitz to Schindler*, Tim Cole writes, 'Before we are taken through the ghettoes of Eastern Europe, into the railway car, under the gateway of Auschwitz, and into the "Concentration Camp Universe", we meet Anne Frank's face.' This Washington 'Anne' is one who is represented as both 'an emblem of lost potential and a beacon of hope'. Forty-five years after the publication of the diary and the wild success of the Broadway play and following decades of debate, visitors encounter both versions of Anne Frank: 'The universal liberal "Anne", made in 1950s America, lives alongside the Jewish, Holocaust "Anne" made in contemporary America.'

Historians and those most involved in preserving Anne's legacy may care about the contradictions, but it seems ordinary people do not. Decades have passed since the first publication of the diary, but our appetite to know more about its author remains insatiable, and it appears that her work and life still have layers of secrets to reveal.

In 2018, researchers at the Anne Frank House used photo-imaging software to uncover the text behind two pages of Anne's diary that she had pasted over with brown paper. The covered sections included dirty jokes and conversations Anne had shared with Otto about grown-up topics like prostitution. 'All men, if they are normal, go with women, women like that accost them on the street and then they go together,' she wrote. 'In Paris they have big houses for that. Papa has been there.' Calling her mother 'the old nanny goat', Anne also complained about Otto's vulgarity and fondness for talking about farting and going to the toilet.

Was it right, critics wondered, to reveal such personal things that Anne herself had wanted to remove? For Ronald Leopold at the Anne Frank House in Amsterdam, the missing pages reveal more of the essence of Anne – the real, precocious teen-age girl, rather than the icon. Today, he says, more than half of the visitors to the Anne Frank House are under thirty. They are often four or five generations removed from the Second World War, with no knowledge of the Holocaust. Anne's unique legacy is that through her writing she can 'meet young people where they are, in their own lives'. In a world where so many young people are now struggling to find and express their identities, Anne has never been more relevant, Leopold believes. In April 1944, Anne wrote, 'If only I could be myself I would be satis-fied.' She didn't say, 'I want to be a woman, I want to be Jewish, I want to be Dutch, or German,' Leopold says. As the Anne Frank House seeks to build a new international youth network, fulfilling Otto's vision, it is because 'Anne shares a longing for the freedom to discover who she is' that she still connects with young people around the world. If politics and tyrants have forced *The Diary of Anne Frank* upon their citizens and twisted her words, it is that individual connection that gives it enduring power and meaning.

'Statistics play no role,' Otto told a reporter, discussing how people responded to tragedies, wars and disasters. Tens of thousands of children could die in a famine or war and nobody would ask any questions. 'But individuality, which has gained so much attention through my daughter's diary, captures the imagination of the average person more than any numbers can.'

He concluded that the popularity of the diary had less to do with the persecution of the Jews than the universal human story: 'The fact that the book has been translated into Persian or Bengali does not stem from interest in the persecution of the Jews in the Netherlands during the war. The reason is purely the human aspect. Otherwise it would not have been this popular.'

Houses are expensive to maintain and ultimately fall into disrepair. Archives are lifeless, dry papers handled only with gloves or viewed under glass. Even trees, like Anne's chestnut tree, eventually die. For decades the chestnut tree survived threats to its existence, including plans to remove large parts of its roots, an oil spill and battles over ownership. There was name-calling when a member of the foundation created to save the tree allegedly compared the contractors who had 'killed' it to those who had killed the Jews. Despite all efforts, the tree eventually crashed down in a storm on 23 August 2010 and was no more.

If Anne Frank is only an icon or a folk hero, these physical relics are irreplaceable. People must fight for them, preserve them or mount vigils to save them. But without relics, as Ronald Leopold says, 'It is just her diary that is here as the silent messenger when she's not there any more.' Anne is remembered in Amsterdam at the Anne Frank House. Anne will be remembered in Frankfurt at the Frank Family Center at the Jüdisches Museum Frankfurt. But Anne Frank is much more than just an icon, and her ultimate meaning will live on not through museums, houses or foundations but in the written word. As Otto would have wished, Anne's legacy lives on through her words in *The Diary of Anne Frank*.

ACKNOWLEDGEMENTS

After many delays due to Covid-19, I would like to thank Stephanie de Hoog, an absolutely excellent researcher and translator, who worked extensively to find information about the first publication of *The Diary of Anne Frank* and those involved, as well as Otto Frank's subsequent court cases, in the Literatuurmuseum, and the Institute for War, Holocaust, and Genocide Studies at the NIOD in the Netherlands.

Secondly, once again I called upon the superb research and translation skills of Paula Kirby, an experienced German translator with a deep knowledge of the GDR in particular. Paula translated a vast amount of primary archive material and secondary literature from German into English for me and helped me make sense of it.

I gratefully acknowledge the Anne Frank Foundation in Basel for permission to quote from Otto Frank's private family letters and diary, and Yves Kugelmann for his help and discussions about *The Diary of Anne Frank*.

Of the many people who co-operated, helped and agreed to be interviewed, I would particularly like to thank Gertjan Broek at the Anne Frank House in Amsterdam, who went out of his way to answer my questions and help as much as possible, even when Covid narrowed our world. I would also like to thank Jan Erik Dubbelman and Ronald Leopold for talking with me and agreeing to be interviewed.

In the US I would particularly like to thank Joshua Rubinstein for helping me find out more about the publication of the diary in Russia, as well as Hasia Diner and Doyle Stevick for giving me their perspective on the diary in the Jewish community and the southern states.

In South Africa I'd like to thank Myra Osrin for speaking to me at length about her work and sending me much valuable information, as well as Youk Chhang in Cambodia and Aimable Mpayimana in Rwanda.

I'd also like to thank Martin van Gelderen, a highly esteemed historian and scholar on Anne Frank, for giving me some advice and direction, and Alain Lewkowicz for taking the time to talk to me about his work on Anne Frank in Japan.

As ever, I have to thank my agent Gaia Banks for helping me think through how this book might work and then shepherding it through a series of hurdles, as well as Alba Arnau and the team at Sheil Land. I'd also like to thank Olivia Beattie at Biteback for being so patient, flexible and determined, and editor Lucy Stewardson.

Finally and most importantly, I remember my mother Margot Ann Bartlett, who supported and believed in this book, and all my books, but did not live to see it completed. Her absence is profound.

FURTHER READING

Although Covid-19 disrupted many of my original plans to conduct archive research, it was possible for my researcher Stephanie de Hoog to access the material in the Literatuurmuseum and the Institute for War, Holocaust, and Genocide Studies at the NIOD, both in the Netherlands. In addition, there were many texts that helped me piece together the story of *The Diary of Anne Frank*. This is not a scholarly review of all the literature available about Anne Frank or the diary but a selection of some of those I thought were interesting for certain parts of the story.

If you are interested in finding out more about the life of Otto Frank and a fascinating theory about the betrayal of the Frank family, I recommend reading Carol Ann Lee's *The Hidden Life of Otto Frank*, as well as her book about Anne, *Roses from the Earth: The Biography of Anne Frank*. Melissa Müller has also written a fascinating book called *Anne Frank: The Biography*, and you can read more about the whole Frank family in *Treasures from the Attic: The Extraordinary Story of Anne Frank's Family* by Mirjam Pressler.

There are many books by Anne's friends and people who knew her, but in the context of this book I found the following particularly helpful: *Anne Frank Remembered* by Miep Gies; *Anne Frank the Untold Story: The Hidden Truth about Elli Vossen, the Youngest Helper of the Secret Annexe* by Jeroen De Bruyn and Joop van Wijk; *The Last Seven Months of Anne Frank: The Stories of Six Women Who Knew Anne Frank* by Willy Lindwer; and *After Auschwitz*, my own book with Eva Schloss.

For information about *The Diary of Anne Frank*, its publication and reception, I recommend *Anne Frank: The Book, the Life, the Afterlife* by Francine Prose; *The Phenomenon of Anne Frank* by David Barnouw; *The Diary of Anne Frank, The Critical Edition*, published by the NIOD; and *Anne Frank: The Collected Works*, published by the Anne Frank Fonds.

Other books which contained essays and reflections on the diary included *Selling the Holocaust: From Auschwitz to Schindler* by Tim Cole; *Anne Frank: Reflections on Her Life and Legacy*, edited by Hyman Enzer and Sandra Solotaroff-Enzer; and *Anne Frank Unbound*, edited by Barbara Kirshenblatt-Gimblett and Jeffrey Shandler.

For anyone interested in the United States, I would suggest Hasia Diner's excellent book *We Remember with Reverence and Love: American Jews and the Myth of Silence after the Holocaust, 1945–1962*. Tony Kushner also contributes an excellent chapter on the reception of the diary in the UK in *War and Memory in the Twentieth Century*, edited by Martin Evans and Ken Lunn.

Although it is only available in German, I recommend *Anne Frank und die DDR: Politische Deutungen und Persönliche Lesarten des Berühmten Tagebuchs* by Sylke Kirschnick, as well as *East German Film and the Holocaust* by Elizabeth Ward, which is in English.

For more on the story of Meyer Levin, his obsession with Otto Frank and his own life and career, read Ralph Melnick's *The Stolen Legacy of Anne Frank: Meyer Levin, Lillian Hellman, and the Staging of the Diary* and *An Obsession with Anne Frank: Meyer Levin and the Diary* by Lawrence Graver.

I also found Gillian Walnes Perry's book *The Legacy of Anne Frank*, about her own work founding the Anne Frank Trust UK and the international history of the exhibition, fascinating and full of useful information and insights.

For information about other children who kept diaries, I suggest *Children in the Holocaust and World War II, Their Secret Diaries* by Laurel Holliday and *Salvaged Pages: Young Writers' Diaries of the Holocaust* by Alexandra Zapruder.

Finally, although the story of the diary covers so many decades and countries, and therefore so much background reading, I would like to pick out two further books I found helpful. *Tangled Loyalties: The Life and Times of Ilya Ehrenburg* by Joshua Rubinstein helped me understand more about the context in Russia and was also a hugely enjoyable and informative read. And *Ashes in the Wind: The Destruction of Dutch Jewry* by Jacob Presser is always a book I return to, to know more about the Netherlands in the lead-up to the Second World War.

In addition, there are a few articles I would like to highlight:

'Translating Anne Frank's *Het Achterhuis*' by Simone Schroth, which has fascinating information and context on translations.

'Survivor, Agitator: Rosey E. Pool and the Transatlantic Century'. This PhD thesis by Lonneke Geerlings can be found in the archives of the Anne Frank House in Amsterdam.

'"Why Does the Way of the Wicked Prosper?" Teaching the

Holocaust in the Land of Jim Crow' by Theodore Rosengarten is included in *As the Witnesses Fall Silent*, edited by Zehavit Gross and E. Doyle Stevick.

'Ania's Diary: The Polish Translation of the Diary of Anne Frank: Its History, First Publication, and Reception in Post-Stalinist Poland' by Iwona Guść provided invaluable information about the diary in Poland.

INDEX

Yad Vashem Holocaust Remembrance
    Center, Jerusalem 175, 244
Yamamuro, Ryuichi 221
Yevtushenko, Yevgeny, 'Babi Yar' 202
Young, James E. 263

van Zeeland, Paul 138
Zimmerman, Barbara 73–6, 98, 103, 106–7,
    115–16, 130–31, 258–9
Zweig, Arnold 159–61